The Elements of Economic Policy

The Elements
of Economic Policy

Burgess Cameron
The Australian National University

 HODDER AND STOUGHTON (AUSTRALIA) PTY LTD
for
 UNIVERSITY OF LONDON PRESS LTD

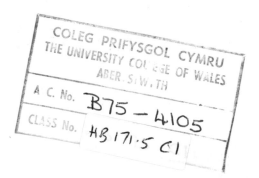
ISBN 0 340 15970 7

Hodder and Stoughton (Australia) Pty Ltd
Cnr Bridge Road and Jersey Street, Hornsby, NSW 2077, for
University of London Press Ltd.

Set in Monotype Times Roman and printed in Singapore by
Tien Wah Press (Pte.) Ltd

Contents

Preface

The aim in writing this book has been to give an understanding of economic policy issues in a modern society. That aim has dictated that this should be a *macro economic* text in the fullest sense, i.e. a book about over-all national economic policy.

The contents are arranged so that each succeeding chapter will help the reader to understand some additional aspect of economic policy. This is brought out in the questions at the end of each chapter where questions numbered 1 to 10 revise basic concepts, those numbered 11 to 20 are quantitative, and finally questions numbered from 21 explore broader problems of analysis and policy. Worked answers are at the back of the book.

The method of reasoning in each chapter is based on the concept of an *economic system*, which is set out as a model consisting of three logic blocks ⊟ in the opening chapter. The continued use of this basic concept gives an integrated view of the analysis of policy issues.

This book arose out of an attempt to expand an introductory university course on Keynesian macroeconomics into a course that would enable students to study the economic policy issues of all nations—rich and poor, planned and unplanned. In order to ensure that the student did not lose sight of the wood for the trees, it was decided: firstly, to use as few of the techniques of economic analysis as was consistent with efficient presentation; secondly, so far as possible, to treat the economy as a single *aggregated* industry, and to represent relationships by *straight lines*. It is in this sense that this is an introduction to economics. One of the benefits of this approach, as it turned out, was that the formal reasoning could be summarised in algebraic statements about sums and straight lines. The reader will find that this simple algebra is succinct, versatile and helps to crystallise ideas. There is no differential calculus in the text.

An instructor wishing to give a shortened one-year course could omit part II. Similarly the reader coming to economics for the first time may find it helpful to omit part II on a first reading. (In several chapters more difficult material is asterisked so that the reader may omit it if he wishes.)

My debt to my colleagues is great. In particular I must thank D. W. Stammer, J. Logan, C. Walsh, S. Bambrick, and J. Coat. Isobel Everitt managed the typing with fortitude.

And I should like to thank Helen, Ian and Fiona for their patience when I might have gone fishing.

Part I—The National Income

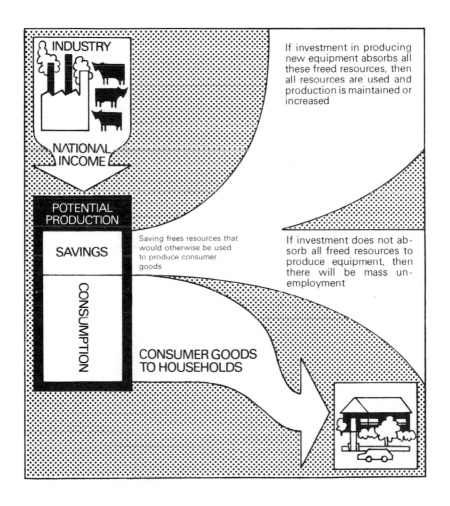

INDUSTRY

NATIONAL INCOME

POTENTIAL PRODUCTION

SAVINGS

CONSUMPTION

CONSUMER GOODS TO HOUSEHOLDS

Saving frees resources that would otherwise be used to produce consumer goods

If investment in producing new equipment absorbs all these freed resources, then all resources are used and production is maintained or increased

If investment does not absorb all freed resources to produce equipment, then there will be mass unemployment

The Economy
as a Physical System

Given physical data on available resources and technology together with profit mark-ups and final demand, we deduce: the nation's potential production, income distribution, and the commodity-composition of production.

1. Building an economy

Imagine that a group of colonists arrives in a new land, having brought with them a capital stock of seed, livestock and implements. Land in the new region is abundant and fertile.

How will the colonists make best use of the available physical resources? They must decide in what proportions to produce consumer goods. In a colony where primary needs are for food and warmth, this decision is presumably not a difficult one.

What methods of production will the colonists use? It is likely that they will initially adopt the traditional technology of the land from which they came and that decisions to change that technology will come only later.

What provision will they make for the future? The colonists will soon realise that as well as producing grain, meat and fibres for food and clothing, they also need to build more capital equipment so that as their children come of age they will have additional tools to till the land and process the crops. Moreover, in addition to producing such equipment to add to their equipment stock, they also need to replace old equipment as it wears out. Calculation of the size of such needed investment in capital equipment goes like this:

Suppose that the population and work force of the colony are expected to grow 2 per cent annually. This means that in order to equip the annual growth in the work force with the traditional amount of equipment per worker, new equipment will have to be built each year equal to 2 per cent of the total stock of capital equipment at the start of the year. Regarding the replacement of worn-out equipment: if equipment has a 25 year life, then in the long run replacement investment in any year must equal the production of equipment 25 years earlier. It can be calculated that this replacement of equipment in any year must be equal to 3 per cent of the equipment stock.[1] Thus in total a volume of equipment must be produced each year equal to 5 per cent of the total equipment stock.

Suppose, now, that a census of the size of the capital stock shows that it would take the entire resources of the community 4 years to reproduce the existing capital equipment stock. In other words if the entire labour force were devoted to building equipment (and none devoted to producing food) then the national product at the end of the year would be an amount of equipment equal to just one-quarter of the initial capital stock. This can be summarised by saying that the ratio of the capital stock to the annual national product is 4, or simply that *the capital/output ratio* is 4.

Summary

THE SIZE OF ANNUAL INVESTMENT
i.e. PRODUCTION OF CAPITAL EQUIPMENT

Net investment to equip an annual 2 per cent rise in work force at traditional technology   = 2 per cent of capital stock

Replacement investment if equipment has a 25 year life   = 3 per cent of capital stock

Hence *total* (or gross) *investment* needed is 5 per cent of the capital stock. If the capital stock is 4 times the annual national product, it follows that annual investment needed is equal to 20 per cent of the annual national product.

From this we conclude that if the colony is to equip the annual growth of the work force at the traditional equipment/labour ratio, as well as replace worn-out equipment, then (5 per cent × 4 =) one-fifth of the national product must be saved. In other words only four-fifths of the national resources can be devoted to producing goods for consumption. The remaining one-fifth represents the use of resources in the industries producing equipment (e.g. coke, limestone, iron ore, pig iron, steel, heavy engineering).

The purpose of this opening illustration has been to show how one may probe into the essential characteristics of an economy — in this case the probe has drawn attention to the relation between the

[1] See below, chapter 2.

savings-income ratio and a set of physical characteristics, namely the population growth rate, the equipment/output ratio and equipment life. This specific case will be taken up again in chapter 2. However, in order to probe the nature of an economy effectively, a clearly defined concept of the economic system is now needed.

2. The economic system ▤

The nation's economy is a physical system comprising a collection of resources that are employed in industry to produce commodities for final use. The subject matter of economics is the study of how these resources are used and hence to show what determines:

    (a) the production potential of the nation;
    (b) the distribution of the nation's production as between income groups;
    (c) the actual production of the nation, and also the commodity-composition of that production.

To illustrate, consider a very simple example:
Imagine that the nation's labour force is 2 million men; and that each man can produce annually 3 tons of wheat, which is the only commodity produced. Suppose also that land is plentiful (so that land-rent is zero); and that the price of wheat is set by applying a 50 per cent profit mark-up to operating costs, i.e. in this case to wages paid. Finally, households spend 90 per cent of their income on current consumption of wheat; and a government agency buys up the balance of production for stockpiling.

From the information in this example we readily deduce:
    (a) potential production is 6 million tons of wheat annually;
    (b) wages are two-thirds of national income because the farmer sets the price of wheat by putting a 50 per cent mark-up on every dollar of wage costs; i.e. for each amount of wheat sold at $1.50, $1 goes to wages and 50 cents to profit;
    (c) since total production can be sold, actual production can be expected to equal potential production; and 90 per cent of production is currently consumed, the remainder representing the nation's *investment* in adding to stocks of wheat.

These deductions could be made because the example provided

three sets of information on:

(a) resource supplies (2 million men) and technology (3 tons per worker);

(b) profit mark-up (50 per cent) so that, since the price of wheat is wholly exhausted by wages and profit, the distribution of income is deduced;

(c) final demand (all production saleable, 90 per cent for consumption).

It is convenient to call each bit of information a *relation* and the relations are summarised in figure 1.1. Here, in the businessman's terminology, the statement that 'the value of wheat is the sum of profits and wages' is called the *cost account*. (It can be regarded as a definition of profit: the difference between the value of wheat and wage-costs.)

FIGURE 1.1   THE ECONOMIC SYSTEM

To ascertain	Relations	Example
Potential production	Resource supplies Technology	Work force = 2 million men Each man can produce 3 tons of wheat per annum.
Income distribution	Cost account Profit mark-up	Value of wheat $\equiv$ wages + profit Profit = 50 per cent of wage bill
Size and composition of production	Final demand	Households spend 90 per cent of income on wheat Unsold production is stockpiled

This simple numerical example displays the logical structure of our later analysis of the economy. For the information in the example describes the economy in terms of a set of relations. This set of relations is called a *model* of the economy, by which is meant that it is a coherent set of ideas specifying our conception of the nature of the economy. To be quite specific, the model is now set out in figure 1.2 in a three-block form that will henceforth be used as a standard layout.

FIGURE 1·2   MODEL OF THE ECONOMIC SYSTEM

Potential *production* *block*	Resource supplies Technology	: :	the work force $= W$ $aX = N$
Price *formation* *block*	Cost account Profit mark-up	: :	$XP - N.P_n + V$ $V = v(N.P_n)$
Demand *block*	Consumption demand Investment demand	: :	$C = cX$ $I = (1-c)X$

Note: $W = 2$ million $v = 0.5$
　　　　　 $a = \frac{1}{3}$ 　　　　　　　 $c = 0.9$

Legend: W work force C consumption demand (volume)
　　　　　　 X output 　　　　 I investment demand (volume)
　　　　　　 N employment 　 P price
　　　　　　 V profit 　　　　　 P_n wage-rate

For a full list of symbols refer page 311.

Our simple example has now been called a 'model' and restated using symbols in figure 1.2. The reader is entitled to wonder whether this sophistication is necessary or whether it is rather an algebraic charade. The answer is that such emphasis on logical structure, while unnecessary in such a simple example, is an invaluable aid to reasoning as our discussion becomes more realistic. For greater realism involves an increase in the volume and variety of basic information. A sound logical structure enables us to marshal this information with comparative ease.

Summary

In order to explain the size, distribution and composition of the nation's production, information is needed as to:

— physical resources
— technology
— degree of competition (measured by profit mark-ups)
— final demand

(Information may also be needed regarding social institutions, e.g. religion, land inheritance.)

When we speak of 'the economic system' we will now have in mind a model such as that set out in figure 1.2, and this model will be used again and again throughout this book (occasionally adding bits as we proceed). Representing an economy in this way has two signal advantages: first, it is quite explicit as to what is being asserted about the economy; second, it allows elementary arithmetical procedures to be used in deducing the characteristics of the economic system. Thus in figure 1.2 we deduce that potential production is W/a, and that the wage-share is $1/(1+v)$. A diagrammatic version of the model is given in figure 1.3.

FIGURE 1·3   THE ECONOMIC SYSTEM

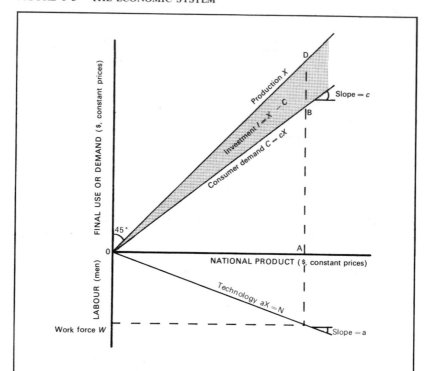

Working from the bottom: by employing the work force W, a national product of OA can be produced. The graph is charted so that $AD=OA$; AD then is divided into AB consumption and BD investment. (In this model, investment is simply a residual obtained by subtracting AB from AD.)

3. The national income

In practice the national income is calculated by drawing up a set of national income accounts. In principle this procedure involves the summing of the cost accounts of all productive enterprises in the community and then closing off the accounts by recording each transaction as both a payment and a receipt. To illustrate, the following sets out the annual cost accounts of a nation aggregated into two sectors: farm, and non-farm, industry. These two cost accounts are now aggregated into a single consolidated account, cancelling out sales between the two sectors for simplicity.

FARM INDUSTRY: COST ACCOUNT ($M)

Costs		Sales to	
Non-farm inputs	1,568	Non-farm industry	940
Wages	282	Households (consumption)	1,212
Surplus*	1,746	Exports	1,660
Indirect taxes	130		
Imports	86		
TOTAL COSTS	3,812	VALUE OF OUTPUT	3,812

*i.e. non-wage income (profit, rent, interest).

NON-FARM INDUSTRY: COST ACCOUNT ($M)

Costs		Sales to	
Farm inputs	940	Farms	1,568
Wages	7,031	Households (consumption)	9,388
Surplus	5,020	Government	2,133
Indirect taxes	1,469	Private investment	
Imports	2,961	in equipment	2,802
		Stock rise	68
		Exports	1,462
TOTAL COSTS	17,421	VALUE OF OUTPUT	17,421

It is useful to pause here and comment. First, imports and exports have been included for realism.[2] Second, the farm industry cost account is itself a consolidation of many individual farm accounts, and inter-farm sales of inputs (e.g. hay sold for feed) have previously

[2] Note that non-farm industry includes the 'industry of importing final consumer goods'.

CONSOLIDATED ACCOUNT ($M)

Costs		Sales to	
Wages	7,313	Household consumption	10,600
Surplus	6,766	Government demand for	
Indirect taxes	1,599	goods and services	2,133
Imports	3,047	Private investment,	
		fixed capital	2,802
		Stock rise	68
		Exports	3,122
	18,725 ·		18,725

Note: In order for the national income produced to be estimated, a further sum of $1,463m must be added to the left hand side for civil servants' salaries, and an equal entry on the right hand side as government demand for labour services:

Wages	1,463	Government demand for	
		labour	1,463
TOTAL SUPPLIES	20,188	TOTAL DEMAND	20,188

been cancelled out. The same applies to the non-farm sector. Third, the items on the right-hand side of the final consolidated account record the *end-use of commodities flowing into final demand.* Now let us consider some major concepts.

In economic analysis a distinction is drawn between the 'value of output' and 'value produced' for an industry. In the present example the value of farm output (excluding imports and indirect taxes on sales) is (3812 − 130−86 =) $3,596m, i.e. the value of grain, livestock, etc. actually turned off the farm. But the value produced by farms is defined as equalling the total incomes (wages and surplus) paid to factors employed in the industry, i.e. $2,028m (= 282 + 1,746). The difference between value of output and value produced is the $1,568m value of material inputs (fertilisers, gasoline, etc.), which themselves represent value produced in non-rural industry.

The usefulness of the concept 'value produced' lies in the fact that it avoids double-counting of processed materials. Thus the sum of

Double-counting processed materials

The $940m farm products sold to non-farm industry includes such items as milk sold to butter factories. If this $940m were included in the official estimates of national production, then that milk would be counted twice—once as milk and once as part of the value of butter. Our definitions and consolidating procedure avoid this double-counting.

the value produced in all industries is called the national product and this by definition equals the *national income*, which is the sum of incomes received by factors of production in all industries.[3] Thus in the consolidated account the sum of the value produced in all industries is wages $7,313m and surplus $6,766m, to which we add a further $1,463m for the wages of public servants to obtain a national product of $15,542m.

The national product so defined includes provision for depreciation of equipment, for this item is part of surplus. It is possible in principle to subtract depreciation, but the sheer difficulty of doing this with any accuracy is the reason why frequent use is made of the above concept of national product, which is commonly called *gross national product* since it is gross of (i.e. includes) depreciation.

This concept of production is called more fully gross national product *at factor cost* and if we add to it net indirect taxes ($1,599m sales tax, purchase tax, etc. less commodity subsidies), we have the gross national product *at market price* ($17,141m). This, together with the value of imports ($3,047m) gives the ($18,725m + $1,463m =) $20,188m of total supplies at market price available to satisy final demand. Final demand itself has four major components:

—consumption by households
—private investment
—government use of goods and services
—export

The word *investment* refers to physical accumulation of equipment, buildings and inventories (i.e. stocks). This contrasts with ordinary usage in which 'investment' also means a transfer of legal ownership (e.g. 'investing' in shares in a company). Finally, government use of goods and services can be subdivided into current consumption (bombs, milk for schools) and investment (roads, hospitals).

A set of national income accounts consists in essence of the above consolidated account together with the receipts and expenditure

[3] Not all incomes are included in the national income. Thus social service cash benefits (including pensions) are treated as a transfer of income from taxpayers in *productive* activity. To include them in national income produced would be regarded as double-counting of incomes: once when they are earned by productive factors and then once again as social service benefits.

accounts of the transacting sectors, i.e. households, government and foreigners. In these three further accounts we find the $6,766m income surplus allocated to:

HOUSEHOLDS ($M)

Outlay		Income	
Consumption	10,600	Wages—industry	7,313
Personal income tax	1,400	—public servants	1,463
Foreign travel	50	Dividends, interest	
Savings	1,192	and unincorporated	
		income	3,416
		Social service benefits	1,050
	13,242		13,242

GOVERNMENT ($M)

Outlay		Income	
Goods and services	2,133	Indirect taxes	1,599
Wages	1,463	Company tax	750
		Personal income tax	1,400
		Social service benefit	−1,050
		Budget deficit	897
	3,596		3,596

OVERSEAS ($M)

Outlay		Income	
Exports	3,122	Imports	3,047
Increase in		Dividends, interest and	
foreign indebtness	375	profits accruing to	
		foreigners	400
		Foreign travel	50
	3,497		3,497

households $3,416m (including dividends, interest and the receipts of self-employed farmers, doctors, builders and other unincorporated enterprises); company tax $750m; profits accruing to foreigners $400m. The balance of $2,200m includes undistributed profit and depreciation charges.

To close off this set of accounts, we add a Capital Account so that all transactions are recorded both as receipt and payment. The significance of this account is that it shows the sources of finance for investment.

CAPITAL ACCOUNT ($M)

Use of funds		Source of funds	
Investment	2,802	Undistributed profit	2,200
Stock rise	68	Personal savings	1,192
		Government surplus	—897
		Increase in foreign indebtedness	375
	2,870		2,870

Summary

The national product is defined to equal the national income. The national income is the sum of all wages, rent, interest and profits paid to the owners of productive factors (labour, land, equipment) for their services in producing the current year's volume of output.

Each of the following concepts of national production has its equivalent national income concept—since the value of production is defined to equal the incomes paid to productive factors for their services:

Example	$ million
Gross national product at market price	17,141
less indirect taxes (net of subsidies)	1,599
Gross national product at factor cost	15,542
less depreciation provision (say $1,000m)	1,000
Net national product at factor cost	14,542
less incomes accruing to foreigners (net of incomes received from overseas)	400
Net national product on a residential basis (= residential net national income)	14,142

Each of these concepts, save the last, refers to the national product (and income) of a geographic region. The final deduction of net incomes accruing to foreigners changes the concept of income from a *geographic* to a *residential* basis.

The word *gross* as applied to national product means 'total' national production before making any allowance for wearing out capital equipment. The deduction of the accountants' 'provision for depreciation' yields the estimated 'net national product'.

Major transactions are recorded in the national income accounts. The Consolidated Account shows three things: the size of the national product; its distribution between wages and other incomes (or 'surplus'); the relative size of the several parts of total final demand (consumption, investment, exports, government absorption of goods and services). The Capital Account shows how the national investment programme is financed.

These last five accounts comprise a set that gives an over-all view of the size and distribution of the national income and of the sources of saving. One way of obtaining a feel for important magnitudes in an economy is to express all the items in the Consolidated Account and in the Capital Account as percentages of the national income (here $15,542m[4]).[5]

Summary

§1. 'Economic decisions' are decisions as how best to use the nation's physical resources in order to satisfy the wants of the population. Such decisions include:
— in what relative proportions to produce consumer goods (chapters 9, 10);
— what technology to use, e.g. more or less labour intensive methods (chapters 6, 7);
— how much capital equipment to produce (chapter 2).

§2. Economics analyses the influences determining the nation's production potential, income distribution and the size and composition of production.

Basic information is required as to physical resources, technology, profit mark-up and final (consumption and investment) demand.

This information is assembled in a set of relations, i.e. in a model, from which deductions are made as to:

production potential (W/a), determined by resources and technology;
wage-share ($1/(1+v)$), determined by profit mark-up.

§3. National income and national product are defined as equal. The national income accounts record the major transactions in the economy.

---

[4] The concept of gross *geographic* national income has been used here. By subtracting net profits and interest accruing to foreigners ($400m), we obtain gross *residential* national income.

[5] For this purpose it is often acceptable as a first approximation to treat households as paying all indirect taxes. Household consumption at factor cost would then be $(10,600 - 1,599 =)$ $9,001m, which with government use ($3,596m), private investment ($2,802m), stock rise ($68m) and exports-net-of-imports ($75m), exhausts the national product ($15,542m).

Further reading

The official National Income Accounts.

A.J. Brown, *Introduction to the World Economy* (London: Allen & Unwin, 1965).

R.T. Gill, *Economics and the Public Interest* (Pacific Palisades, Calif.: Goodyear Publishing Co., 1968).

Evolution of Modern Economics (Englewood Cliffs, N.J.: Prentice Hall, 1967).

P.A. Samuelson, *Economics*, 7th ed. (New York: McGraw-Hill, 1967) part I.

Questions

1. What do you understand by the term 'economic system'?
2. Explain the aims and methods of economic analysis.
3. In chapter 1 section 3, what is the value produced in non-farm industry? What is the value of non-farm output entering final demand? Explain their inequality.
4. Define: final demand, investment, national product, residential national income. Does the national income include old age pensions?

11. In the model in figure 1.2, suppose the constants were $W = 3$ million; $a = \frac{2}{3}$; $v = 1$; $c = 0.8$. What conclusions can you draw? (Write your conclusions in words, not symbols.)
12. The value of national consumer expenditure deflated by the price level is a constant proportion of the sum of the nation's factor incomes, also deflated by the same price level (or index of prices). Write out in symbols and simplify.
13. There are three industries in the economy: wheat farming, flour milling, and bakeries. Information is provided on each as follows in $m:

> Wheat farming: total cost of wheat produced is 50, broken into wages 40, depreciation 5 and distributed profits 5.
> Flour mills: total cost of flour produced is 59, broken into wages 5, wheat 50, depreciation 2 and distributed

profits 2. Of total output valued at 59, 15 is stockpiled and the remaining 44 sold to bakeries and households.

Bakeries: total cost of bread produced is 50, broken into wages 8, flour 30, dividends 6, undistributed profit and depreciation 6.

What is the value of the national product? What are the levels of household savings and of corporate savings (including depreciation)?

14. Suppose the dairy industry produces $10m of milk of which $6m is sold to households and $4m to the butter industry, which makes $6m of butter to sell to consumers. What is the value of the national product if there are no other industries?

21. Obtain an official set of national income accounts, if possible last year's. Express the major sources of investible funds as percentages of the national product. Break down the nation's investment into major categories, and express as percentages of the national product. Similarly express exports, imports and the international flow of capital as percentages of national production.

If you feel able, calculate the shares of major income groups in the national income, before and after income transfers.

22. To what do you attribute the rise in national production over the past century?

23. Can the burden of a rise in military expenditure be lightened by raising a government loan among the nation's people?

24. Do you think that the economic problems of India are the same as those of the United States?

2

Capital Accumulation

A nation has to save in order that part of its resources are used to produce equipment: firstly to equip the annual growth of the work force; secondly to replace old equipment. If the nation wishes to raise long-run living standards by increasing the amount of equipment per worker then savings must be raised further.

Example: A nation whose population and work force are growing 2 per cent annually has a capital/output ratio of 4, and equipment has a 25 year life. Assuming constant scale returns we deduce: one-fifth of the national product must be saved in order to maintain existing living standards.

1. Increasing resources

Since the maximum national product attainable depends on the available resources and state of technical knowledge, it is natural to ask whether the national product can be increased by increasing resources or knowledge.

So far as knowledge is concerned, a significant amount of resources is devoted by governments and private firms to both research and education, i.e. to the creation and dissemination of knowledge. Important as this topic is, it will not be pursued here.[1]

Let us then seek to increase resources, say by land reclamation as in the following example. Some of the terms used to describe technology are set out in the box.

Example: Suppose that the nation's production is simply food, and that each labourer's production adds 0.09375 tons of food to the annual national product, i.e. the marginal product of labour is 0.09375 tons. Imagine also that the proposal to reclaim one acre of land requires that $13\frac{1}{3}$ men must be transferred for a year from food production to land reclamation. This means that food produc-

---

[1] Refer J. Jewkes et al., *The Sources of Invention* (London: Macmillan, 1958).

Technology

In order to produce a good it is usually necessary to employ inputs, not just of labour but of other productive factors as well. Production terminology describes two sorts of situation:

(a) Where the input of *only one* factor is changed:
The *marginal product of labour* is the rise in total output when one more labourer is employed, with no change in the input of other factors.
The *marginal product of land* is the rise in total output when one more acre is employed, with no change in the input of other factors.

(b) Where the input of *all* factors is changed by the same proportion:
Then if output rises by that proportion, it is said that 'scale returns are constant';

e.g. a 2 per cent rise in employment of all productive factors is called:
constant scale returns	if output rises 2 per cent
increasing scale returns	if output rises more than 2 per cent
diminishing scale returns	if output rises less than 2 per cent

---

tion must fall by $(0.09375 \times 13\frac{1}{3} =)$ 1.25 tons for that year. Finally, suppose also that the marginal product of land is 0.125 tons of food. Then if an acre of reclaimed land is permanently productive, it follows that land reclamation yields an annual rate of return of 10 per cent (since for a cost of 1.25 tons of food we obtain a return of 0.125 tons annually for ever). Of course, from the viewpoint of raising national food production, the physical form of the new resources created might just as well be tractors as reclaimed land.

Now suppose that, for whatever physical reason, the reclaimed land has a productive life of 25 years (instead of infinity). The compound rate of return is then calculated to be 8 per cent per annum.[2] To illustrate the significance of the *limited life*, imagine that the $13\frac{1}{3}$ men are transferred *permanently* from farm production to land reclamation. Thus they will reclaim one acre a year for 25 years to increase resources by 25 acres, after which each acre they reclaim in succeeding years will merely replace one acre that goes out of production. The resulting time profile of production of consumer goods is shown in figure 2.1 on the assumption that the marginal

---

[2] This figure can be checked by using it as the rate of discount that equates the sum of the present values of the annual marginal products over the ensuing 25 years to the initial cost, i.e.:

$$1.25 = \frac{0.125}{(1+r)} + \frac{0.125}{(1+r)^2} + \ldots + \frac{0.125}{(1+r)^{25}}$$

in which the rate of discount r is found to be 0.08.

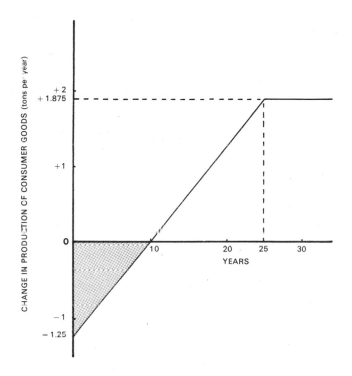

FIGURE 2.1 THE EFFECT ON NATIONAL PRODUCTION OF CONSUMER GOODS OF PERMANENTLY TRANSFERRING A BATCH OF $13\frac{1}{3}$ MEN FROM FARMING TO RECLAMATION

The diagram shows the cumulative effect of reclaiming one acre annually, assuming constant marginal productivity of land. The dotted area measures the loss of consumption (i.e. saving) which enables the rise in consumption after the tenth year.

product of land is constant over this range. The transfer of $13\frac{1}{3}$ men permanently from farming to land reclamation (i.e. from producing consumer goods to producing capital equipment) implies a 1.25 ton fall in consumption at the outset; in ten years consumption is back to the old level, and in twenty-five years production is 1.875 tons higher than would have been the case if no labour had been transferred. *In order to maintain this higher level of production, the 13⅓ men must continue to produce 'replacement' land indefinitely.*

Summary

The higher productivity of capital-intensive processes is a source of long-term rise in consumption and living standards. For example, the transfer of 13⅓ men from food production to land reclamation involves an immediate annual fall in food production of 1.25 tons but a long-term annual rise of 1.875 tons. (For the time-profile see figure 2·1).

It is a basic assumption of the ensuing discussion that there do exist such capital-intensive processes capable of raising production of consumer goods.

With this example in mind, it is apparent that a community faces three problems in the matter of capital accumulation:[3]

(a) First, most communities have an increasing population and so a proportion of the total work force must be kept at producing new capital equipment in order to equip the annual rise in the work force at the traditional technology and so maintain living standards.

(b) Second, every community has an inheritance of capital equipment, which must be maintained and replaced. In other words a proportion of the work force must be kept at producing replacement capital equipment in order to maintain living standards.

(c) Third, the community has to decide whether to increase its stock of capital equipment, relatively to the work force, in order to raise consumption in the future at the cost of lower consumption in the present.

These are the three topics discussed below in sections 2, 4 and 5.

2. Population growth

Plan of argument

Modern discussion of capital accumulation stresses the tendency of population growth to depress living standards if capital equipment

[3] It is assumed in this chapter that resources are fully employed (unless otherwise stated).

cannot grow as rapidly as population and work force. It is true that living standards depend on:

— natural resources
— technical knowledge
— managerial efficiency
— income distribution
— social institutions
— the availability of foreign credits

However, in a world characterised by population growth, capital accumulation takes on a critical role.

If we assume two factors of production, labour and equipment, and constant scale returns in production, then in order to achieve a specified target rate of growth of production, an equi-proportional growth of labour and equipment is needed. In other words the growth of production is limited by:

(a) Labour availability: *the rate of growth of work force,* which depends on natural reproduction and migration, and is initially assumed to be constant (*w*);
(b) Equipment availability: the rate of growth of capital stock, which depends on the *average propensity to save,* or savings-income ratio (*s*).

It is this role of the average propensity to save, or *savings-income ratio,* which is examined first, under the heading 'the feasible growth rate of production'. In this discussion the *capital/output ratio* (*b*) is assumed to be constant.[4] Now, so long as capital stock and the employed work force grow at the same rate, output will also grow at the same rate (given constant scale returns), so that the capital/output ratio is indeed constant. However, if the capital stock grows faster than the employed work force, then we must assume that output per worker rises at the same rate as capital per worker in order to obtain the result that the capital/output ratio is again constant. Hence this assumption will later be reviewed.

The second stage of the argument is to compare the growth rate of work force (*w*) with the growth rate of production (*n*) which is feasible in terms of the savings-income ratio.

[4] Refer page 2 where the capital/output ratio *b* = 4.

The feasible growth rate of production

Suppose that in order to increase the volume of the national product by \$1m it is necessary to build increased plant capacity valued at \$$b$ million (e.g. $b = 4$). We can express this by saying that the *capital/output ratio* associated with a rise in national production is b. So, using X to designate national product and ΔX to designate an increment in production, we can say that: to produce an extra amount of output ΔX requires investment $b.\Delta X$. In other words investment *requirements* expressed as a proportion of current national product are $b.\Delta X/X$. Since this cannot exceed the proportion of resources *available* for investment (which are measured by s the savings-income ratio), it follows that:

$$\frac{b.\Delta X}{X} \leqq s$$

By assuming that the limit is operative, we may ignore the inequality and write that:

$$n \equiv \frac{\Delta X}{X} = \frac{s}{b}$$

the feasible growth rate of production (n) *is* s/b.

In other words if the national product is to grow next year by an amount n per cent, then (assuming no excess capacity) there must be investment during the year of b *times* n per cent. Plainly this cannot exceed s per cent of national production. So we can express the limit to the growth rate of production in the form:

$$s = b.n$$

Example: If $s = 10$ per cent and $b = 4$, then the production growth rate cannot exceed $2\frac{1}{2}$ per cent.

The work force growth rate

If the rate of growth of population and work force is w, consider the three possibilities: that w is equal to, greater than, or less than, n, the feasible growth rate of production.

(a) *If* $w = n$, *then living standards can be maintained* using the traditional equipment/labour ratio to equip the annual increment in the work force. The supporting argument is as follows (let $w = n = 2\frac{1}{2}$ per cent per annum, $s = 10$ per cent, $b = 4$): if the employed work force rises $2\frac{1}{2}$ per cent in the year and the capital stock also rises $2\frac{1}{2}$ per cent through physical investment, then, assuming constant scale returns, national product will also rise $2\frac{1}{2}$ per cent. (Observe that this is consistent with assuming the capital/output ratio constant.) It follows that the volume of net investment must be four times the $2\frac{1}{2}$ per cent rise in the national product. This can be met from the savings-income ratio $s = 10$ per cent, and consumption per head can be maintained.

It does not follow, however, that the case where $w=n$ presents no problem for government economic policy in a poor country. For even though savings are sufficient to equip the annual growth in the work force with the traditional technology, nonetheless if technology is primitive then labour productivity and living standards will be low. Thus their problem is how to raise the equipment/labour ratio in order to raise labour productivity. This is a basic policy issue and is explored in section 5 below.

(b) *If* $w > n$, say because work force is growing at the higher rate of 3 per cent compared with a $2\frac{1}{2}$ per cent feasible growth rate of national production, it is obvious that *existing living standards are endangered.* For, in order to equip a 3 per cent growth rate of work force at the traditional equipment/labour ratio, a 3 per cent growth rate of capital stock would be required, which would raise national product 3 per cent—but the *volume* of investment needed for this is 12 per cent of the national product, which exceeds the investible resources made available by saving.

Such a situation might be resolved by:
— rapid technological advance
— foreign aid to increase available savings
— emigration or family planning to reduce the population growth rate (w)

Or it might be resolved by measures to raise the savings-income ratio by redistribution or forced savings—an alternative examined in section 5. In the short run, however, the situation may be resolved in a wholly unsatisfactory way by a rise in unemployment and a fall in living standards. A rise in *complementary unemployment* will occur to the extent that it is not possible to equip all the rise in the work force with the complementary tools and equipment to work productively. The *fall in living standards* will occur to the extent that equipment is spread more thinly among the workers, i.e. the equipment/labour ratio falls and so labour productivity and living standards fall. Since the unemployed must live, *both eventualities represent a fall in average living standards.*

(c) *If* $w < n$, say because the work force growth rate is only 2 per cent, *then the opportunity exists to raise living standards* because investment needs to equip the 2 per cent work force growth rate at the traditional equipment/labour ratio are only 8 per cent of the national product, compared with a savings ratio of 10 per cent. However, *if this opportunity is not taken, then unemployment will develop* because aggregate demand is less than the nation's productive capacity. Workers will be disemployed from the equipment-goods industries and this unemployment will spread into a business recession, as discussed in the next chapter. It is to be observed that *in this situation it is deficiency of demand (not shortage of complementary equipment)* that is the cause of unemployment.

It is also interesting to note that one of the means of eliminating such unemployment is an immigration programme, which raises the work force growth rate and stimulates aggregate demand.

Example: A group of immigrants who enter the country during the year and, being given employment, raise the national product by a $\frac{1}{2}$ per cent in the year, stimulate a volume of investment equal to 2 per cent of national product (if $b = 4$), while their consumer demand also rises (since only 10 per cent of the rise in national product is

Summary

An annual work force growth rate of $2\frac{1}{2}$ per cent would require an annual $2\frac{1}{2}$ per cent increase in the stock of capital equipment in order to maintain constant living standards under constant scale returns.

If the capital/output ratio is constant at 4, such an annual $2\frac{1}{2}$ per cent increase in capital stock equals 10 per cent of annual national product.

Hence required savings are 10 per cent of national income.

Three possibilities exist:

   (a) Savings are 10 per cent of national income. (But living standards, though constant, may be lower than desired. See section 5.)

   (b) Savings are less than 10 per cent of national income. There are several possible outcomes, but living standards are likely to fall.

   (c) Savings exceed 10 per cent of national income. Then it is possible to increase equipment per worker and so raise output and living standards.

saved) so that total consumption plus investment demand rises by more than production. If this annual migration is sustained, this consequent higher level of demand will move the economy back towards full employment.[5]

3. Review: the use of savings

If the community were determined to spend its entire national income on consumer goods, then the national product would consist only of food, clothing and other consumer goods. It is only because the community is prepared *not* to consume its entire income—i.e. is prepared to save—that resources are available[6] for the production of investment goods including buildings and machinery. The three main sources of the motive to invest are:

—replacement of old equipment,

—growth of population and work force who need equipment and factory buildings,

—innovation, i.e. the use of new methods of production (often involving an increase in the amount of equipment per worker).

The total level of investment in the nation may be called *gross investment*, and if replacement investment is subtracted from gross investment, we have *net investment*, i.e. the addition to the nation's stock of capital equipment.

It is often convenient to use a similar terminology for saving; i.e. gross saving is total saving, of which one part makes resources available to carry out replacement investment,[7] and the remainder, which we may call 'net saving', makes resources available for adding to the stock of capital equipment.

For the moment let us simplify by ignoring replacement, and

---

[5] Thus if a nation with an immigration programme experiences temporary unemployment due to deficiency of demand, it is an error to propose to eliminate this 'labour surplus' by a long-term cut in the immigration programme, for such a measure will cause a cut in investment and a further rise in unemployment.

[6] The availability of resources to produce investment goods does not always imply that those investment goods will be produced. Except where otherwise stated, it is assumed in this chapter that resources available for the production of investment goods are in fact used for that purpose. In the two following chapters this assumption is discarded and the possibility of resources not being employed is explored in detail.

[7] Corporations call their savings made for this purpose 'provision for depreciation'. The relation between provision for depreciation and replacement is discussed below.

suppose also that the third innovation motive is inoperative; i.e. we concentrate on those resources released by net saving to equip the annual growth of work force with tools and equipment. Imagine then that we can control w, the work force growth rate.

If we set w high and 'overshoot' n, then we have the problem of the poor countries: either falling living standards because the available equipment has to be spread more thinly among the workers; or rising 'complementary' unemployment due to inability to productively equip the new workers with complementary tools.

If we place w at any level less than n, there will be *demand-deficiency* unemployment, i.e. unemployment due to the fact that at full employment planned investment is less than available savings, so that demand (investment plus consumption) is less than total production (which, being equal to national income, equals consumption plus savings).[8] This is a situation sometimes called 'secular stagnation': society's institutions are geared to provide net savings but there is insufficient motive to invest to absorb those savings. So there is unemployment—which will rise owing to the positive feedback effect known as the national income multiplier.[9] Now, however, consider the role of *innovation*—defined as the introduction of new methods of production. Innovation includes introducing methods that raise the amount of equipment per worker and so it is seen that the innovatory motive to invest can ensure both full employment and rising living standards. However, innovation is also the process whereby new scientific and technical knowledge is applied in industry, and this also has great significance for living standards. In summary, it is easy to imagine (as a first approximation) that the innovation motive to invest not only raises the capital/labour ratio but also raises factor productivity so that the output/labour ratio rises by the same proportion.[10] Thus at full employment all savings can be absorbed by investment, and both output and capital equipment grow at the same rate (n). (Refer figure 2.2.). For the rest of this chapter it is assumed that all resources made available by saving are in fact employed to build investment goods.

---

[8] This is the subject of detailed discussion in chapter 3 and especially in section 4 of chapter 4.

[9] See below, chapter 3.

[10] i.e. constant marginal returns through time to capital.

FIGURE 2·2   TWO ASPECTS OF INVESTMENT

Given the savings-income ratio, then maintaining the level of investment:
(a) maintains full employment;
(b) raises output per worker

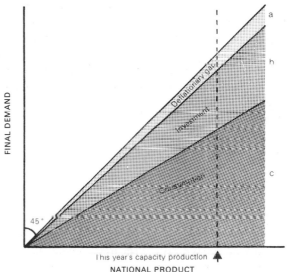

Notes: Not to scale.
   a 2 per cent deflationary gap.
   b Investment to equip a 2 per cent work force growth rate, since *b*
      =4, equals 8 per cent of production.
   c Consumption =90 per cent of production.
  If the work force growth rate is 2 per cent p.a. and the capital/output ratio
is 4, then investment to equip the annual work force growth is 8 per cent of
national income. If the savings-income ratio is 10 per cent, consumption is
90 per cent of national income. So total final demand is 98 per cent of national
income—leaving a 2 per cent gap or excess of production over demand, which
will result in unemployment.
  If innovatory motives result in total investment rising from 8 per cent to 10
per cent of national income, there are two results:
   (a) Current demand equals current production and so demand-deficiency
        unemployment is avoided;
   (b) The extra investment raises the nation's capacity to produce. In the
        simplest (not necessarily most common) case in which the equipment/
        labour ratio is raised by this innovatory investment and the output/
        labour ratio rises in the *same* proportion, then the capital/output ratio
        is unchanged at 4, so that capacity production grows at 2½ per cent per
        annum.

4. Replacement investment[11]

The discussion in the preceding section has covered only net investment in adding to the capital stock and has ignored the need to replace old equipment. The argument can be expanded to include *total* (both *net* and *replacement*) *investment* as follows.

It has been shown that (ignoring replacement), in order for the national product to grow at an annual rate n, there must be an annual volume of investment $b.n$ (as a proportion of production), where b is the constant capital/output ratio. It will now be shown that (recognising replacement), for the national product to grow at rate n, the annual volume of gross investment (as a proportion of production) must be $(b'.n)$ where b' is defined as:

$$b' \equiv \frac{b}{1 - \dfrac{1}{(1+n)^m}}$$

and m is equipment life in years.

The argument is that since the national product is to grow at rate n and the capital/output ratio is constant, then the capital stock is also to grow at rate n. We now wish to calculate the size of annual gross investment and show that it also grows at rate n. Current net investment (I^*)

net investment $I^* = n.K_t$

equals a constant proportion n of the start-of-year capital stock K. Since capital stock is growing at rate n, net investment is also growing at rate n. It will now be shown that replacement investment (R) is a constant proportion $[1/\{(1+n)^m - 1\}]$ of net investment and so is also growing at rate n.

Replacement investment in the current year t equals total investment m years previously, where m is the length of life of equipment. That total investment m years previously had two parts, net investment and replacement investment, and the latter part was equal to total investment *another* m years before that. To summarise, replacement investment in the current year t can be expressed:

---

[11] It is assumed throughout that the efficiency of equipment is constant during the whole of its productive life. Since maintenance is a normal activity and maintenance typically depends on the intensity of usage of equipment, this simple assumption seems realistic for most situations.

replacement$_t$ = net investment$_{t-m}$ + replacement$_{t-m}$

but :

replacement$_{t-m}$ = net investment$_{t-2m}$ + replacement$_{t-2m}$

So, if the capital stock has been growing steadily over a very long period of time, we can continue the reasoning to read:

$$R_t = I^*_{t-m} + I^*_{t-2m} + I^*_{t-3m} + \ldots + I^*_{t-km} + R_{t-km}$$

over periods 1, 2, 3, ... k, so that if the constant k is indefinitely large (say dating back to Domesday), then R_{t-km} approximates to zero and the rest of the expression can be treated as an infinite sum. Since net investment has been growing at rate n, so that:

$$I^*_t = I^*_{t-m}(1+n)^m \text{ and } I^*_{t-m} = I^*_{t-2m}(1+n)^m$$

we can simplify:

$$R_t = \frac{I^*_t}{(1+n)^m} + \frac{I^*_t}{(1+n)^{2m}} + \frac{I^*_t}{(1+n)^{3m}} + \ldots \text{ to infinity}$$

i.e.:

$$R_t = \frac{I^*_t}{(1+n)^m - 1}$$

Thus replacement investment is a constant proportion of net investment and so is also growing at rate n.[12]

It also follows that total current investment (I_t), which equals net investment plus replacement, can be expressed:

$$I_t = n.K_t + \frac{n.K_t}{(1+n)^m - 1}$$

i.e.:

$$I_t = \frac{n}{1 - \dfrac{1}{(1+n)^m}} . K_t$$

---

[12] So annual gross investment is growing at rate n also. Hence current replacement investment, which equals total investment m years ago (I_{t-m}):

$$R_t = I_{t-m}$$

$$= \frac{I_t}{(1+n)^m}$$

This enables us to express replacement as a proportion of total investment. (It could also be used to derive the result in the next paragraph.)

and since $K_t = bY_t$, the result is that total investment expressed as a proportion of national product Y is:

$$\frac{I_t}{Y_t} = \left[\cdot \frac{b}{1 - \dfrac{1}{(1+n)^m}} \right] \cdot n$$

in which b' may be written to stand for the expression in square brackets.

Example: For $n = 2$ per cent, $m = 25$ years, $b = 4$, total annual investment is 20.49 per cent of the national product.

From the above reasoning we conclude that if the capital stock has been growing for a long time at a constant rate n, then both net investment and replacement investment are constant proportions of the capital stock and of the national product. What happens if the rate of growth of the capital stock changes, assuming as before that the capital/output ratio is constant?

If (n) the rate of growth of capital stock is now doubled (from say 2 per cent to 4 per cent), then net investment and so the net savings-income ratio[13] must be doubled, as indicated by the original relation presented in section 2:

net savings-income ratio $= b.n$

Replacement investment does not have to rise until m years after the date on which the capital growth rate is doubled. Throughout that period national production has also risen at the higher growth rate. Because of this time-lag of m years, *replacement investment* (though it rises absolutely) *declines as a proportion of the national income.* Thus, in the long run, raising the target growth rate of capital and production from 2 per cent to 4 per cent requires the net savings ratio to double but the total or gross savings-income ratio rises by only about one-quarter as calculated in figure 2.3 (e.g. in the second column, a rise from 0.2049 to 0.2563).

---

[13] Net savings are defined in section 3 above as savings that make resources available for *adding* to the capital stock. Net savings, *plus* savings that make resources available to *replace* old capital equipment, sum to total (or gross) savings.

FIGURE 2.3 THE SAVINGS-INCOME RATIO

The level of the total savings-income ratio (s) where the capital/output ratio (b) equals 4, for designated levels of the annual growth rate (n) of capital stock and the length of life of equipment (m) in years.

Annual growth rate (n) of capital stock	Life of equipment in years (m)			
	20	25	30	35
0.01	0.2222	0.1824	0.1556	0.1366
0.02	0.2447	0.2049	0.1786	0.1600
0.03	0.2694	0.2302	0.2044	0.1865
0.04	0.2947	0.2563	0.2315	0.2145

Example: At an equipment life of 25 years and an annual growth rate of capital stock of 2 per cent (i.e. 0.02), the ratio of savings to income is 0.2049 to 1. This is expressed either by saying that the savings-income ratio is 0.2049 or that savings are 20.49 per cent of income.

This 0.2049 has two components. The first component is savings made to permit addition to the stock of capital equipment, and this is calculated by multiplying the growth rate $n = 0.02$ by the capital/output ratio (which is 4 for the whole table) to obtain the net savings-income ratio of 0.08. The second component is savings to permit replacement investment, which by subtraction is $0.2049 - 0.08 = 0.1249$.

If the rate of growth of capital stock were subsequently halved to the original level (2 per cent), then the sequence of events is reversed. That is, the net savings-income ratio halves immediately, but after a lag of m years the ratio of replacement investment to national income converges on the original value (corresponding to a total savings-income ratio of 20.49 per cent in the example).

Summary

An annual work force growth of 2 per cent would require an annual 2 per cent increase in the stock of capital equipment in order to maintain constant living standards under constant scale returns. If the capital/output ratio is 4, this means that net savings must be 8 per cent of national product. If equipment has a 25 year life, replacement investment equal to 12.49 per cent of national product is also required. Hence total savings required are 20.49 per cent of national product. (See figure 2.3).

If the annual growth rate of national product were doubled to 4 per cent, then net savings must double from 8 per cent to 16 per cent of national product. But replacement requirements fall from 12.49 per cent to 9.63 per cent of national product, for, by the time replacement is to be made, the national product has grown. Hence total savings needed rise from 20.49 per cent to 25.63 per cent of national product as shown in figure 2.3.

Throughout the above analysis of replacement investment there has been no mention of *financial provision for depreciation.* It is to be be noted that, in a growing economy, financial provision for depreciation is *not* a measure of replacement investment because depreciation reserves are built up now for replacement that will only be required in future years. For since total investment is rising, this year's replacement of a volume of plant I_{t-m} built m years ago is necessarily less than this year's provision for depreciation, which (on straight line depreciation) is

$$\frac{1}{m}(I_{t-m} + I_{t-m+1} + \ldots + I_{t-1})$$

one mth part of the growing stream of equipment built over the past m years. Thus any practical estimate of replacement investment should be based not on depreciation provision but on the relation already derived: that *replacement, as a proportion of gross investment, is* $1/(1+n)^m$, assuming total investment has been rising steadily at an annual rate n for a period equal to the m-year life of equipment.[14]

5. Capital accumulation to raise long-term living standards

Living standards may be raised (or prevented from falling) by:
— foreign aid
— emigration
— income redistribution
— improved technical knowledge
— a rise in the savings-income ratio

This last is discussed here. It is envisaged that a rise in savings in the current year enables resources to be transferred from producing consumer goods to producing equipment—and that this increase in the equipment stock results in an annual rise in production henceforth.

Consider then the aim of pursuing ever higher living standards in a situation in which technical knowledge is constant. We start from an initial situation in which savings are sufficient to raise the stock of capital equipment at the same rate as the work force. Since we assume constant scale returns, it follows that national production also grows at this same rate, and so living standards are constant.

Example: If the life of equipment is 25 years and the capital/output ratio is 4, then the savings-income ratio (s) required to

[14] Refer footnote 12 in this chapter.

maintain an annual growth rate of production (n) of 2 per cent is specified by

$$s = b'.n$$

where, using the expression on page 28, we calculate $s = 0.2049$ as in figure 2.3. If the annual growth rate of work force (w) is also growing at 2 per cent per annum, it follows that this savings-income ratio of 0.2049 ensures that production per worker (i.e. 'living standards') is maintained constant.

Now suppose that the target figure for the annual growth rate of production (n) is raised from a level equal to the work force growth rate (w) to some higher figure ($w + p$). Then the savings-income ratio must be raised to achieve this target.

Example continued: With the annual growth rate of work force (w) constant at 2 per cent per annum, suppose that the target annual growth rate of production (n) is raised to 3 per cent. This is equivalent to saying that production per worker is to rise by 1 per cent annually (i.e. $p = 0.01$). It is plain from figure 2.3 that to achieve this rise in the annual growth rate of production (n), the savings-income ratio will have to rise from 0.2049 to 0.2302. (The net savings-income ratio rises immediately, but savings required for replacement rise only after 25 years.)

The logic underlying such a rise in the savings-income ratio is as follows. We begin in an initial situation where savings are just high enough to increase the stock of capital equipment at the same annual rate as the increase in the work force—in other words the annual increment in the work force is being equipped at the traditional equipment/labour ratio. If now the community will cut the proportion of the national income that it devotes to spending on consumption goods—*i.e. the community raises the savings-income ratio*—then resources can be transferred from producing consumer goods to producing equipment. The use of this extra equipment means that the amount of equipment per worker is increased and so production per worker rises. Since the new lower consumption-income ratio or average propensity to consume is sustained, a rise in the

the consumption-income ratio or average propensity to consume	= =	unity − the savings-income ratio $1 - s$

equipment/labour ratio occurs in each successive year. It follows that the annual growth rate of production (n) is sustained at a figure higher than the work force growth rate (w).

The heart of the matter is illustrated in figure 2.4, where for simplicity the need to carry out replacement investment is ignored. There it is seen that the pursuit of the aim of raising the annual growth rate of production by raising the savings-income ratio clearly requires a fall in immediate living standards because the proportion of the national income that is consumed falls. But that cut-back in the average propensity to consume makes possible a transfer of resources to producing equipment, so that equipment per worker rises, and so the growth rate of national production and national

FIGURE 2.4 THE PURSUIT OF EVER HIGHER LIVING STANDARDS. POPULATION GROWTH 3 PER CENT PER ANNUM.

A rise in the net savings-income ratio from 12 per cent to 18 per cent results in an initial fall in consumption. However, assuming the capital/output ratio is constant at 4, the annual growth rate of national income rises from 3 per cent to 4½ per cent. Hence, after the sixth year, consumption is higher than under the old savings-income ratio.

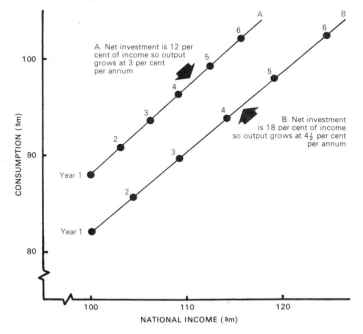

Notes: Before the rise: position A   After the rise: position B

	A	B
Savings-income ratio	12%	18%
Capital/output ratio	4	4
Output growth rate	3% p.a.	4½% p.a.

Year	Output		Consumption	
	A	B	A	B
1	100	100	88.0	82.0
2	103	104.5	90.6	85.7
3	106.1	109.2	93.4	89.5
4	109.2	114.1	96.1	93.6
5	112.5	119.3	99.0	97.8
6	115.9	124.6	102.0	102.2

The difference between output and consumption measures investment.

In the diagram the slope of a line equals the average propensity to consume; the horizontal spacing between points shows the absolute annual growth of national production.

For a more detailed analysis refer I. Tinbergen, *Development planning* (London: World University Library, 1967) p. 83.

income is higher. In this example the figures used give the result that, after six years, total consumption is higher than would have been the case at the old lower savings-income ratio.

In applying the above argument to the world around us, we should treat two matters with caution. The first is that if a large part of the nation is already living at subsistence level, then the casual phrase 'raise the savings-income ratio' may in fact imply intolerable suffering and deprivation—which could cause social and political upheaval. The second matter is to evaluate the relevance of our assumption that the capital/output ratio remains constant (for example $b=4$). For if technical knowledge is indeed constant, then for every one per cent rise in the volume of equipment per worker we may find that production per worker rises by something less than 1 per cent, with the result that the capital/output ratio rises. If that did occur, it is plain that ultimately a point would be reached at which the annual growth rate of production would fall back to equal the annual growth rate of the work force.

Example: In figure 2.4, the rise in the savings-income ratio to 18 per cent enables the output growth rate to be raised to 4½ per cent, only so long as the capital/output ratio is 4. If over a long period the capital/output ratio drifted up to 6, then from then onwards the output growth rate would be back at the old figure of 3 per cent, which is the same as the population growth rate.

However, we may end on an optimistic note by pointing out that in reality technical knowledge does change, and it could be that the nature of changing technical knowledge (as well as some opportunities for increasing scale returns) might be such as to reproduce through time the effect of constant marginal returns to equipment, and thus maintain the capital/output ratio constant.

Summary

Many governments aim at a *permanent transition* state, i.e. at raising production per head indefinitely. Arithmetically this requires a total savings-income ratio (s) equal to the modified capital/output ratio (b') times the target growth rate of national product (n)—which by assumption is
$$s = b'.n = b'(w + p)$$
greater than the work force growth rate (w) by some positive figure (p).

The two natural queries about such a policy are: what sacrifice is involved in the higher level of the savings-income ratio? and, is the capital/output ratio likely in fact to remain constant?

6. The economic system ⊟

The demands made by population growth on a nation's potential production can be summarised by setting down the demand block of our three-block model, in which all resources are employed; the

$$C = (1 - s)X, \quad \text{Consumption}$$
$$I = b.\Delta X, \quad \text{Investment}$$
$$X = C + I \text{ in equilibrium}$$

average propensity to consume is constant and investment needs are determined by the growth of national product. This has the solution:

$$n \equiv \frac{\Delta X}{X} = \frac{s}{b}$$

specifying the feasible growth rate of production (n). (It has been shown that this can be expanded to include replacement investment, i.e. by replacing b by b'.) Clearly if the population and work force growth rate w is greater than s/b, living standards will fall if there is no remedial action.

In order to show that the discussion can be extended to a more realistic representation of the economy that explicitly distinguishes the industries producing consumption goods and investment goods, we can rewrite the demand block of equations as follows, here measuring all outputs in quantities purchasable for $1m in the base year.[15]

$$C = (1-s)X$$ Consumer demand

$$I = b_c.\Delta X_c + b_i.\Delta X_i$$ investment demand

$$X_c = C \text{ in equilibrium}$$
$$X_i = I \text{ in equilibrium}$$ } commodity market equilibrium

$$X \equiv X_c + X_i$$ definition

Legend: C consumption demand
I investment demand
X_c output of consumer goods
X_i output of investment goods
X national product (or income)
s, b_i, b_c constants

From this set of relations we deduce:

$$X = (1-s)X + b_c\Delta X_c + b_i.\Delta X_i$$
$$= (1-s)X + b_c(1-s)\Delta X + b_i.s.\Delta X$$

hence: $n \equiv \dfrac{\Delta X}{X} = \dfrac{s}{b_c(1-s)+b_i.s}$

(which equals s/b if $b_c = b_i = b$). The conclusion is that the attainable growth rate of national production equals the savings–income ratio divided by the weighted capital/output ratio. These weights are the relative sizes of the two industries.[16] This result can be manipulated to show the level of s required by a target growth rate of production n:[17]

[15] The last equation of the block states that the national product is the sum of individual industries' products entering final demand.

[16] Note that this simple weighting can only be used because all industries are growing at the same rate.

[17] This analysis can be extended to more industrial sectors and also to two or more consuming sectors to allow income distribution to affect the national savings–income ratio.

$$s = n . \frac{b_c}{1 - n(b_i - b_c)}$$
$$= n . b$$
if $b = b_i = b_c$

This relationship enables us to explore the implications of the fact that the investment-goods industry not only has to produce equipment to expand the capacity of the consumer-goods industry but also to expand its own capacity. For while farms need tractors, tractor factories need foundries and machine shops. Moreover it is common for the capital/output ratio—i.e. the ratio of the value of capital stock to value produced in the industry—to be relatively high in the equipment industry itself.

Suppose for example that the capital/output ratio is 7 in the equipment industry—and only 3.25 in the consumer-goods industry. What net savings-income ratio is needed to achieve a 5 per cent annual growth rate of production? The answer is a savings ratio of 20 per cent, whereas if the equipment

Calculation

$$s = 0.05 \left(\frac{3.25}{1 - 0.05(b_i - 3.25)} \right)$$
If $b_i = 7$, then $s = 0.2$
however:
if $b_i = 0$, then $s = 0.14$

industry did not need to produce any equipment to expand its own productive capacity, then the savings-income ratio required would only be 14 per cent.

7. The rate of return on investment

The concept of the rate of return on investment has only been briefly mentioned. This concept is now considered in relation to the material in this chapter.

The calculation of the rate of return on an investment project is based on the assumption of the annual reinvestment of proceeds as follows: We have the sum of $2,580 to invest in a project expected to yield $1,000 at the end of each year for three years, after which the equipment will be worn out. The present value of the $1,000 at the end of the first year is $1,000 (1+r), where r is the unknown rate of return, which is another way of saying that to invest $1,000/(1+r) at the start of the year will yield $1,000 at the end of the year. The present value of the $1,000 at the end of the second year is $1,000/(1+r)^2; the argument being that the investment of $1,000/(1+r)^2 at the start of the first year yields $1,000/(1+r) at the end of the first year and the reinvestment of this yields $1,000 at the end of the second year. Thus the rate of return r is the rate of discount r which,

$$2,580 = \frac{1000}{(1+r)} + \frac{1000}{(1+r)^2} + \frac{1000}{(1+r)^3}$$

when applied to the series of prospective yields,[18] equates the sum of their present values to the cost of the project. In this example the rate of return is 8 per cent per annum approximately.

Now, if in a fully employed economy the national level of planned investment is less than planned savings, then it seems natural (paralleling a fall in land-rent when land is in surplus) to suggest that, by dropping the level of the rate of interest, investment projects with lower rates of return would be stimulated. Note that this line of reasoning implies that the rate of interest has two functions:

(a) to control the national total of investment so as to equate it to savings at full employment;

(b) to sieve individual investment projects, screening out those whose rate of return is too low.

However, the historical record shows that in many capitalist countries the rate of interest has not performed the first of these functions successfully. Various reasons have been given for this. But one basic reason seems to be that if the rate of interest changes slowly, then its effects may be swamped by change in the national income. Thus if the effect of planned investment being less than planned savings is for employment and national production to fall, these changes can engender expectations of further falls in production— which is not a climate in which businessmen readily expand planned

[18] These prospective yields are total sales receipts less operating costs. That is, the prospective yield includes depreciation provision but excludes wages and materials used in the factory; e.g. in a brewery project one would subtract the cost of sugar, malt, hops and labour in the brewery.

CALCULATING THE RATE OF RETURN ON AN INVESTMENT PROJECT

Imagine that you can buy or build a piece of equipment today at a cost of $3,000. The equipment has an expected life of 3 years. After paying for all operating costs (including cost of labour to tend the machine and cost of materials processed by the machine) it is expected to yield:

$1,100 at the end of the first year
$1,210 at the end of the second year
$1,331 at the end of the third year

after which its scrap value is nil.

These figures imply an annual rate of return of 10 per cent. This rate of return is also called the *marginal efficiency of capital* invested in this project. This rate of return, or marginal efficiency, is the discount rate that equates the sum of the present values of the annual prospective yields (1,100; 1,210; 1,331) to the cost (3,000) of the equipment.

Calculation

$$3000 = \frac{1,100}{(1+10\%)} + \frac{1,210}{(1+10\%)^2} + \frac{1,331}{(1+10\%)^3}$$
$$= 1,000 + 1,000 + 1,000$$

One can imagine carrying out this calculation for every proposed investment project and charting the result for the nation in the form of this 'schedule of the marginal efficiency of capital', showing the volume of investment that will

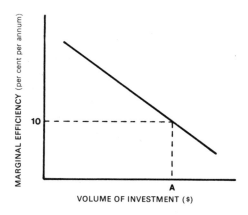

yield a rate of return at least equal to any chosen figure (such as 10 per cent per annum). This is a short-term 'investment demand schedule' inasmuch as it shows how firms' demand to carry out investment will contract as the required rate of return rises.

investment. All of this suggests the need for government intervention (as discussed in the next chapters) to manipulate the nation's total level of savings and/or of investment.

Businessmen naturally try to estimate the expected rate of return of alternative investment projects. In recent decades governments have increasingly been moved to copy this practice because of the large volume of resources involved in government-sponsored projects for irrigation and water storage, electric power, virgin lands, or transportation systems. If the choice is between expanding cotton production in either Eastern or North-Western Brazil and government public investment in irrigation is required, then a rational approach from the national viewpoint is to calculate the rate of return on the *total* (public and private) investment to be made on the alternative projects.

Summary

§1. Transferring $13\frac{1}{3}$ men for one year from farming to land reclamation results in a drop in farm output this year of 1.25 tons, but the acre of land reclaimed will yield 0.125 tons annually for ever. This is a 10 per cent annual rate of return.

If the land has a life of only 25 years, the annual rate of return falls to 8 per cent. If the $13\frac{1}{3}$ men are kept at reclaiming land, then they will finally produce 25 acres; farm production, which initially fell by 1.25 tons, will ultimately rise 1.875 tons (net) provided reclamation is continued. (The calculation assumes constant marginal productivity of land over the range.)

The process of capital accumulation (including land reclamation) produces resources:

   (a) to equip the growth in the work force (§2)
   (b) for replacement of old equipment   (§4)
   (c) to increase equipment per worker   (§5)

§2. If the savings-income ratio is 10 per cent and the capital/output ratio is 4, then only sufficient capital equipment can be produced for a $2\frac{1}{2}$ per cent annual growth rate of national production.

§3. So, if the work force growth rate equals $2\frac{1}{2}$ per cent, living standards can be maintained; whereas if the work force is growing more rapidly, living standards are in danger of falling.

If the work force is growing more slowly, the opportunity exists to increase equipment per worker and so living standards—but failure to take this opportunity can result in unemployment due to inadequate demand.

§4. If equipment has a life of 25 years, replacement investment must be added to previous calculations. Thus if the target growth rate of production is only 2 per cent annually, and the capital/output ratio is 4, then the total savings-income ratio required is 20 per cent, of which more than half is for replacement.

§5. A typical policy aim is a target growth rate of national production of 4 per cent, i.e. a permanent 2 per cent rise in income per worker—since the work force is already rising at 2 per cent. In order for this objective to be attained there must be an increase in the total savings-income ratio as illustrated in figure 2.3. But there is the difficulty that, as the amount of equipment per worker is increased, the productivity of capital equipment falls. So the capital/output ratio may rise, unless this is prevented by better technical knowledge.

§6. A model of the economic system both summarises the analysis and enables the consumer-goods and equipment industries to be distinguished. Thus if the capital/output ratio is 7 in the equipment industry and only 3.25 in consumer industry, then the net savings-income ratio needed to achieve a 5 per cent annual growth rate of production can be calculated (viz. 20 per cent).

§7. The rate of return on investment is analysed.

Further reading

J. Bhagwati, *The Economics of Underdeveloped Countries* (London: World University Library, 1966), ch. 11.

J. Tinbergen, *Development Planning* (London: World University Library, 1967), ch. 6.

W. A. Eltis, *Economic Growth* (London: Hutchinson, 1966), ch. 8.

J. Tobin, *National Economic Policy* (New Haven, Conn.: Yale University Press, 1966), ch. 9.

H. Myint, *Economics of the Developing Countries* (London: Hutchinson University Library, 1967).

R. T. Gill, *Economic Development: Past and Present* (Englewood Cliffs, N.J.: Prentice Hall, 1969).

Questions

1. What are the motives to capital accumulation?
2. Explain the meaning of 'capital/output ratio'.
3. Explain how it is possible to raise living standards by capital accumulation.
4. Does provision for depreciation measure current replacement?
5. 'Given a constant capital/output ratio, a fall in the rate of growth of consumer demand from 5 per cent to 3 per cent implies an absolute fall in investment'. Explain.

11. In Pindina the net savings-income ratio is 6 per cent. The capital/output ratio is 2, and population is growing at 4 per cent annually. Comment. (Assume constant scale returns and no technical change.)
12. In the previous question now suppose that the net savings-income ratio is not 6 per cent but 10 per cent. Comment.
13. Explain in figure 2.3 why, in the last column, the proportion does not double from row 0.02 to row 0.04.
14. Comment on the significance and validity of the assumption that average output per worker rises at the same rate as the amount of capital equipment per worker rises.
15. A farmer plans to buy a harvester, which he expects will raise his gross profit by $500 annually for two years, after which it will be worn out. Since he will have to buy with money borrowed at an interest rate of 10 per cent, how much would he be prepared to pay?
16. The national capital stock (excluding land) is valued at an undepreciated value of $400m. The annual national product is $100m; labour employment is 15,000 persons, annual wage per person is $3,000, total wage bill $45m; land-rents are $15m; the remaining $40m of national income is imputed as an annual gross return to capital. Assume equipment has constant efficiency through its 25 years life. Summarise the situation with respect to the return on capital.

21. Consider the political and social implications of a poor nation seeking to raise its long-term living standards by a rise in the savings-income ratio.

22. Explain the role of savings in the economy. Is it true that un-employment of labour can result if savings are either too high or too low?

23. 'A poor nation with a high population growth rate is in a dual difficulty: because it is poor its savings-income ratio is low, but because of the high population growth rate it needs a high savings-income ratio'. Discuss and illustrate the relation between the savings-income ratio and population growth.

24. (a) Explain how, for any investment project for which there is a confidently known life, annual prospective yield and initial cost, one can calculate a 'rate of return over cost' (also called the 'marginal efficiency of capital').

   (b) Imagine that *every* potential investment project for the coming year was subjected to such a calculation and 'tagged' with its rate of return over cost. If such information were sorted and graphed cumulatively, what would the resulting schedule look like? Does this suggest a role for the interest rate?

25. Is there an optimum size to a nation's population?

26. Consider possible different interpretations of the policy aim: 'Maximise living standards'.

Aggregate Demand

Part of the work force may be unemployed owing to deficiency of demand for goods. Government action, however, can raise aggregate demand and move the economy towards full employment.

1. Introduction

One of the perhaps unexpected features of a modern economy is that aggregate final demand may fluctuate independently and so cause either inflation or recession. Moreover, as we shall see, such fluctuations are self re-enforcing. Consequently once a nation has made long-term decisions affecting population growth and capital accumulation as discussed in the previous chapter, it is a task for short-term government economic management to control the level of aggregate demand whenever demand fluctuations tend to cause the economy to diverge from the long-run growth path.

If total demand tends to *exceed* potential production, then the pressure of demand may threaten to squeeze some categories of demand which are government targets: for example maintaining the investment programme, maintaining consumption standards of low income groups, or military preparedness. If the allocation of supplies is to conform with government policy aims, then the government may need to restrict some categories of demand.

On the other hand demand may be *insufficient* to clear the market of current production when the work force is fully employed, in which case there will be mass unemployment. The required government action will then be to boost demand.

The plan of this chapter is as follows:

§2. examines the influences causing fluctuations in investment;

§3. analyses the multiplier effect of such fluctuations;

§4. introduces the concept of personal disposable income to give greater realism to the discussion;

§5. analyses how the government can control the level of final demand;

§6. shows how the discussion can be extended when there is foreign trade;

§7. discusses more fully the influences affecting the level of consumer demand, and shows that fluctuations in consumer demand, like fluctuations in investment demand, can set in train a multiplier mechanism affecting the national income;

§8. then extends the analysis from a discussion of equilibrium situations to the time-path of national income.

It is to be noted that, throughout the following discussion, all concepts of consumption, investment, saving, spending and production are to be interpreted as amounts per year or per calendar quarter. For example a reference to the level of consumer spending refers to total consumption spending in a year.

2. Investment demand

The nation's requirements for capital goods for long-term growth have been explored in the previous chapter. However, the actual level of investment in capital equipment that business firms seek to undertake (i.e. 'investment demand') in any year is subject to a variety of influences. The level of investment demand is affected by:

(a) *Long-term influences* such as population growth, replacement requirements, and innovation. *Innovation* is applied here to encompass any investment to satisfy markets emerging from changing situations, whether the change is a new commodity (colour television), a new industrial process, or a change in consumer tastes.

(b) *Short-term influences* that cause long-term investment plans to be delayed or brought forward. Three examples are:

(i) *The internal financial liquidity of a firm.* Some firms may follow a self-imposed policy of financing a large part of all investment from accumulated internal reserves (i.e. undistributed profits). Thus during a business recession accumulated profits tend to be low and so investment falls off—even if other sources of finance are available.

(ii) *Short-term profit expectations.* Some firms may time their investment to fit an expected boom in sales in order to write off plant as quickly as possible.

(iii) *Surplus capacity* or 'investment over-run'. Investment has typically to be planned ahead of market demand. However, it would be surprising if market demand always grew at precisely the expected rate. Thus if market demand for a firm's product has grown *less than expected* over the past few years, this implies some surplus capacity, which will depress investment in the immediate future below the level it would otherwise have been. This can be summarised by saying that at any time planned investment depends not only on expected market growth, but also on the excess of actual capacity (i.e. capital stock) over needed capacity. Thus investment may fall or rise merely because of inability to forecast perfectly the growth of the market.

The actual level of investment demand that is ultimately realised depends also on the supply of resources for investment. In other words the realised investment demand depends on the mechanism that equates the demand to the supply. *This rationing mechanism may take the form of varying the level of the interest rate.* For example the Japanese banking system has tended to change the ruling interest rate by a substantial amount whenever the demand for investible resources has been greater or less than the supply. Alternatively the rationing mechanism may take the form of some allocation of credit by the banks or by a central planning agency without altering the interest rate. Australia illustrates an in-between case since, when the demand for investible resources exceeds the supply, the banks tend to ration credit at relatively stable interest rates.

In summary, the level of investment depends on a number of variables listed above, ranging from population growth to the rate of interest. Moreover, by its very nature it may fluctuate as the creation of new plant capacity runs ahead (or falls short) of the growth of market sales of consumer goods.

Faced with this variety of influences on investment, economists have occasionally attempted to present a simple 'theory of investment'. Two examples are now given to illustrate such simplification.

A simple theory of investment is that the current year's net investment (i.e. ΔK, the rise in the capital equipment stock during the year) equals b times the rise in this year's national product over last year (ΔX), i.e.:

net investment, $\Delta K = b.\Delta X$

where b is the nation's capital/output ratio. The reasoning behind this proposition is that if $b = 3$, and if the national product rises by $1m this year, then extra capital equipment valued at $3m must be constructed to provide the needed additional productive capacity. This is known as the 'naive accelerator theory' because for historical reasons the capital/output coefficient b is known as the *accelerator coefficient*.[1] However, the theory is unsatisfactory because it:

— ignores surplus capacity;
— fails to recognise that much investment is undertaken in *anticipation* of a rise in demand (not after consumer demand and production have risen);
— assumes that the capital/output ratio is unvarying;
— fails to recognise other influences on investment that are in fact found to be important.

Another simple theory of investment proposes that in the short run all influences on the level of investment other than the rate of interest can be regarded as constant; i.e. in the short run:

Investment = $h-k$ (interest rate)

where h, k, are constants.

There is no reason why this relation has to be a straight line, but such a relation is illustrated in figure 3.1. This short-run investment demand schedule is also known as the *schedule of the marginal efficiency of capital*—for the reason that, for any level of the interest rate set by the monetary authorities, one can read off the volume of investment comprising all those investment projects yielding a marginal efficiency (or rate of return) at least equal to that interest rate. However, such an investment-demand schedule *does* assume that all other influences on investment are constant and unchanging in the short

[1] The origin of this phrase is as follows: Imagine the cargo-carrying industry uses 100 ships, each of 20 year life, so that on average 5 ships are replaced each year. Then, if the volume of cargo carried is constant, the shipbuilding industry will build 5 ships annually. Now suppose that consumer demand, and so cargo carried, rises 5 per cent annually. This means that ship production must *double* from 5 to 10 ships (i.e. 5 replacement, 5 new). But cargo carried is only rising 5 per cent annually, so ship production (investment) has accelerated.

Observe too that if consumer demand next year grows only at 3 per cent (instead of this year 5 per cent) then ship production will fall *absolutely* from 10 to 8 ships (i.e. 5 replacement, 3 new). This absolute fall in investment resulting from a slow-down of the rate of growth of consumer demand was the basis for early accelerator theories of business cycles.

run. It will be argued in the next chapter that this may very likely not be a valid assumption.

FIGURE 3·1   A SHORT-RUN INVESTMENT DEMAND SCHEDULE

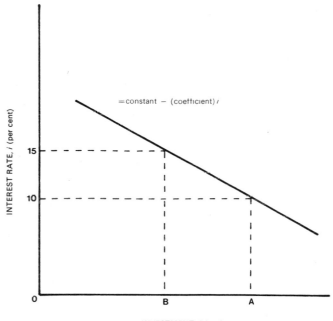

INVESTMENT, *I* (yen)

Source: Klein and Shinkai, 'An Econometric Model of Japan 1930-59' in *International Economic Review* (January 1963).

In their econometric model of Japan the authors set out the relationship:

$$I = 0.051 \, K + 0.478 \, V - 0.678 \, i.K$$

I net investment
K year-end capital stock
V non-wage income

} billions of 1934–6 yen

i interest rate

In the short run, in which *V* and *K* may be taken as known constants, this investment demand schedule becomes the straight line in the diagram.

It is apparent that if the monetary authorities raise the annual interest rate from say 10 per cent to 15 per cent, then investment will fall from *OA* to *OB*.

Summary

The level of investment in capital equipment during the year depends on:
(a) long-term influences: population growth, replacement, innovation;
(b) short-term influences: internal liquidity, profit expectations, surplus capacity;
(c) availability of investible resources, which may be rationed by the interest rate or by credit controls.
An examination of these influences suggests that the level of investment may fluctuate.

Having seen how the level of investment may be expected to fluctuate, we shall consider in the next section the effect of such a change in investment.

3. The national income multiplier

A fall in any category of demand—e.g. in demand for investment goods—will result in a fall in production of such goods and so a fall in the incomes of the workers producing them. This initial fall in national income will result in a fall in consumer spending by the disemployed workers, and so cause a further fall in production and employment in the consumer-goods industry. Thus the *initial* fall in investment demand results in a cumulative or *multiplied* fall in national income. This phenomenon is called the national income multiplier process. In order to analyse it, we must first point out that the major single influence on the level of consumer demand is the level of the national income; i.e. consumer spending rises and falls with a rise or fall in the national income.

One might simply assume that national consumer demand is a fixed proportion of the national income since this simple relation works fairly well for some nations. Here, however, we will initially make the less restrictive assumption that: *total consumer demand depends linearly upon national income*. Expanding this statement, we assume that: national real consumption C (i.e. consumption expenditure at constant prices) is a straight-line function of real national income X, for which the slope of the line is called the marginal propensity to consume. The *marginal propensity to consume* is the ratio $(\Delta C/\Delta X)$ of the increment in real national consumption (ΔC) to the increment in real national income (ΔX), and is 0.8 in figure 3.2.

It is common practice for governments to survey investment plans throughout the nation and to issue a forecast for the level of national

FIGURE 3·2   EQUILIBRIUM NATIONAL PRODUCT

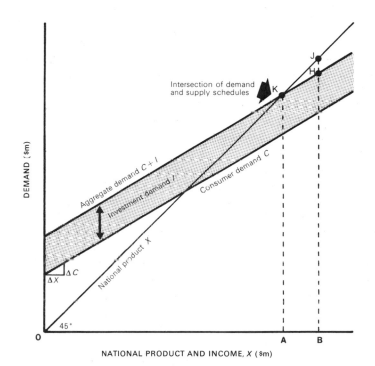

Intersection of demand and supply schedules

DEMAND ($m)

Aggregate demand C + I

Investment demand I

Consumer demand C

National product X

ΔC

ΔX

45°

O   A   B

NATIONAL PRODUCT AND INCOME, X ($m)

Notes: All magnitudes are in $m at constant prices.
       X National product, i.e. Supply.
      $C + I$ Aggregate demand schedule.
      I Investment demand = 50.
      C Consumer demand schedule = $100 + 0.8X$

Equilibrium production is at OA even though maximum national production may be OB. For at OB, national production exceeds aggregate demand by HJ, which is the annual rate at which unsold commodity stocks accumulate, and such a situation is not tenable for business enterprise. In order for an equilibrium at OB to be established, the aggregate demand schedule would have have to be raised to intersect the 45° line at J.

*

In this diagram, because the consumer-demand schedule does not pass through the origin, the average propensity to consume (total consumption divided by total income) is not equal to the marginal propensity to consume (the slope of the consumer demand schedule, $\Delta C / \Delta X$).

planned investment. It is seen from figure 3.2 that if this given level of investment is added vertically to the consumption-demand schedule (or consumption-income function), we obtain an *aggregate demand schedule*, showing the level of aggregate demand at all levels of the national income. The intersection of this aggregate demand schedule with a line drawn through the origin at 45° specifies the level of national product OA at which demand equals production. Thus OA is called the equilibrium level of national production. In summary, it is seen that equilibrium production can be calculated from a knowledge of the consumption demand schedule and the level of investment demand. Now consider what happens when demand changes.

The immediate effect of a sustained autonomous fall[2] in investment demand of $10m per quarter is a $10m fall in quarterly production of equipment, accompanied by unemployment of labour. The incomes of workers in the equipment industry will fall $10m per quarter. If their marginal propensity to consume ($\Delta C/\Delta X$) is 0.8, then consumer spending in the current quarter falls by $8m per quarter, and this results in an $8m rise in stocks of unsold consumer goods in that quarter. Businessmen in the following period will reduce production of consumer goods by $8m to match this lower demand; so they will disemploy a further batch of workers (from industries producing consumer goods) whose incomes were $8m. Since these workers have lost this income, consumer demand in this second period will fall by a further ($8m × 0.8=) $6.4m, so that we can expect a further fall in production of consumer goods in the next quarter equal to this fall in demand. It is seen then that the national income and *national product will fall progressively in successive periods* by amounts (in $m):

10, 8, 6.4 .. ,

so that the total fall in national income over a long run of periods will be:

$$10 (1 + 0.8 + 0.8^2 + 0.8^3 + \ldots \text{ to infinity})$$

which equals 10 times $\dfrac{1}{1-0.8}$ or $50m.

---

[2] The word 'sustained' means that investment falls (say from $50m to $40m) to a new lower level *and stays there*. The word 'autonomous' means that the fall in investment is due to some revision by businessmen of their investment needs, and is *not* due to some prior change in demand or in national income.

Summary

An autonomous sustained fall in investment demand will result in a *multiplied* fall in national income. The size of the multiplier is equal to

$$\text{National income multiplier} = \frac{1}{1 - \frac{\Delta C}{\Delta X}}$$

the reciprocal of unity minus the marginal propensity to consume $\Delta C/\Delta X$. The size of the national income multiplier is seen to be determined by the marginal propensity to consume because the latter determines the ratio of successive increments of income in the above sequence.

We now recapitulate, paying particular attention to the concept of equilibrium. Market equilibrium refers to a situation where aggregate demand equals aggregate production offered for sale. An economy might be at full employment and yet demand may be less than production. For example if we are at a full-employment equilibrium and planned investment demand then falls, this causes a multiplied fall in national income, i.e. a movement of the economy further away from the initial position. The economy may then settle down at an equilibrium level of production characterised by large scale unemployment (unless the government stimulates demand).

4. Personal disposable income

In the previous section it was supposed that total consumer expenditure was linearly dependent on the level of national income. The reality, however, is that consumer expenditure depends not on the level of national income but on the level of personal disposable income. *Personal disposable income* is defined as the amount of national income that households ultimately receive after a number of transfers of income have taken place. These transfers include: dividend payments (but not undistributed profits, which are held by corporations); and taxes (as well as cash social service payments, which are negative taxes).

To illustrate, imagine that 60 per cent of the national income is paid in wages, the remaining 40 per cent being surplus. Of this surplus, however, suppose that one-half is paid in dividends. Thus households receive an income equal to 80 per cent of the national income; but this is now subject to an income tax, which (after allowing for some gross tax revenues being paid back in social service payments) is a net tax of 20 per cent of householders' income receipts, so that income after deducting this income tax is $(80-16=)$ 64 per cent of national income. So far, then, households are left with a proportion $(1-q)$ of national income, where q (or $100-64=36$ per cent) accrues to corporations and to government. But we have not finished. For suppose that households' tastes are such that people choose to spend a proportion c of their income $(1-q)Y$ on consumer goods,[3] where this figure c has to cover not only the price of the goods at factor cost but also a sales tax levied at rate $i=15$ per cent. In other words national consumer expenditure at factor cost $(C.P)$ plus the sales tax $(i.C.P)$ is a proportion c (say $c=0.9$) of household income $(1-q)Y$; i.e.:[4]

> where C, X are the volume of consumption, national production
> P is the price level at factor cost (not including indirect tax)
> Y is the national income and equals $X.P$
So $X = Y/P$ measures real national income, i.e. at constant prices

$$C.P + i.C.P = c(1-q)Y = c(1-q)X.P$$

$$C = c\left[\frac{(1-q)}{(1+i)}.X\right]$$

The expression in square brackets is called 'personal disposable income' and may be written for brevity as $(1-t)X$, where t is the proportion of real national income transferred to governments and firms. So we can summarise:

$$C = \{c(1-t)\}X$$

where the whole of the expression in curled brackets describes the slope of the consumption-demand–national-income schedule, and is therefore also the marginal propensity to consume out of national income. In this example:

$$\{c(1-t)\} = c.\left(\frac{1-q}{1+i}\right) = 0.9\left(\frac{0.64}{1.15}\right) = 0.5$$

---

[3] Y is the national income and is defined equal to the national product $X.P$, where X is the volume of production and P is the price level at factor cost.

[4] The last step is illustrated if the sales tax is 50%: Then with a weekly income of $90 one can buy (before the sales tax is introduced) 90 loaves at $1 a loaf. But when the sales tax of 50% is introduced one can buy only 60 loaves at $1.50 a loaf. Hence real disposable income is $1/(1+i)$ of pre-tax income, where $i(=0.5)$ is the rate of sales tax on consumer goods.

This marginal propensity to consume out of national income determines the size of the national income multiplier because it determines the size of the ratio of successive income increments in the national income multiplier process. For a marginal propensity to consume out of national income of 0.5, the national income multiplier is 2. This arithmetic, although the figures used are imaginary, also shows how *a relatively low figure for the national income multiplier results from a substantial proportion of the national income being transferred to government and corporations.*

Summary

   A proportion t of the real national income accrues to government and business enterprise (as taxes and retained profits). Thus the proportion accruing to households is $(1-t)$. This is called personal disposable income.

   If households spend a constant proportion c of their personal disposable income on consumer goods, then the relation between the volume of total consumer spending (C) and the real national income (X) is:

   $$C = c(1-t)X$$

In this relation the expression $c(1-t)$ is the marginal propensity to consume out of national income, and it specifies the size of the real national income multiplier k as:

   $$k = \frac{1}{1-c(1-t)}$$

It will be convenient in the following discussion to refer to personal disposable income as a proportion $(1-t)$ of the real national income, since the method of ascertaining t has been set out in this section. In section 5 it will be assumed that consumers' tastes are such that the proportion of personal disposable income spent on consumption is constant at c, but that the ratio of personal disposable income to national income $(1-t)$ can be changed by government action. In section 7 we discuss the further possibility of a shift in the consumption–personal-disposable-income schedule resulting in a change in the proportion c of personal disposable income spent on consumption (see figure 3.3).

5. Fiscal measures to control aggregate demand

   The central government can control the level of aggregate demand by a variety of monetary and fiscal (i.e. budgetary) measures. Thus the level of aggregate investment spending can be raised:

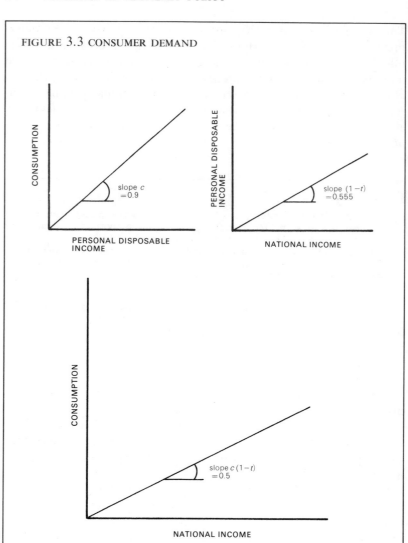

FIGURE 3.3 CONSUMER DEMAND

The first two diagrams yield the lower diagram showing the consumption-national-income schedule. It follows that this schedule can be shifted upwards by shifting either the first or second schedules upwards: e.g. exhorting people to save less—to raise c; or cutting income tax rates—to raise $(1-t)$.

—by increasing government spending on the public works programme, or by subsidising private investment projects (e.g. shipbuilding);
—by reducing overdraft interest rates trading banks charge;
—by reducing taxation rates on companies.

The Swedish government in particular has experimented with measures for controlling fluctuations in private investment spending.[5] Yet another approach, as already noted, is:
—to raise the immigration programme.

The purpose of this section is to examine fiscal measures for controlling aggregate final demand and so for preventing large scale unemployment due to a deficiency of demand. For this purpose we rearange the budget of a typical central government from the form:

GOVERNMENT BUDGET

Receipts		*Payments*	
Tax revenues	100	Expenditure on goods and services	
		Civil service salaries	25
		Bombs, milk, paperclips	45
		Social service cash payments	
		Pensions, welfare payments	30

into the form:

GOVERNMENT BUDGET

Receipts		*Payments*	
Taxes net of transfer payments	70	Expenditure on goods and services	70

on the grounds that the right hand side shows the absorption of real resources by the government, while the left hand side shows the net result of financial transfers *to* the government (taxes) and *from* the government (social service payments). (The figures used in the example are imaginary and do not have to balance.)

This rearrangement of the central government budget lays a foundation for drawing attention to the two basic ways in which the budget can be used to control aggregate final demand. *First, the government can reduce the net tax rate* (either by reducing the actual tax rate or by increasing social service payments). This increases personal dis-

[5] Refer A. Lindbeck, 'Theories and Problems in Swedish Economic Policy in the Postwar Period', *American Economic Review* (Supplement to June 1968), p. 1.

posable income and so raises consumer spending—which will then have an upwards multiplier effect on the national income. *Secondly, the government can increase its own spending on goods and services,* e.g. more spending on public works or on defence. This too will have an upwards multiplier effect.

Before exploring these two types of measures in numerical terms, we should point out that it is not necessary for the central govern- to balance its budget (i.e. equate net taxes to spending on goods and services). There are two senses in which balancing the budget is not necessary. First, it is not necessary as a policy aim—for a rational policy will be judged on the criterion of making the best use of physical resources. Second, it is not necessary as a matter of fact, because the government can borrow any funds it needs from the central bank (or from the public or the trading banks).

Suppose now that the government decides to eliminate some unemployment caused by inadequate demand. Now, private consumption spending by households is the largest single category of final demand. The volume of such spending can be controlled by varying the rate of tax levied on individuals' income or spending. Because of the prevalence of the pay-as-you-earn method of collecting income tax, it is especially simple to control consumer spending by varying rates of income tax. This can be illustrated as follows: If the average rate of taxation on all individuals collectively is $t = 25$ per cent, then out of a national income at constant prices (X), an amount (tX) is collected in tax revenue and only $(1-t)X$ accrues to the private sector as after-tax income. Suppose, now, that the nation spends a proportion $c = 90$ per cent of this after-tax income on consumer goods. Then this may be summarised by saying that total consumption spending at constant prices (C) is 67.5 per cent of real national income.

$$C = c(1-t)X$$

If $c = 0.9$ and $t = 0.25$, then:

$$C = 0.9(0.75)X$$
$$= 0.675X$$

where X is defined to equal the real national income (Y/P). If the government now reduces the tax rate from 25 per cent to 20 per cent, then total consumer spending rises to

$$C = 0.9(0.8)X$$
$$= 0.72X$$

72 per cent of national income. This can be represented graphically as an upward shift in the consumption-demand–national-income schedule.

Instead of cutting the rate of income tax, the government of course could decide to increase its quarterly rate of spending on the nation's public works (i.e. public investment). This would shift the aggregate demand schedule upwards by the amount of the quarterly rise in public works (in just the same way as would a rise in private investment spending).

In summary, the government can raise (or lower) the level of either investment or consumer demand, and both can be graphed as an upwards shift in the aggregate demand schedule in figure 3.2. Such an upward shift will set in train an income multiplier effect because the workers who are newly employed as the *immediate* result of the rise in demand will themselves now raise their consumer spending, and so this process will continue. The size of the multiplier effect is calculated from the expression:

$$\frac{1}{1 - m.p.c.}$$

where *m.p.c.* is the marginal propensity to consume out of national income.

The discussion can be illustrated by a simple example in which the existing level of annual national income of $1,000m could be raised by about one-sixth to absorb unemployed workers. Suppose the average income tax rate for the nation to be 25 per cent and that consumers spend 90 per cent of their after-tax income. The government then announces a cut in the tax rate to 20 per cent. The immediate effect of this is to raise consumer spending from $675m to $720m, i.e. a rise of $45m. We assume quite realistically that neither investment demand nor government spending on goods and services falls.[6] Thus the $45m is a net rise in annual spending. This will be subject to a national income multiplier, which is $1/(1 - 0.72)$, i.e. 3.57. Hence the national income will ultimately rise by $160.7m (= $45m × 3.57) to $1,160.7m (refer figure 3.4). Referring to figure 3.5, in summary it is

[6] The government can finance a budget deficit by central bank credit, and private firms commonly finance investment from trading bank advances and accumulated undistributed profits.

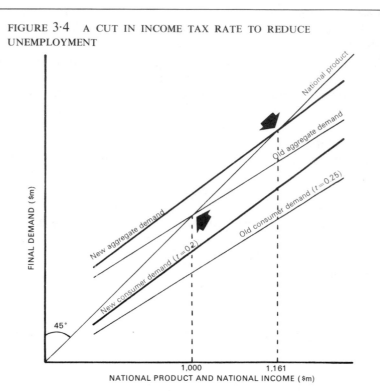

FIGURE 3·4   A CUT IN INCOME TAX RATE TO REDUCE
UNEMPLOYMENT

Notes: All values are at constant prices.
    ▶ indicates intersection of supply and demand schedules.
  Initially consumption spending is 67.5 per cent of real national income and
planned investment plus government spending on goods and services is $325m,
yielding an equilibrium national income of $1,000m. A cut in income tax rate
from 25 per cent to 20 per cent shifts the consumer-demand schedule upwards:
an initial upward shift equal to $45m at existing national income sets in train
a multiplier process raising national income to $1,160.7m.

seen that the $45m rise in consumer demand caused a *consequent*
rise in national income of $160.7m, of which 72 per cent was allocated
to consumption, i.e. a further rise in consumption of $115.7m. Thus
the final level of consumption is (675 + 45 + 115.7 =) $835.7m.
  Alternatively the government might leave the tax rate unchanged
at 25 per cent so that the basic figures are still $c = 0.9$ and $t = 0.25$;
in which case:

FIGURE 3.5 THE RISE IN NATIONAL PRODUCT

End-use of national product	Initial market equilibrium	Initiating rise in demand	Final market equilibrium
	$m	$m	$m
Consumption	675	+45	835.7
Investment	75		75
Government[a]	250		250
National Product	1,000		1,160.7

Note: a Government use of goods and services including labour of public servants, public works, armaments.

$$C = 0.9(0.75)X$$
$$= 0.675X$$

So the national income multiplier is:

$$k = \frac{1}{1 - 0.675}$$
$$= 3.077$$

In order to achieve a target rise in real national product of $160.7m, the government will need to raise its quarterly rate of public works spending by approximately $52.2m since this will be subject to an income multiplier of 3.077.

Since there are many fiscal, monetary and other measures by which the government may stimulate (or restrict) aggregate demand, it is worth emphasising that they all have the same basic logic, namely:

*the target rise
in national   =   the national
income
multiplier   ×   the sustained
initial rise
in demand*

If the first two items are specified then the third can be deduced. Thus in the above tax-rate cut example, to achieve a target rise in national income of $160.7m required a cut in tax revenues on budget day of $50m in order to cause a rise in consumer spending of (90 per cent of $50m=) $45m at that level of the national income; since the income multiplier was 3.57, the target was achieved ($45 × 3.57 = 160.7$). Using the alternative of a rise in public works required a rise of $52.2m of government spending on goods and services because the national income multiplier was lower at 3.077 (owing to the higher marginal rate of tax).

Summary

1. Since inadequate demand may cause unemployment, the government must have power to control the level of demand.
2. Such powers include the use of the government budget to control demand: either by cutting tax rates or by increasing government spending on goods and services. Such measures increase total demand and have a calculable multiplier effect on the national income.
3. A budget is simply a package of financial measures. The criterion of the success of those measures is a physical one; namely, whether the government has achieved its objectives with respect to high employment and living standards.

Once there is a recognition of the central government's ability to control the level of demand, attention focusses on the merits of the alternative methods of doing this—the main methods (in a non-trading economy) being:

— government spending on goods and services;
— tax rates;
— credit control.

The choice between the fiscal techniques of raising government spending on goods and services (e.g. public works, defence) and cutting tax rates must depend on their administrative efficiency (especially the time-lags before the measures take effect) and on the social priority attached to the alternative forms of resource use. Thus public works spending plans will not immediately employ people if land needs to be resumed or blueprints prepared, or if provincial governments have to be persuaded to spend the funds provided by the central government; likewise a cut in tax rates has no effect on spending so long as households simply increase their savings because of a fear of themselves becoming unemployed. Measures by the central bank to make bank loans more freely available and to reduce interest rates are a valuable adjunct to fiscal measures, but may initially fail to raise investment spending if businessmen expect unemployment to continue. A government may often seek to use all these fiscal and monetary measures since they complement one another.

Further comments on fiscal measures *

The following comments are intended to explore some further implications of the preceding discussion.

One corollary of the above analysis applies to a situation in which a fall in national investment causes a fall in both national income and in income tax revenues, so causing a budget deficit. In such a situation, appropriate action for the government is to cut tax rates (in order to stimulate demand for goods), not to increase tax rates (in an attempt to balance the budget).

A second point of note is that the government is a big enough economic organisation to affect its own income by its own spending. Thus a rise in public works has a multiplier effect on the national income, which increases the government's income tax revenues.

A third point sometimes asked is whether the government can follow a 'neutral' policy with respect to the level of demand. A ground for giving a negative answer to this general question is that the sheer existence of the taxation system affects the level of demand. Thus a rise in private investment has a multiplier effect, which is automatically modified by the existence of the income tax rate.

The previous question can be posed in a more specific form, however: does the fact that the budget is balanced imply that the government is pursuing a neutral fiscal policy with respect to demand? The answer to this is in the negative, as can be illustrated: Suppose that compared with last year, the government is raising public works $100m and raising tax revenues through tax-rate increases also by $100m. Now the latter reduces personal disposable income and so reduces consumer demand by say $80m, and reduces savings by $20m. So there has been a net rise in aggregate demand of $20m, i.e. a rise in investment of $100m less the fall in consumption of $80m. Thus the casual observation that the budget is balanced does not allow one to draw any conclusion as to whether the government is influencing the level of aggregate demand.

This last argument suggests that a government whose budget is initially balanced could eliminate growing unemployment, by both raising tax rates and increasing government spending on goods and services in a manner that raised total demand, and yet still leave the government budget in balance. Why has this possibility not been explored in more detail in the above discussion? There are

* These coments can be omitted on a first reading.

two answers to this. First it is basically irrational for a central government to aim at balancing its budget—an irrationality that is high-
lighted by the proposal to raise tax rates (even if public works are
to rise also) when there is unemployment due to inadequate demand.
Secondly, an examination of the arithmetic shows that a high increase
in tax rates would be required—so high that it would run into serious
disincentive problems. These answers explain why the 'balanced
budget' path to high employment has not been used in practice.

6. The open economy

The discussion of fiscal measures has been limited to a closed
economy, i.e. one not engaging in international trade. Although
a detailed analysis of trade is not undertaken until part III, it is easy
to show how the previous argument can be extended to an open or
trading economy in simple situations.

The significance of trade in this discussion is that exports are
an additional category of final demand and imports are an additional
source of supplies. Now, imports are likely to be a proportion m
of national product. While that proportion may vary, owing for
example to changes in the ratio of import prices to home prices,
it will be assumed here that the period under discussion is sufficiently
short to suppose that m is constant. It follows that, of total supplies
coming on the market, a proportion $m/(1+m)$ are imports and a
proportion $1/(1+m)$ are home production.

> *Example:* If imports are one-quarter of home production, then
> of each $1m of supplies, one-fifth are imports and four-fifths
> are home production.

The basic argument concerning the national income multiplier

$$\begin{matrix} \text{rise in} \\ \text{national} \\ \text{income} \end{matrix} \quad = \quad \begin{matrix} \text{sustained} \\ \text{initial rise} \\ \text{in demand} \end{matrix} \quad \times \quad \text{multiplier}$$

is now affected in two ways. First, when there is a sustained initial
rise in, for example, investment demand of say $100m, then part of
that is a 'leakage' into demand for imports, so that only the part
that is a demand for home production will have an income multiplier
effect at home. Second, a similar argument applies to the size of
the multiplier, which is determined by the size of the marginal pro-

pensity to consume *home-produced* goods out of national income—since it is only the demand for the produce of home labour that keeps the multiplier process going.

Example: Imports are one-quarter of home production—this applies to both consumer goods and investment goods. So four-fifths of both investment and consumer demand is satisfied by home production, one-fifth is satisfied by imports.

Given that the marginal propensity to consume out of national income is 0.75, it follows that the marginal propensity to consume home-produced goods is four-fifths of this, i.e. 0.6. Hence the national income multiplier is:

$$k = \frac{1}{1 - 0.6} = 2.5$$

Now suppose that there is a sustained autonomous rise in investment demand of $100m per quarter. Only $80m of this is a rise in demand for home-produced goods, the remaining $20m being regarded here simply as a 'leakage', i.e. part of income not spent on the produce of home factors of production.

Hence the ultimate rise in national income will be $(2.5 \times 80 =)$ $200m.

It will be apparent that the only novelty in this analysis is the need to ascertain *the home-produced content of each category of demand*. With this modification, the analysis is readily applicable to fiscal measures. For example in the example just worked out, the rise in investment demand of $100m could well have been a rise in public investment by the government.

7. Consumer demand

The relationship between households' expenditure on consumer goods on the one hand and households' disposable income on the other not only reflects the tastes of householders (i.e. their propensity to allocate income between consumption and savings) but also reflects a variety of objective factors. Changes in these objective factors can shift the consumption–disposable-income schedule, and it is therefore worth while listing some of the more important objective factors.

The level of consumer spending then not only depends on personal disposable income, but may also depend on:

(a) *income distribution;* e.g. a redistribution from wages to profits will cause the consumer demand schedule to shift down if the marginal propensity to spend of profit-receivers is lower than for wage-earners.
(b) *assets.* Some investigators have emphasised the potential importance of holdings of liquid assets (money, and perhaps also government securities) as influences on spending.
(c) *consumer credit.* If more finance is available for consumer credit, it seems probable that the consumption-income schedule will shift upwards, and conversely.

Moreover if households operate at a maximum acceptable ratio of repayments to income, it follows that the onset of a recession implies that the repayments/income ratio is above the acceptable level (since income has fallen). In order to get the ratio down to the acceptable level households must reduce their total debt by reducing new borrowings below repayments (unless the debt repayment period is lengthened). In effect this is 'negative credit' and the consumption-income schedule will shift downwards, thus worsening the recession.
(d) *stocks of durable commodities.* It is useful to distinguish consumption of motor vehicles, and other household durable goods, from the bulk of consumer spending. Some evidence has been found to support the hypothesis that the demand for durable consumer goods is inversely related to households' stocks of such goods.
(e) *interest rate.* In modern industrialised nations the interest rate seems to have little importance as a *direct* influence on decisions whether to spend on consumer goods. This may well be due to the fact that movements in the interest rate are small.

A rather different approach to the discussion of influences on the consumption–disposable-income schedule is *the distinction between the short-term schedule and long-term shifts in that schedule.* Thus it has been variously suggested that the short-term relationship between consumption spending and disposable income may be systematically shifted by:

(a) long-term changes in income distribution due to more progressive tax schedules, higher inheritance taxes and greater educational opportunity;

(b) innovation in the range of goods available (from the T model Ford to the colour television set), which induces households to spend today rather than save for tomorrow;

(c) an asymmetry in the response of households to falls in disposable income compared with rises in disposable income. The central idea here is that over the long run households may tend to raise consumer spending proportionately with disposable income, but that in the short run when a recession interrupts the long-run growth of living standards, then households are reluctant to squeeze their living standards and tend to squeeze current savings instead. This argument can be applied both to people who actually become unemployed and to those whose incomes merely fall. Thus in the aggregate, as figure 3.6 shows, we obtain a short-term consumption schedule (for each recession) as a spur off the long-term consumption schedule.

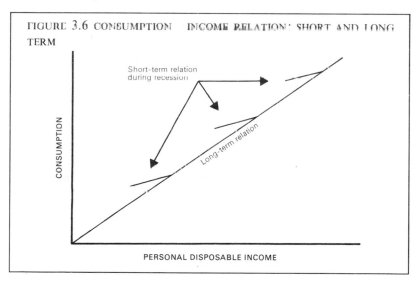

FIGURE 3.6 CONSUMPTION—INCOME RELATION: SHORT AND LONG TERM

Yet another approach to analysing the influences affecting the level of consumer spending is the hypothesis that, rather than actual current income, it may be households' concept of their 'normal income' (or 'permanent income') that determines their level of consumer spending. It is easy to see that this is a reasonable hypothesis to apply to income groups whose income is highly variable, for example farmers producing cash crops for export. In effect the hypothesis is that, in the face of fluctuating incomes, farmers 'smooth out' their spending in accord with some notion of normal disposable income. There is convincing statistical evidence of the usefulness of this hypothesis.[7]

Summary

A simple linear relationship between consumer spending and personal dispos-able income usually furnishes a good approximate explanation of short-run changes in consumption—especially if modified by the 'normal income' concept for fluctuating income groups such as farmers.

However, other influences on consumer spending are significant:

— income distribution
— consumer credit
— liquid asset holdings
— commodity stocks
— desire to maintain living standards

The recognition of such influences enables us to improve our explanation of changes in consumption. It is convenient to regard such influences as shifting the consumption–personal-disposable-income schedule by a measurable amount. The multiplier effect of such change on the national income can then be analysed.

There is no shortage of hypotheses concerning the influences on consumer spending. For example it has been suggested that if people save in their youth and dissave in their old age, then the proportion of the national income consumed will depend on the age distribution of the population. Hence if the population growth rate rises, there will be proportionately more young poeple over the next thirty years and so a fall in the nation's average propensity to consume will result. Our only way of discriminating between these and other hypotheses is to submit them to statistical testing and to reject those that do not pass the tests.

[7] Two methods of testing have been used with success. The first asserts that farm consumption depends on non-farm income (which is relatively stable) owing to social emulation. The second asserts that farm consumption, although dependent on current disposable farm income, also depends on farm consumption in the previous period; the effect of this last is that, even though current income falls, current consumption falls less than proportionately because it depends on past consumption. Both approaches 'smooth out' fluctuations in consumer spending. Refer L.R. Klein, 'The Friedman-Becker Illusion', in *Journal of Political Economy*, LXVI, No. 6 (1958).

8. The time-path of national income

The discussion so far has concentrated on examining the effect of a sustained autonomous change in aggregate final demand on the *equilibrium* level of national income. In practice, however, it takes time for the national income to react to a change in demand and, before equilibirum national income is reached, demand may well have changed again. Hence it is likely to be more useful practically to know the time-path of national income   i.e. the level of national income in each successive quarter—rather than the ultimate equilibrium position. In order to obtain this information, we need to know the time-lags with which people respond.

Thus if we review the national income multiplier sequence, it will be seen that if a group of workers are newly employed in the investment-goods industry, there are three time-lags in the immediate sequence of events. First, a period of time elapses from the day on which they are employed to the day on which they (and other productive factors) are paid their income; second, a further period of time elapses from the date of receipt of income to the day on which they may be regarded as spending their income on consumer goods; third, a still further period elapses between this last date (which represents a rise in sales of consumer goods) and a subsequent date on which businessmen producing consumer goods decide to raise production to meet the higher consumer demand, and so employ a new batch of workers in the consumer goods industry. *This sequence of lags is known as the factor-income lag, the consumer-spending lag and the output-decision lag.* Clearly these three lags constitute a single round in the national income multiplier process, and so they may be regarded as collectively constituting an *income propagation period* (refer figure 3.7). On this view the successive increments in the national income previously

10, 8, 6.4, . . .

discussed are the cumulative income increments in successive income propagation periods. There is some statistical evidence to suggest that such a period is of the order of a calendar quarter in some countries. In order to fit the analysis into this period as simply as possible, let us here imagine that the factor-income lag and the consumption-expenditure lag are initially zero and that the output-

FIGURE 3.7 THE INCOME FLOW

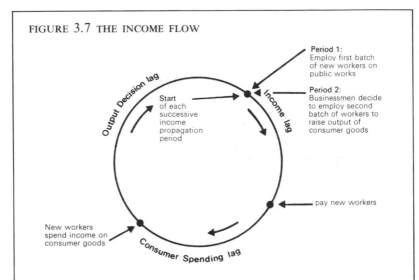

The sequence of events depicts the income flow. The time taken to go round is the income propagation period. Thus if the stock of money in active circulation is $1,000m and the annual national product is $4,000m, then on average each dollar does the circuit four times annually; i.e. the average income propagation period is a calendar quarter. (Note: money in active circulation does not include money held as a stock of idle balances.)

decision lag is 3 months. In other words when new workers are employed they are paid immediately and they spend these incomes immediately, but it takes three months for businessmen producing consumer goods to raise production to match the higher demand. This simple set of assumptions will mean that a $10m rise/fall in investment will result in a time-path of national income as shown in figure 3.8.

The most interesting aspect of the tabulation in figure 3.8 is that by the fourth quarter the national product has risen to approximately *three* times the sustained autonomous rise in investment, compared with a figure of *five* for the national income multiplier in ultimate equilibrium. However, if the marginal propensity to consume out of national income is relatively low, say 0.5, then the ultimate figure for the income multiplier is approached relatively quickly, since this is a property of a convergent sequence. This is illustrated in figure

FIGURE 3·8   SEQUENCE TABLE: MULTIPLIER IS 5

| Quarter | All figures are changes over the initial situation ($m) | | | | Change in stock of consumer goods over previous quarter |
| | Producers' Outlays | | | Consumption Spending | |
	on Consumer Goods	on Investment Goods	TOTAL (National Product)		
1		10	10	8	−8
2	8	10	18	14.4	−6.4
3	14.4	10	24.4	19.52	−5.12
4	19.52	10	29.52		

3.9, where the amount of 18.75 is relatively close to the 20 given by a multiplier of 2.

FIGURE 3·9   SEQUENCE TABLE: MULTIPLIER IS 2

| Quarter | All figures are changes over the initial situation ($m) | | | | Change in stock of consumer goods over previous quarter |
| | Producers' Outlays | | | Consumption Spending | |
	on Consumer Goods	on Investment Goods	TOTAL (National Product)		
1		10	10	5	−5
2	5	10	15	7.5	−2.5
3	7.5	10	17.5	8.75	−1.25
4	8.75	10	18.75		

Sequence tables such as those just used are capable of handling any combination of lags we care to feed into them.[8] Suppose for example that, noting the cumulative run-down of inventories in the last column of figure 3.9, we now add to that example the postulate that businessmen try to maintain the base period level of inventories. The implications of this are worked through in figure 3.10, where it is seen that the time-path of national income displays a fluctuation called an 'inventory cycle'. The explanation of this is that when

[8] The reader may care to set up an example of a consumer expenditure lag.

stocks fall in the first quarter owing to the output-decision lag, the rise in production of consumer goods to make good this loss in the second quarter is in effect a *temporary* rise in investment in building up stocks. It is the fact that this is temporary that foreshadows the cyclical movement. The time-path of national income (column 4) shows that it first rises above the long-term equilibrium level given by the national income multiplier and then falls below this level. This example does not claim to describe an actual sequence of events, but aims at showing how readily the sequence table enables us to deduce the implications of chosen assumptions about business behaviour for the time-path of national income.

FIGURE 3·10   INVENTORY CYCLE ($m)

Quarter	1	2	3	4	5	6	7
	Production of		Investment Equipment	National Product	Consumer Demand	Consumer Good Stocks	
	Consumer Goods						
	to meet recent demand $=(5)_{t-1}$	to stock-pile $=-(7)_{t-1}$				change over last quarter $=(1)+(2)-(5)$	cumulated change
1			10	10	5	5	−5
2	5	5	10	20	10	0	−5
3	10	5	10	25	12.5	+2.5	−2.5
4	12.5	2.5	10	25	12.5	+2.5	0
5	12.5	0	10	22.5	11.25	+1.25	+1.25
6	11.25	−1.25	10	20	10	0	+1.25
7	10	−1.25	10	18.75			

All figures show the change over the base period, save for the second last column.

There is a sustained autonomous rise in investment of $10m per quarter in column 3, which results in a fluctuation in national income. Because there is an output lag, stocks fall and to replace these there is temporary investment in new stocks. When the original stock position is re-established in the fourth quarter, national income is about to fall away owing to the fall in investment in new stocks. But owing to the output lag, sales fall ahead of production, so that unwanted stocks build up. Production is then cut back (in the seventh quarter) below the long-term equilibrium level ($20m) in order to dispose of surplus stocks.

Summary

The real national income multiplier process describes an important adjustment mechanism whereby a sustained initial change in demand spreads boom or recession throughout the economy.

In its simplest form the multiplier was calculated for the ultimate change in national income in a new position of equilibrium. But because there are significant lags in the process, the current year's time-path of national income is likely to be of greater interest than any calculation of ultimate equilibrium.

The sequence table is a simple method of calculating this time-path. It is a versatile method because it will handle any possible combination of time-lags.

9. The economic system ☐

The model of the economic system used in this chapter is set out in figure 3.11. Attention has been focussed on the third, demand,

FIGURE 3·11   MODEL OF THE ECONOMIC SYSTEM

Resource supplies	:	Work force W is known
Technology	:	$aX = N$
Income distribution	:	$XP = N.P_n(1+v)$
Demand	:	$C = j + c(1-t)X$
		G, I are known
		$X = C + I + G$ in equilibrium

Constants. a,v,j,c,t
For meaning of symbols refer page 311.

block. The properties of this system include the size of the national income multiplier, which is the coefficient in the solution:

$$X = \frac{1}{1-c(1-t)}. \ [j+I+G], \text{ and hence: } \Delta X = \Delta G. \frac{1}{1-c(1-t)}$$

which states that a sustained autonomous rise or fall in government spending on goods and services ΔG (say a rise in public works) is subject to a multiplier effect in altering the level of national product. In order to ascertain the time-path of national income, we replace the condition of market equilibrium by a statement of the speed of response of output to change in demand. Thus if the sole lag is a one-period output-response lag, the third block reads:

> Consumer-demand response $C_t = j + c(1-t)X_t$
>
> Output response $\qquad X_{t+1} = C_t + I_t + G_t$
>
> where G_t, I_t are known

Many variations are possible. Thus statistics may reveal a one-period consumer-demand response lag:

$$C_{t+1} = j + c(1-t)X_t$$

The policy significance of this analysis has been that the government can influence the level of final demand and that the measures it takes will have an income multiplier effect. Most governments are able to control demand either by budgetary measures (already discussed) or by monetary measures carried out by the central bank (to be discussed in the next chapter). It is worthwhile here reviewing the basic question to be asked of *any* measure that is proposed to reduce unemployment caused by inadequate demand. How will it raise demand for the produce of home labour? To illustrate this reasoning, and because it is important in itself, consider a proposal to reduce unemployment by a nation-wide cut in money wage-rates.* Initially assume for simplicity that there is no foreign trade.

In a non-trading economy, a fall in unemployment will come about only if there is a rise in the volume of demand, so it is necessary to look at each category of demand. Now, consumer demand is the largest single category of demand, but a rise in consumer demand at the existing level of the national income implies an upward *shift* in the consumption-income schedule. The possibility of such an upward shift in the consumption–national-income schedule depends on whether there is an income redistribution.[9] In order to analyse the effects of any such income redistribution, let us rewrite the consumption function in the form:

$$\frac{C.P}{P} = j + b(1-t)\frac{V}{P} + c(1-t)\frac{N.P_n}{P}$$

in which consumption spending at constant prices depends on profits V and wages $N.P_n$ (in each case after tax and at constant prices).

---

*The rest of this section can be omitted on a first reading.

[9] It also depends on the importance of the 'real balance effect'. It is conceivable that the wage-cut might, by lowering prices, increase the real value of money balances and so stimulate consumer spending.

Since the wage-share is $1/(1+v)$ and profit share is $v/(1+v)$, this consumption function can be rewritten:

$$\frac{C.P}{P} = j + b(1-t)\frac{v}{(1+v)}.\frac{X.P}{P} + c\frac{(1-t)}{(1+v)}.\frac{X.P}{P}$$

i.e.: $\quad C = j + b(1-t)\frac{v}{(1+v)}.X + c\frac{(1-t)}{(1+v)}.X$

or: $\quad C = j + \left[c + (b-c)\ \frac{v}{1+v}\right](1-t).\ X$

It follows that this consumption function will not shift in response to such an event as a change in the money wage-rate unless both of two conditions are satisfied, namely:

$$\begin{cases} b \text{ and } c \text{ are unequal} \\ \text{the profit share } \dfrac{v}{1+v} \text{ changes} \end{cases}$$

Even if b and c are unequal (being the amount of an increment in after-tax profits and wages respectively spent on consumption), if the profit share is unchanging then the consumption function does not shift. If in reality time-lags do cause the profit share to change, such a change may be in favour of profits. A review of the several possibilities suggests that a wage-cut, even if practicable, is unlikely to stimulate employment in a closed economy. However, in a trading economy, a wage-cut may make exports more attractive to the foreigner. In that event, exchange depreciation is likely to prove a more efficient tool, as discussed later in chapter 12.

10. Conclusion

This chapter has tacitly assumed that the community uses a monetary commodity of negligible intrinsic value, which is used by individuals as a store of value. For, in a barter economy, physical investment is necessarily the residual between consumption and production, whereas we have assumed that planned investment can vary independently. This implies the existence of a money commodity serving as a store of value so that individuals may plan to allocate the part of their income not spent on consumption either to physical investment or to accumulation of the money commodity.

In a barter economy, unemployment due to deficiency of demand could not normally occur because consumption and investment demand would collectively exhaust potential national production. But in a monetary economy deficiency of demand can and does occur. It is desirable therefore to explore the nature of the monetary system.

Summary

§1. Final demand may fluctuate independently, thus causing inflation or recession.

§2. Various causes may result in fluctuation in the level of investment.

§3. Such fluctuations have a multiplier effect on the national income.

§4. Personal disposable income is the part of real national income ultimately accruing to households. It is a major determinant of consumer demand.

§5. The government can control the level of investment demand and consumer demand by both budgetary and monetary measures; e.g. altering tax rates and availability of bank credit. A change in tax rates alters the relation between disposable income and national income.

§6. The analysis can readily be extended to foreign trade situations by concentrating attention on the home-produced content of each category of demand. (More detailed treatment is in part III).

§7. Consumer expenditure is affected by other influences than disposable income: income distribution, assets, consumer credit, stocks of durable goods, age composition, normal income, and the interplay of short-term and long-term influences. These influences can be regarded as shifting the consumption–disposable-income schedule.

§8. The time-path of national income is analysed by specifying reponse lags and setting up a sequence table.

§9. The model of the economic system can be used to analyse the effects on final demand of fiscal or monetary measures or change in wage-rates.

§10. The analysis has tacitly assumed modern monetary institutions.

Further reading

C.L. Schultze, *National Income Analysis* (Englewood Cliffs, N.J.: Prentice Hall, 1967).

R.T. Gill, *Economics and the Public Interest*.

B.N. Siegel, *Aggregate Economics and Public Policy* (Homewood, Ill.: Irwin, 1960).

D.C. Rowan, *Output, Inflation and Growth* (London: Macmillan, 1968).

M.K. Evans, *Macroeconomic Activity* (New York: Harper & Row, 1969).

For a parlour game approach:

P.H. Lindert, *Macro: A Game of Growth and Policy* (New York: Holt, Rinehart & Winston, 1970).

Questions

1. Explain the distinction between an analysis of the nation's requirements for capital goods and an analysis of the influences affecting the level of investment demand.

2. 'The level of current investment is proportional to this year's rise in consumer demand'. Consider this as an explanation of the level of investment.

3. Explore the usefulness of the idea that long-term influences determine the broad trend of investment volume, and that short-term influences cause fluctuations around that trend.

4. Explain how a situation of full employment can fail to be a state of equilibrium.

5. What qualifications do you attach to the use of the national income multiplier?

6. Explain how the government can raise the level of aggregate demand either by a cut in the income tax rate or by a rise in public works spending.

    Explain how the government can alter its own income by its own spending.

    What criteria would you use to judge between cutting tax rates and raising public works spending?

7. How is the output of the steel industry affected by a cut in the rate of personal income tax?

11. If the marginal propensity to consume out of personal disposable income is 0.8 and the marginal propensity to consume out of national income is 0.6, what is the national income multiplier? If you were now told that imports are one-quarter of home production, how is your answer affected?

12. Explain how the marginal propensity to consume out of personal disposable income can be 0.9 and yet the national income multiplier can be as low as 2.

13. Explain how, if the multiplier is 2 and the income propagation period a calendar quarter, the multiplier indicates approximately the national income level in four quarters.

14. Suppose that there is unemployment due to deficiency of demand, and the government wishes to raise national income by $100m per quarter at constant prices. The government taxes one-quarter of any rise in national income and the marginal propensity to consume out of personal disposable income is 0.8.

    The government might choose to raise its rate of public works spending by $xm per quarter. What is x?

    Now suppose that a political opponent advocates that, instead of public works being raised, the personal income tax rate should be cut so as to both (a) reduce tax collections at the existing level of quarterly national income by $41.625m and (b) reduce the tax rate on any rise in the national income from 25 per cent to 17.5 per cent. What would be the effect of such a proposal?

21. Draw up a list of the influences that may affect the level of consumer spending. Consider whether they have a stabilising or destabilising effect on the national income, i.e. whether they tend to reduce fluctuations in income.

22. Comment on the political objective of balancing the budget.

23. Does the central government raise taxes in order to pay for its spending?

24. 'Short-term economic management' aims, amongst other things, at keeping the economy at a high level of employment. Consider the problems involved, and consider in particular the relevance of time-lags, of growing population, and of technological innovation.

4

Money

The creation of a money commodity brings a great gain in national efficiency. However, it also allows of the possibility of unemployment due to deficient demand. There is no 'natural' tendency for a monetary economy to settle down at full employment equilibrium.

1. Creating a monetary system

The motive for introducing a generally accepted medium of exchange (i.e. *money*) into a hitherto barter economy is simple efficiency. For barter requires each party to a transaction to have what the other wants and to want what the other has. Existence of a money commodity speeds up the operation of the market, allows more resources to be devoted to the actual productive process, and encourages specialisation (i.e. *division of labour*). Even though the existence of money requires some people to operate the banks, there is still a huge net gain in national efficiency.

In a modern economy most of the money supply is in the form of bank deposits, and we will here ignore the existence of a second form of money (bank notes and coin) as being of trivial economic significance in most circumstances. In order to monetise a barter economy, a commercial bank is established whose management lends money to each business enterprise for 'working financial capital', i.e. to pay wages and other costs during the period elapsing until receipts flow into the firm. During this initial period the bank gradually increases business overdrafts over successive weeks until no further increase is needed because financial receipts of all firms equals financial expenditure. (The bank of course secures its overdrafts against the assets of the business firms.) The bank itself survives as an enterprise because it charges an interest rate on overdrafts. In a sense this interest rate is a tax levied by the bank on the national product—a tax that is deemed justified by the efficiency of the financial system that the bank administers.

Businessmen collectively will come to regard an overdraft equal to a fraction of their turnover as standard business practice. We can obtain a feeling for the size of this fraction by recapitulating the events of the initial weeks when money is first introduced:

At the start of the first week workers are employed in industry that at the end of the week will pay their incomes in bank deposits for the first time. Thus on Friday the firms will use their overdraft facilities in order to pay out a volume of money equal to factor incomes produced during the week. Suppose, during the second week, that households spend their money income until by Thursday night all bank deposits have passed back to firms' accounts. This process is endlessly repeated. The money supply then is equal to the factor incomes produced during the income period (the second week) that elapsed between the payout of factor incomes by firms and the eventual receipt of these funds from households.

In reality this income-expenditure cycle of households (and firms) is longer than a week: some incomes are paid fortnightly, some are paid six-monthly. The average period lies in between; it might be two months, for example. If this were the case then, so far as the argument has proceeded, the money supply would need to be equal to one-sixth of the annual national product. The provision of these funds for the financial transactions flow is a social function of the banks and this sum is permanently on loan by the banks to business enterprise.

Now let us recognise that some (say one-fifth) of the national product consists of investment goods and that physical investment is financed by issues of securities (debentures, bonds, notes, shares). If all households directly allocated their current monetary savings to purchasing new securities during the current income period, the foregoing argument would need no modification in principle. For while part of firms' production is now investment goods in the first week for which they pay incomes to employed factors, income receivers would buy newly issued shares or debentures in the course of the second week. So, by the end of the second week, it would still be true that firms had the whole of the money supply back in their hands—some funds being received in exchange for consumer goods and some in exchange for debentures. Hence, in terms of the previous arithmetic, the money supply would still be one-sixth of the annual national product.

However, households (and other savers too for that matter) may not directly allocate the whole of their current monetary savings to purchasing newly issued securities. On the contrary we know that they have a demand to hold idle money balances, which they proceed to accumulate progressively out of their current money savings until money balances rise to some desired level, e.g. a specific proportion of national income (at any given interest rate). Hence if the finance of the nation's investment programme is to continue (and if demand-deficiency unemployment is to be avoided), the banks must step in with *offset finance* to match the monetary savings that are newly added to idle money balances. (This offset finance will rise at a diminishing rate to some specific level.) This is another social function of the banks—the provision of money to firms to finance the creation of physical equipment—and it is a function necessitated by the demand by people for idle money balances. In other words the demand by households for idle money balances requires the banks to perform the social function of providing money *on capital account*.

The provision of these funds on capital account involves the creation of a further volume of money that is permanently on loan by the banks to business enterprise. However, so far as any single investment project is concerned, the loan will normally be of limited duration—the repayment in respect of one past project is matched by a new bank advance for a new investment project, the money supply remaining unchanged. In other words these funds, seen as advances to business enterprise, form a revolving fund.

No general statement is possible as to the size of the extra finance provided on capital account to business enterprise for (as the above argument shows) this reflects the money hoarding propensity of the public. We do know that the ratio of idle money balances to national product can be influenced by the level of interest rates as people seek to switch their holdings of financial assets between money and interest-bearing debentures.

2. The commercial banks

An understanding of the operation of commercial banking is a preliminary to later discussion of the work of the central bank (or reserve bank) in implementing economic policy. Up till now we

Summary

The creation of a monetary system increases the efficiency of the economy both by increasing the efficiency of the market and by encouraging specialisation in production.

Banks lend money to finance the flow of commodity transactions. They lend further money to offset the holding of idle money balances by the public. (They also lend to finance asset transfers, e.g. real estate.)

The quantity of money demanded by the community is a proportion of the value of national production. However, this proportion varies inversely with the interest rate.

have ignored the fact that there are two sorts of money, cash and bank deposits. The central bank typically has the sole right to create cash in the form of bank notes. The bulk of the money supply in a modern industrialised society consists of bank deposits created by the commercial banks. The ability of the commercial banks to create money rests on their having customers who are willing to settle debts on one another simply by transferring ownership of bank deposits. (Thus I pay my liquor bill by writing a cheque, which is a legal instrument for transferring ownership of some of my bank deposits to the liquor store.)

There is a limit to the ability of a commercial bank to create money in the form of bank deposits. This limit stems from the bank's need to keep on hand cash reserves equal to some minimum proportion of deposits it has created. There are three reasons for this.

(a) The bank needs cash for those of its customers who wish to make a withdrawal from their credit at the bank in the form of bank notes.

(b) The bank needs cash to settle any net balance on its daily clearing of cheques with other banks. (A commercial bank holds this cash in the form of a credit at the central bank, and meets any net balance on the daily clearing by transferring some of this credit to another commercial bank. A commercial bank's credit at the central bank could be withdrawn as bank notes and so is regarded as cash.)

(c) In many nations a commercial bank is required by law to have a minimum ratio of cash to deposits, which may be raised or lowered from time to time at the direction of the central bank. This is a basic technique of central bank control as we will see later.

In summary, for reasons of custom and law, a commercial bank must maintain a minimum ratio of cash reserves to deposits—a ratio of 10 per cent for example—and so the system is referred to as *fractional reserve banking*.

Imagine then that the commercial banks of the nation are in an equilibrium where they are lending all they can, as shown in this balance sheet where the cash-deposit ratio is at the assumed minimum 10 per cent, a figure chosen solely for its simplicity.

COMBINED BALANCE SHEET OF COMMERCIAL BANKS ($M)

Liabilities		Assets	
Deposits	40	Cash^a	4
Shareholders' funds	3	Advances^b	39
	43		43

Notes: a Including notes, credit at central bank, and including legal requirement.
　　　　 b Short and long term, on various security, to firms, persons, governments.

Under what circumstances would the commercial banks be able to create more bank deposits in the normal course of business activity? Two situations are of special interest.

The first is that in which *the central government borrows from the central bank in order to finance a rise in its spending on public works or defence.* For the central bank writes a credit to the government's account with the central bank (on the security of a treasury bill or other instrument.) When the defence contractor is paid by the government, he lodges his cheque with his commercial bank, which then presents it to the central bank. The central bank then transfers ownership of this credit from the government to the commercial bank. Thus the commercial bank's cash reserve is increased, its ratio of cash to deposits is also increased above the minimum, and it can now expand advances until the cash ratio falls back to 10 per cent.

Example:

The defence contract is worth $0.1m and is being financed by central bank credit. When the contractor is paid he deposits this with his bank, whose deposits thus rise to 40.1, and his bank is credited by the central bank on presentation of the cheque so that cash reserves are now up to 4.1.

NEW BALANCE SHEET

Deposits	40.1	Cash	4.1
Sharehold	3.0	Advances	39.0

The commercial bank cash reserve ratio is now up to almost 10.25 per cent. If the commercial bank were confident of maintaining the absolute size of its new cash reserve, it could expand advances and so create deposits of $0.9m, which would yield a further balance sheet situation

Deposits	41	Cash	4.1
Sharehold	3	Advances	39.9

in which the cash ratio is back to 10 per cent. In practice the bank's expansion of its activities in this way would result in some erosion of its cash reserve (to both customers and other banks on daily clearing) so that its ability to expand advances would be rather less than the multiplicative factor of 9 used here. (The figure of 9 results from the arbitrary 10 per cent cash reserve ratio.)

The second situation is one in which *the nation experiences a rise in the value of its exports*. The sequence of events parallels the case of central-bank-financed government spending. A $0.1m rise in exports shows up firstly as a rise in deposits standing to the credit of exporters at their commercial banks. Then when the commercial banks sell the foreign exchange to the central bank (which usually holds the bulk of a nation's foreign exchange stocks), the commercial banks are credited with $0.1m to their account at the central bank. As before, this represents a rise in the cash reserve ratio of the commercial banks, which are thus able to expand advances and create money in the form of newly created bank deposits.

3. The central bank

Although legislative provisions vary between nations, the central bank—or reserve bank—is the major monetary arm of the central government. When short-term economic management of the economy is under discussion, whereas fiscal measures refer to action taken

Summary

Commercial banks create the bulk of the money supply in the form of bank deposits. Their ability to create money, however, is limited by the need to maintain a minimum ratio of cash reserves to deposits—hence the term 'fractional reserve banking'.

Two typical situations that increase the ability of the commercial banks to create more bank deposits are: government spending financed by central bank credit; increase in export receipts.

by the Treasury, monetary measures refer to action taken by the central bank.

The reasoning behind the use of fiscal and monetary measures is similar. On the one hand the level of consumer spending depends on after-tax income, which can be influenced by changing tax rates. On the other hand much physical investment is financed by borrowed funds. The commercial banks are a major lender, and so by controlling their rate of lending the central government can seek to control the level of investment spending.

Historically central banks have relied mainly on three techniques to restrict the volume of lending by the commercial banks:

(a) *raising interest rates* (including the rate at which the central bank will lend to the commercial banks);

(b) *raising the legal minimum ratio of cash reserves to deposits* of the commercial banks;

> *Example:* A rise in the legal minimum cash/deposit ratio from 10 per cent to 10.5 per cent will force the commercial banks to contract advances in order to reduce deposits and so achieve the required cash/deposit ratio.

(c) *open market operations;* i.e. the sale of government securities by the central bank on the stock exchange.

> *Example:* If the public buys $1m of securities from the central bank on the open market, a cheque for that sum is paid to the central bank. But only commercial banks (and governments) have an account with the central bank. The central bank will debit the accounts of the commercial banks with itself, thereby reducing their cash reserve by $1m. Thus their cash reserve ratio is reduced.

There can be no doubt but that these are powerful weapons in the hands of a central bank that is determined to hold back demand —presumably because it fears inflationary pressures. And the choice between restricting total demand by a rise in tax rates, by a cut in government spending, or by central bank action, will depend partly on the speed of effect of these measures and partly on which use of resources it is desired to restrict.

However, there is a lack of symmetry in the capability of the central bank in as much as it is easier for it to *restrict* commercial bank lending than to *stimulate* such lending once a recession has already begun and engendered pessimism among potential borrowers. The effectiveness of the central bank in countering recession depends on its willingness to act before the downturn has had time to affect business confidence.

Summary

Just as aggregate demand can be controlled by fiscal measures that alter consumption or government spending (and so shift the aggregate-demand–national-income schedule), so demand can be controlled by monetary measures taken by the central bank that alter investment spending (and shift the schedule).

Choice between these measures depends on their efficiency and on resource use.

4. Saving and investment

Once money is seen to serve as a store of value, people will be motivated to accumulate idle money balances by *saving*. However, if the money commodity has a value that derives only from its general acceptability as money, then accumulation of the money commodity, although it is saving (i.e. non-spending), is not in itself provision for the future in any material sense, i.e. it is not physical investment. This fact that the existence of money as an asset divorces the decision to save from the decision to invest, is emphasised by pointing out that the two sorts of decision are largely made by different people: it is business firms that make the decisions to invest, while both households and firms make decisions to save.[1] The possible effect of this divorce can be numerically illustrated in figure 4.1 by supposing that current national production (in $m) is 100, of which 80 is spent on consumption and 20 is saved; some of these savings are sub-

[1] Households do of course make decisions to invest in residential housing.

scribed to new security issues to finance investment, and some of the savings may be used to add to idle money balances. Now, the level of planned physical investment by businessmen may be any figure at all, for it depends on their long-term expectations of the need for new plant capacity, on short-term influences such as a minor business recession or uncertainty about export markets. Moreover the variability of the possible level of planned investment is emphasised by the ability of firms to obtain financial capital not merely from currently saved bank balances but also from accumulated idle money balances or from newly created overdraft drawing rights, i.e. new money. Suppose the level of planned physical investment is only $15m.

FIGURE 4·1   SAVING AND INVESTMENT ($M)

PERIOD 1

National income		National spending	
Consumption	80	Consumption	80
Saving	20	Investment	15
		Unintended stock rise	5
National product	100	National product	100

Note: It is often convenient to refer to the figures for saving (20) and investment (15) here as *intended* saving and *intended* investment. It will be seen that:
  (a) these need not be equal;
  (b) if they are unequal:
    — this is *equivalent* to stating that intended spending (95) is not equal to national production (100);
    — the level of national product in the next period will differ from what it would have been if they had been equal.
Unnecessary confusion has been caused by: lumping unintended stock rise (5) with intended investment (15); calling this 'investment'; and hence asserting that investment equals savings (20). Clearly this is true by definition if we include, in investment, the stocks of goods the businessman has been unable to sell. Confusion is avoided by calling this concept *'realised* investment' whenever it is used.

It is apparent that this will result in a rise in unsold stocks of $5m. Hence in the ensuing period we may expect a fall in employment and a cut-back in production to $95m to equal the recent level of demand.

What we have just done has been to rephrase the argument of the previous chapter (that demand may be insufficient to clear the market), using the concepts of saving and investment. Six specific points will now be made in order to clarify this optional mode of expression:

(a) The condition of market equilibrium for commodities is:

Consumption demand (C)	$+$	Investment demand (I)	$=$	National product (X)

But by definition national product equals real national income; and also real national income is defined to be equal to consumption (C) plus savings (S)

To summarise:

> in equilibrium $\qquad$ $C + I = X$
> but by definition $\qquad$ $X = C + S$

Hence the condition of market equilibrium can be *equivalently restated* that investment equals savings, i.e.:

> in equilibrium $\qquad$ $I = S$

(b) At this point we emphasise that all the concepts just used—consumption, investment, savings, production—are used in the *causal* sense that they will affect the equilibrium level of production. To denote this causal sense, we say that all these concepts are *intended* or *planned* magnitudes. Hence the conclusion just drawn is that the condition of market equilibrium can be stated in either of two equivalent forms:

(i)   Planned consumption + planned investment = planned production;

(ii) planned savings = planned investment.

(c) Since we believe that the economy is often not in equilibrium (but rather on a path from one equilibrium to another), it follows that we believe that planned savings and planned investment in a period are often unequal.

> *Example:* There is a $10m rise in investment in the current quarter, and, since the marginal propensity to consume out of national income is 0.6, current consumption spending rises by

$6m. But, because of the output-decision lag, production of consumer goods has not yet risen, so the rise in consumption is met by a fall in stocks of consumer goods.

The position in this quarter is clearly not one of equilibrium: since the marginal propensity to save is 0.4, planned savings have risen $4m, which is less than the rise in planned investment of $10m. This excess of planned investment over planned savings is simply a way of expressing the excess of planned demand over planned production. It is apparent that future production will rise over what it would otherwise have been.

(d) It worries some people to be told that planned savings and planned investment can be unequal, because they believe that savings and investment are always equal. However, this belief applies to *realised* savings and *realised* investment. The vital point to grasp here is that realised investment is defined to be equal to the sum of planned (or intended) investment and unplanned stock change. Using this definition, we can see that it is true that realised savings and realised investment are always equal, *as a matter of definition*.

Example. In the above example realised savings are the same as planned savings, i.e. $4m. Realised investment equals planned investment ($10m) plus unplanned stock change (minus $6m), which is also $4m.

The definitional identity of realised savings and realised investment can be set out, using a prime to mean 'realised':

irrespective of whether there is equilibrium:
$$\begin{cases} C'' + I' \equiv X' \\ C' + S' \equiv X' \end{cases}$$
so:
$$S' \equiv I'$$

in which it will be carefully noted that I' includes the sum of planned investment and unplanned stock change (which can only be known after the period is ended).

Since they can have no causal role these 'realised' concepts are of no value in analysis and will not be used in the text. Their sole use is to check on the arithmetic correctness of social accounts, which must show the definitional equality of realised savings and realised investment for any past period.

(e) In reality the existence of both government and foreign trade makes the condition of market equilibrium look more complex— though there are no basic new ideas. Thus, using only planned (or intended) concepts, the *condition of market equilibrium* is that total demand $(C+I+G+E)$ equals total supplies $(X+M)$

$$C+I+G+E=X+M$$

and by definition:

$$X=C+S+T$$

where *E, M* are exports, imports
     G government spending on goods and services
     S, T are savings, taxes

Hence the condition of market equilibrium can be equivalently restated that

in equilibrium $I=S+(T-G)+(M-E)$

in equilibrium intended investment equals the sum of intended savings from three sources: viz. private sector savings, government budget surplus, and the use of foreigners' savings measured by the excess of imports over exports.

(f)   Finally it is possible to pursue the standard national income multiplier analysis using the concept of a planned-savings–national-income schedule. If the reader does use this concept he should bear in mind that an upward shift in the savings schedule is equivalent to a downward shift in the consumption–national-income schedule.

> *Example:* The economy is at full employment with national income at $1,000m. The position is one of equilibrium. Statistical investigation shows that national savings have recently been a constant 10 per cent of national income at all levels of national income.
>
> There is now a sudden concern for the virtues of saving and the community plans to raise the proportion of national income it saves by one-fifth. What is the effect on the national income?
>
> The answer is: that equilibrium national income falls by $(1,000-833=)$ $167m due to the downward shift in the consumption schedule.[2]

---

[2] In equilibrium $Y=(C)+I=(0.88\,Y)+100$
    i.e.:
        $0.12\,Y=100$
    so:
        $Y=833$

Summary

It is the existence of money as we know it that has divorced the decision to save from the decision to invest. In turn this has made possible large scale unemployment due to deficiency of demand.

5. The theory of money

The existence of the institution of money does affect the use of physical resources, and not simply the level of prices. It has already been observed that the existence of money as an asset has resulted in the divorce of the decision to save from the decision to invest, and so makes possible the existence of unemployment due to deficiency of demand. Let us explore the role of money in more detail.

There is a transactions demand for money to serve as a *medium of exchange* which facilitates the production and distribution of the national product. It seems reasonable to suggest that this transactions demand for money (M_T) is proportional to the value of the national product ($X.P$, where X is the volume of production and P the price level). The size of this proportionality constant depends on: firstly, the number of selling stages (t) through which, on the average, the national product must pass, on its path from unprocessed raw materials to a processed product purchased by the final consumer; secondly on the speed or transactions velocity (V) with which money circulates—reflecting the payments habits of the community. In summary, the transactions demand for money

$$M_T = (t/V).(X.P)$$

is a fixed proportion (t/V) of the value of the national product.

While money was historically introduced to serve the transactions function of an efficient medium of exchange (or unit of currency), it was inevitable that, provided money remained reasonably stable in value, it also came to be used as a *unit of account* (or measure of value) and so as a *store of value*. In other words people have a desire to hold assets, and money is such an asset—so there is an *assets demand for money* (M_A), which may be quite substantial and which is additional to the transactions demand for money (M_T). The *size* of this assets demand for money depends not only on the level of the national income ($X.P$) but also on the relative attractiveness of money compared with alternative assets that individuals may hold. Let us illustrate by supposing that there are two kinds of asset: money and debentures (i.e. fixed interest securities that businessmen issue when they wish to finance physical investment).[3] Then we could advance the simple hypothesis that a rise in the market interest rate on debentures makes them a more attractive asset relatively to money since the debentures yield a higher income (and conversely for a fall in the interest rate). On this view, for any chosen level of the interest rate, the assets demand for money may be a constant proportion of the national product $(X.P)$; but when the interest rate changes, the assets demand for money would move inversely. Summarising, we have two demands for money:

transactions demand $M_T = \dfrac{t}{V} X.P$

assets demand $\qquad M_A = \dfrac{k}{i} . X.P$

$\qquad\qquad\qquad$ where k is some constant
$\qquad\qquad\qquad\qquad$ i is interest rate

and adding these:

total demand for money $M_d = \left(\dfrac{t}{V} + \dfrac{k}{i}\right) X.P$

of which a simple imaginary example is:

$$M_d = \frac{0.03}{i} (X.P)$$

showing that at an interest rate of 5 per cent the total demand for money is 60 per cent of the value of national production.

Having so far in this chapter explored the influences affecting the demand for and supply of money, we are now able to analyse further the effect of the institution of money. In embarking on this analysis, various monetary theorists have made any of three different assumptions:

(a) that the level of physical national production (X) is constant at full employment output (X_{fe});

(b) that the price level (P) is constant; or

---

[3] In reality other assets include equities and also physical assets.

(c)   that both national product (X) and price level (P) are free
to vary, and accordingly some other information must be
introduced in order to allocate effects between the two; (i.e.
how much of a rise in expenditure results in a rise in physical
production and how much in rising prices). Such a piece of
information would be a postulate concerning the manner
in which the money wage-rate, and hence the price level,
changes.

It is of course a question of fact which of the three assumptions is
valid in any specific historical situation. *We shall now examine each
of the three cases in turn.*

Consider the case in which we have a stationary economy with
national production constant at a specified full-employment level
(X_{fe}). From a knowledge of the consumption–national-income
schedule we can read off the level of physical consumption (C), and
hence the residual (i.e. the difference between X_{fe} and C) is physical
investment, which is also constant. Now, using a short-run investment demand schedule as in figure 3.1, it follows that we could read
off the constant level of the interest rate that corresponds to this
fixed level of investment.

Example: Imagine that full-employment production is \$1,000m,
and that consumption is 0.9 of this, so that investment is \$100m.
If investment (I) is related to the interest rate (i) by the short-
run relation:

$$I = 300 - 1,300i$$

then by inserting $I = 100$ it follows that the interest rate is 15
per cent approximately. (Note that output, consumption and
investment are being measured at constant prices, say of the
year 1950.)

Turn now to the total demand function for money. In monetary
equilibrium the known money supply (M) created by the banking
system must be equal to the total demand for money (M_d), i.e. using
our previous example:

$$M = \{M_d =\} \ \frac{0.03 \ X.P}{i}$$

i is interest rate

Now, in this relationship, not only is X constant at X_{fe} but also we
have just shown that this implies that the level of physical invest-

ment (I) and hence the interest rate (i) are also constant. So for any given level of the money supply (M), we can calculate the price level.

Example: Continuing the same example and substituting the values $X = 1,000$, $I = 100$ and $i = 0.15$ we obtain:

$$M = \frac{0.03\ (1,000)\ P}{0.15}$$

$$= \frac{(1,000)\ P}{5}$$

If we are now told that the money supply is \$600m then, by substitution, the price level (P) is three. Since the base year was 1950, this concludes that the price index now is three times the price level in the base year.

Moreover it is apparent that if the money supply M is increased say by one-half, then, since the other variables in the money equation are constant, the price level (P) must also increase by one-half. *Thus in this first case, which assumes constant physical production, the price level is proportional to the money supply in equilibrium.*[4]

Monetary theorists in the first third of this century tended to the view that this first case was the important one in practice. It was generally believed that if unemployment developed and national product fell, then the interest rate would fall to stimulate investment (and consumption) spending and thus re-establish full-employment output (X_{fe}). We know, however, from historical observation of the sequence of boom and depression in capitalist nations through the nineteenth and early twentieth centuries that this belief was not well founded. In fact the physical national product can fluctuate, as was discussed in the previous chapter. Hence this first case of the monetary theorists is of limited application.

In 1936 J.M. Keynes launched a vigorous intellectual assault[5] on the classical view just described, which believed that the economy tended to settle down in full-employment equilibrium and that any

[4] A modern example of the importance of this proposition is the ill-fated attempt by the U.K. Labour Government following World War II to force down the interest rate by increasing the money supply. The attempts by the Chancellor of the Exchequer Dr Dalton to force down the interest rate were unsuccessful—the increasing money supply instead fed an inflationary boom.

[5] *The General Theory of Employment, Interest and Money* (London: Macmillan, 1936).

movement from that equilibrium would be quickly reversed. It was Keynes who clearly recognised that a consequence of the divorce of the decision to invest from the decision to save was that the economy could either settle down at an under-employment equilibrium, or experience a fluctuating level of employment and production as autonomous changes in demand were magnified by the income multiplier mechanism—as set out in the previous chapter. Keynes then was successful in providing a convincing basis for explanation of the historical sequence of boom and depression. His analysis falls into the second of our three categories of monetary theory, for in effect he generally assumed that the price level was constant. The rationale for doing this was his concern with analysing the sequence of events when a fall in demand resulted in the economy moving into recession. He proposed that the money wage-rate was difficult to reduce significantly, if at all, because of trade union resistance— and indeed there is some evidence to support this view. Thus if the money wage-rate could be regarded as virtually constant, and prices are determined by a fixed percentage profit mark-up on labour costs, then, in the short-run in which labour productivity may also be assumed constant, it follows that the price level is constant. Moreover this assumption could reasonably be made not only for a down-ward movement into recession but also for the recovery phase as the national product rose—at least so long as the volume of un-employment was still high enough to prevent a move for raising the money wage-rate.

Consider then the implications of Keynes' assumption of a constant price level when, assuming there is a large amount of unemployment due to inadequate demand, the central bank takes the initiative of increasing the money supply (M), say by buying government securities from the public on the stock market. Such open market operations by the central bank increase the money supply, raise the market price of government securities and reduce the market interest rate. Interest rates are then likely to fall generally. If it is assumed that there is nothing else occurring that deters businessmen from bor-rowing, these lower interest rates can be expected to stimulate the level of physical investment, which will then set in train a multiplier sequence with rising physical production and employment. The price level of course does not rise at all.

However, Keynes' analysis does not stop at this point. For the rising volume of national production raises the transactions demand for money. *Compared with the effect of the original increase in the money supply in reducing interest rates, this increase in the demand for money has the opposite or 'countervailing' effect* of limiting the fall in the interest rate, and so of course limiting the stimulus to physical investment.[6]

In summary, Keynes' argument is seen to have two phases. First, *the increased money supply depresses the interest rate, and this stimulates physical investment and so, through the multiplier effect, the national product. But, second, this course of events is restrained by the countervailing effect of an increased demand for money for transactions purposes*—which limits the fall in the interest rate. The argument can very readily be illustrated arithmetically.

Example: Continue the previous illustration with one modification, namely that the existing level of national production $X = \$1,000$m at 1950 prices is a situation of substantial unemployment so that real national production can be raised.

Summarising the information:

Consumption $C = 0.9X$
Investment I $= 300 - 1300i$
Demand for money $= 0.03\ X.P/i$

The initial situation is one in which:

$X = 1,000$ $P = 3$
$I = 100$ $i = 0.15$
$M = 600$

Now suppose that the central bank increases the money supply by one-half to \$900m. Recall that the price level is assumed to be constant. Consider the effects:

By equating this increased money supply to the demand for money, we deduce that in equilibrium the interest rate falls towards 10 per cent (i.e. $900 = 0.03(1000)3/i$). By substituting $i = 10$ per cent in the short-term investment demand function we deduce that investment I rises to \$170m at constant prices,

---

[6] The course of events can be described in this way: The initial purchase of government securities by the central bank depresses the market interest rate. At this lower interest rate businessmen wishing to expand physical investment may then offer new debenture issues. Competition for funds will cause the interest rate at which these debentures are floated to rise. The ultimate interest rate will be lower than the level before the central bank's operations but not so low as we would conclude if the increased transactions demand for money had been ignored.

which is a rise in investment of $70m. Since from the consumption function we deduce that the national income multiplier is 10, this suggests that the national product at constant prices is going to rise by $700m to $1,700m.

However, if we marshal the basic information we find that:

(a) a situation of equilibrium in the commodity market is one in which output (X) equals the sum of consumption (C) and investment demand I, i.e.:

$$X = 0.9X + 300 - 1,300i$$
$$= 3,000 - 13,000i$$

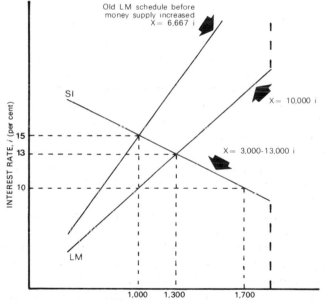

FIGURE 4·2   A KEYNESIAN MODEL

The SI (savings-investment) schedule shows, for each level of production X, the interest rate at which planned savings and investment are equal (i.e. commodity market equilibrium). The LM (liquidity-money supply) schedule shows for each level of production X, the interest rate at which the demand for money equals the given money supply (i.e. monetary equilibrium).

The broken lines show the full employment boundary. In reality the schedules may be curved rather than straight lines bending sharply at the boundary.

(b) a situation of monetary equilibrium with the money
supply at the new level of $900m yields the relation:

$M = 900 = 0.03(X)$. $(3)/i$

Hence:

$X = 10,000i$

reflecting the fact that a rise in the national product (X)
requires more money in the transactions flow and, with
a given money supply M, the interest rate must rise in
order to persuade people to hold fewer idle money balances
(and more debentures), and thus 'siphon' money from
idle to active balances.

These two relations:

$X = 3,000 - 13,000i$

$X = 10,000i$

yield the equilibrium interest rate of 13 per cent and national
product of $1,300m (figure 4.2). The reason why this figure is
lower than $1,700m lies in the 'countervailing effect': The rise
in investment of $70m sets in train a multiplier sequence, but
this rising national income requires more transactions money,
which can only be obtained (the money supply being constant
at $900m) by raising the interest rate. This interest rate rise cuts
back investment and so 'countervails' the multiplier sequence.
At an equilibrium interest rate of 13 per cent the level of investment is $131m, not $170m. (It is very doubtful whether the
countervailing effect is ever numerically as large as in this simple
example.)

Keynes argued that a capitalist economy could have large or
fluctuating unemployment due to inadequate or fluctuating demand,
and that governments could handle this either by fiscal measures or
by changing the money supply. This doctrine has had great impact on
government policy. A further refinement of his doctrine will be
examined in the next section of this chapter. In the meantime consider the third of the three categories into which we have classified
monetary theory.

The world in which we live is usually more complex than either
of the relatively simple cases postulated by the classicists and by
Keynes. It is a world in which both physical production (X) and
price level (P) are free to vary. Specifically, since capitalist nations
have now largely been successful in eliminating large-scale unemploy-

ment, a rise in final demand—whether initiated by fiscal measures or by open market operations raising the money supply and reducing interest rates and so stimulating physical investment—can be expected to *raise both physical production and the price level. How will the rise in demand be allocated between the two?* A fairly simple approach would be to assert that at high levels of unemployment (say 5 per cent of work force unemployed) there is no rise in the wage-rate or price level, but that, as unemployment falls, there is increasing competition for labour so that the wage-rate is bid up and prices are marked up, until, when finally full employment is reached, the whole of any rise in final demand (i.e. actual expenditure) is allocated (or 'dissipated') in rising money wage-rates and so in rising prices.

Such a hypothesis is illustrated for an imaginary case in figure 4.3, where the proportion of a $1m rise in demand at *current* prices that results in a rise in physical output falls linearly from unity (when

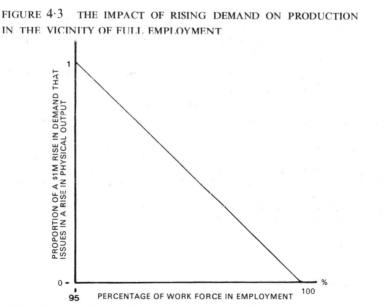

FIGURE 4·3   THE IMPACT OF RISING DEMAND ON PRODUCTION IN THE VICINITY OF FULL EMPLOYMENT

PROPORTION OF A $1M RISE IN DEMAND THAT ISSUES IN A RISE IN PHYSICAL OUTPUT

1

0 -

95   PERCENTAGE OF WORK FORCE IN EMPLOYMENT   100   %

When 5 per cent of the work force is unemployed, a $1m rise in demand at current prices results in a $1m rise in physical production. But as unemployment falls, the proportion of a $1m rise in demand that is dissipated in rising prices increases, and the proportion that results in a rise in physical output falls.

unemployment is 5 per cent) to zero (when full employment is reached). Putting the same thing in order words we can say that the proportion of a $1m rise in demand that is dissipated in rising wage-rates, and so rising prices, rises from zero to unity over the same range.

It then becomes a matter for practical enquiry to calculate how much of the effect of a rise in the money supply is allocated between rising production and rising prices. However, it is to be noted that the real national income multiplier (at constant prices) can no longer be constant but falls towards zero as aggregate demand approaches full-employment capacity production.

Some theorists have been concerned not with the effect of the money supply on rising prices (P) and production (X) separately but with the relation between rising money supply and rising value of national product ($X.P$). If we take as our time-span the annual level of the money supply and value of national product over a decade, we would be most unwise to assume that their ratio is going to be found constant.[7] For such an

> *Example:* In the previous worked example, the 50 per cent rise in the money supply resulted in a 30 per cent rise in the value of national product.[8]

assumption carries the corollary that a rise in the money supply is necessary if the value of the national product is to rise. However, an upward shift in the short-term investment-demand schedule is capable of raising interest rates and 'siphoning' idle money balances

---

[7] Thus, in Australia, the ratio of the money supply to national product fell during 1954 to 1964 from 62 per cent to 55 per cent; during this period borrowers offered progressively higher interest rates in order to attract idle money balances into active circulation and the yield on 2 year government securities rose relatively markedly from 3.55 per cent to 4.36 per cent. (Even at 55 per cent, it seems possible that as much as two-thirds of this represents idle money balances.)

[8] For the simplest Keynesian model,

$$C = c.X$$
$$I = h - k(i)$$
$$M = j.(X.P)/i$$

c, h, k, j are constants

equilibrium in the commodity and money markets exists when:

$$X = \frac{h}{(1-c) + (k.j.P)/M}$$

$$= \frac{h.M}{(1-c)M + k.j.P}$$

In this case, since P is a constant, the ratio X/M cannot be constant.

(subscribed to new debentures issued to finance investment) into the transactions flow. Thus rising investment can result in a multiplier process and rising value of national product without any change in money supply at all. The longer-term relation between money supply and value of national product is still the topic of active debate.

This review has proposed three situations:
— constant production
— constant price level
— variable production and price level

as a convenient way of understanding the relationship between the work of various theorists who have explored the impact of money on the economy. However, in the first and third categories—in both of which the price level is free to vary—there are two further complications, which ultimately have to be recognised. The first complication is that expenditure may rise as a result of rising prices; e.g. if businessmen plan to maintain their physical volume of invest-ment, then as wage-rates and prices of materials rise, so also will their investment demand rise when expressed at current prices. Similar argument may be applied to other categories of demand which also become variables because of rising prices. The second com-plication is that wage-rates do not respond passively to rising com-modity demand but may behave autonomously in various ways not so far explored. For example, as full employment is approached, trade unions may demand ever higher annual increases in money wage-rates so that full employment may be inconsistent with the concept of prices being constant at any level at all. The discussion

Summary

The demand for money, including a transactions and assets demand, depends on both the value of the national product and on the interest rate.

The effects of change in the money supply have been analysed under three different assumptions:

(a) Constant physical production: in which case the price level was found to be proportional to the money supply.

(b) Constant price level: in which case the volume of production rises. The ultimate result reflects both a multiplier sequence and the countervailing effect of changing interest rates. The volume of production is not pro-portional to the money supply.

(c) Both the national product and the price level vary. Here some new as-sumption is needed concerning the behaviour of wage-rates and prices; (see next chapter).

of these ideas is held over to the next chapter. The following section is devoted to concluding the discussion of Keynes' analysis, which assumed a constant money wage-rate and price level.

6. The stability of the economy

Much of our argument in preceding sections has been concerned with the manner in which the level of the physical national product *responds* to any *autonomous* change impinging on the economy. Such autonomous change may be a change in the money supply, or it may be a shift in the short-term investment-demand schedule (reflecting a changed attitude by businessmen to investment opportunities) or some other change in tastes or in government action. Attention has been drawn to two response mechanisms. The first was the national income multiplier sequence. The second was the countervailing effect of a changing interest rate. These two mechanisms are always present in some degree and they are opposed to one another in their effect on production. Putting the point in another way: when any autonomous change impacts on the economy (e.g. a fall in investment demand), the multiplier sequence re-enforces that impact (a positive feedback); but the countervailing sequence limits that impact (a negative feedback). *Thus the countervailing sequence is seen to have a stabilising effect on the economy, and it is a matter of political importance to assess the significance of this stabilising effect.* Consider then the case of a sustained autonomous fall in defence expenditure on goods and services. (The reader should satisfy himself that the argument applies equally to an autonomous fall in private investment—both events initiate a recession).

In the preceding chapter we argued that, starting from maximum national production, a fall in defence or investment spending would not only directly imply a fall in employment and production in the defence or investment-goods industry, but also would set in train a multiplier process whereby the level of income and employment fell further in the consumer-goods industry until ultimately a recession equilibrium is reached which can be calculated from the size of the national income multiplier.

J. M. Keynes argued that a countervailing monetary process reduces such a fluctuation in national income, i.e. has a stabilising effect. The argument is as follows: as the recession develops, less money is needed in the transactions flow so that (assuming the money supply is constant) more money will be available for buying securities, and so the market interest rate will fall. Given such a fall in the interest rate, it is proposed that there will be a consequent rise in physical investment since it is presumed that there will be a larger number of investment projects whose rate of return can match the lower interest rate. Such a rise in investment will limit the downward income multiplier process in as much as it represents a countervailing movement.[9]

This argument is illustrated in figure 4.4 where there are three parts. The first shows, for any chosen volume of national product X, how the demand for money M_d varies inversely with the interest rate in accord with the relation:

$$M_d = \frac{0.03}{i} (X.P)$$

which has been chosen for its simplicity. It is convenient, for the moment, to assume the price level P to be constant, and it can thus be equated to an index of unity. The fixed money supply M is shown as a vertical line.

The second part uses the investment demand function due to Klein and Shinkai in an econometric model of Japan,[10] since the flexibility of interest rates in that nation make it a good subject for the Keynesian countervailing hypothesis. In this relation, if both K and V are held

$$I = 0.051K + 0.478V - 0.678i.K$$

where I net investment
K year-end capital stock } billions of
V non-wage income } 1934-6 yen
i interest rate

constant, then investment (I) falls linearly as the interest rate (i) rises. The third part shows the equilibrium level of national production

---

[9] Refer J.R. Hicks, 'Mr Keynes and the Classics' in *Readings in the Theory of Income Distribution* (Philadelphia: A.E.A. Blakiston Press, 1949) p. 461; also A.H. Hansen, *Monetary Theory and Fiscal Policy* (New York: McGraw-Hill, 1949), ch. 5.

[10] Klein and Shinkai, 'An Econometric Model of Japan 1930-59', in *International Economic Review* (January 1963).

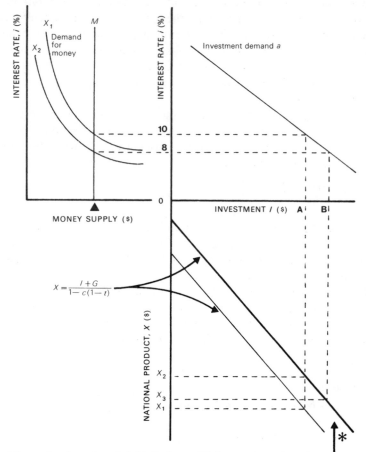

FIGURE 4·4 THE SUGGESTED COUNTERVAILING SEQUENCE IN A RECESSION

The national product is initially in equilibrium at X_1. There is then a fall in government defence spending on goods and services (G) resulting in a shift in the bottom schedule as shown by the starred arrow. The national product then falls towards X_2.

The countervailing hypothesis is that this fall in national production releases funds from the transactions flow with a consequent fall in interest rates, thus stimulating investment to rise from OA to OB and so limiting the fall in national production to the level X_3.

Note: a $I = 0.051K + 0.478V - 0.678i.K$
          V, K being constant

$$X = \frac{I + G}{1 - c(1 - t)}$$

as a function of investment (I), assuming government spending on goods and services (G) and the marginal propensity to consume out of national income ($c(1 - t)$) to be both constant.

The initial situation in figure 4.4 is characterised by a 10 per cent interest rate, at which the demand for money equals the supply (i.e. on balance there is no attempt to exchange money for debentures, or conversely). At this interest rate the level of physical investment is A and the equilibrium national product is X_1.

This situation is now disrupted by a sustained fall in government defence spending so that the equilibrium national income line shifts —showing that, at an investment of A, the national income falls to X_2 as a result of the national income multiplier process.

However, at a national income of X_2, transactions demand for money shifts down as in the upper left diagram. Thus money balances are freed from the transaction flow, which will result in some bidding to purchase fixed interest debentures. Thus the market interest rate will fall[11]—until it reaches a level at which the demand for money equals the supply.[12] This is shown as 8 per cent.

Since the investment demand schedule is downward sloping, investment rises from A to B, with a consequent countervailing effect that shifts the national product back towards X_3. *It is this countervailing effect that is now challenged.*

For the above argument oversimplifies the true situation by assuming that profits V are constant, when in fact they are falling during the recession. This can be recognised, as in figure 4.5, by showing the investment demand schedule shifting down from the initial position when profits are V_1 at national income X_1, to a lower position when

[11] A debenture or government security whose redemption (i.e. face) value is $100 pays a fixed annual sum by way of interest, e.g. $5. If the current *market* price of the debenture is bid up to $125, then the fixed interest payment represents a *market* annual interest rate of 4 per cent, i.e. the market price and the market interest rate move inversely.

[12] In this example the supply of both money and debentures is constant. The interest rate changes as a result of buying pressure for debentures, until the public no longer wish to exchange money for debentures. Paradoxically it is just possible that no actual debenture sales occur—and that the market price of debentures just moves to a position at which the lower market interest rate leaves people content to hold the money (freed from the transactions flow) in the form of idle money balances.

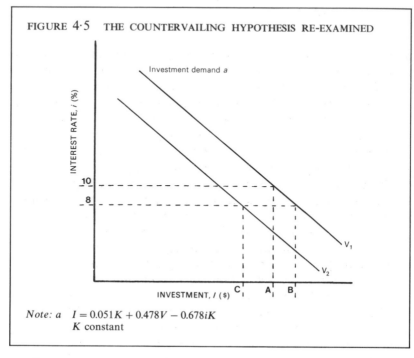

FIGURE 4·5   THE COUNTERVAILING HYPOTHESIS RE-EXAMINED

Note: a $I = 0.051K + 0.478V - 0.678iK$
      K constant

profits are V_2 at national income X_2. It is now seen that while it is true that a fall in the interest rate alone would raise investment to B, in fact the simultaneous fall in profits causes a downward shift in the schedule, and investment may decline to C.

In sum, Keynes' countervailing argument runs into the objection that, while a recession may bring with it a fall in interest rates, it also brings lower sales, lower corporate profits and a more dour view of the immediate future. Moreover there is another line of challenge to the countervailing argument, based on questioning the assumption that the money supply is constant. For a movement into recession is a situation in which the money supply is most likely to contract; e.g. banks may not make new advances for investment as old advances are repaid. In that event the downward pressure on the rate of interest may be much less than the countervailing argument assumes.

The threads of the discussion may now be brought together. It is assumed that there has been a sustained autonomous fall in some component of final demand; (such as a fall in defence spending or in consumer demand for durable goods). We know that this will result in a downward multiplier sequence as falling income causes falling consumption. The question is what happens to investment demand? Drawing on the list of influences affecting investment set out in chapter 3, we now seek to simplify by considering three only:

(a) secular influences including population growth, replacement and innovation—which might be collected as a single variable: 'the expected long-term growth rate of national product';

(b) the rate of interest;

(c) profits.

It is apparent that these three influences pull in different directions:

(a) if population is growing steadily then this tends to sustain the level of investment planned;

(b) the fall in production, by reducing the volume of money needed for transactions, may bring about a fall in the interest rate, which tends to sustain the level of investment;

(c) the fall in profits may, however, cause some currently planned investment to be postponed, so investment is lower than it would otherwise be.

It would be unwise to ignore any of these effects even though this means that no general statement can be made about the short-run behaviour of the level of investment demand. The relative importance of these influences on investment can only be established by statistical analysis.

Summary

The notion has a long history that, if the economy moves into recession, a countervailing or stabilising force will automatically put a brake on the recession. A modern version of this notion has been set out and criticised on the ground that it incorrectly assumes important variables to be constant, namely profits and the money supply.

A second countervailing argument is based on the proposition that consumption and investment spending depend on the real value of money balances (as well as on other influences already discussed). The effect of this during a business recession in which commodity prices fell, would be to raise the real value of money balances and so to stimulate spending on commodities and limit the decline in production and employment. There is evidence to support this proposition, but it is uncertain as yet as to how significant the *real balance effect* has been in promoting economic stability in capitalist economies generally.[13]

7. The economic system ⊟

The model of the economic system used in the foregoing discussion is shown in figure 4.6.

FIGURE 4·6   THE MACROECONOMIC MODEL

Work force W is known Technology	:	$aX = N$, for a given capital stock
Distribution	:	$XP = N.P_n(1 + v)$
Demand	:	$C = c(1 - t)X$ $I = 0.051K + 0.478V - 0.678i.K$ G is known $X = C + I + G$ in equilibrium
Money	:	$\dfrac{M_d}{XP} = \dfrac{0.03}{i}$
Money supply	:	$M = M_d$ in equilibrium

The capital stock K, the wage-rate P_n, and the money supply M, are all assumed constant.

For meaning of symbols refer page 311.

The purpose of this section is to consider the financial aspects of this model. Consider first the supply of money.

A simple, superficially attractive, approach to the supply of money is to assert that it is proportional to the value of national production. On this view an increase of say 50 per cent in the money supply by the banks over a length of time will result—since in equilibrium the demand for money must equal the given supply—in a 50 per cent rise in the value of national production. The extent to

[13] D. Patinkin, *Post Keynesian Economics* (Evanston, Ill.: Row Peterson, 1957), ch. 5.
D.B. Suits, *Impact of Monetary Policy* (Englewood Cliffs, N.J.: Prentice Hall, 1964), p.32.

which that 50 per cent rise is split between a rise in real production and general price inflation presumably depends on how close the economy is to capacity production. Two comments may be made on this 'theory of money', and both are important. The first is that, while it asserts a conclusion (viz. 50 per cent rise in value of production), it does not state the mechanism by which this result is reached. Suppose we assume that the mechanism is that the rise in money supply takes the form of increased bank loans for investment, which set in train an income multiplier process—in sum both investment demand and consumption demand rise. The lesson of this is that one needs to ask how a change in the money supply affects commodity demand. The second comment is that we do know that the demand for money depends also on the interest rate (as in figure 4.4), and this is important because it means that within limits the national product can rise even in the face of a fixed money supply. The mechanism is that if businessmen wish to expand investment, they can float debenture issues at higher interest rates in order to persuade the holders of idle money balances to switch their asset holdings from money to debentures. Businessmen then have the funds to spend on their investment programme even if the banks are unwilling to increase the money supply. Indeed this rise in investment spending will then cause a price inflation if the economy is close to capacity production.

Let us turn now to a second topic—the rate of interest. There is little evidence in industrialised nations to suggest that households will decide to consume less (i.e. save more) *directly* because of a rise in the interest rate. But the rate of interest does turn up at two other points in our conceptual model of the economy: first as a rationing device influencing the level of investment demand; second as a determinant of the demand for money (i.e. a determinant of the composition of asset holdings, money *versus* securities).

In summary, the rate of interest:

(a) appears not to influence directly the level of savings;
(b) does screen out individual investment projects on which the rate of return is less than the interest rate;
(c) does influence the public's willingness to hold their financial assets in money as compared with interest-bearing securities.

So much for the specific functions of the rate of interest. Does it, however, perform any broader role in the administration of the nation's resources?

The nineteenth century belief that the interest rate stimulates investment to absorb the supply of savings available at full employment is historically incorrect. For if there is an autonomous fall in investment, rather than a fall in the interest rate restimulating the level of investment, the major sequence of events is a downward multiplier cumulatively reducing the size of the national income. The matter is worth restating as follows:

In any period of time part of the national income is spent on consumption and part is saved. The savings then are a 'leakage' from the income flow in as much as they are not spent on consumption goods. However, business firms 'inject' their demand for investment goods into the income flow. If these investment 'injections' equal the savings 'leakage' then the economy is in equilibrium since aggregate demand (consumption plus investment) equals national production or income (consumption plus savings); see figure 4.1. If there is now an autonomous fall in investment, classical economists, correctly realising that for equilibrium to be re-established then planned investment and planned savings must once again be equal, incorrectly asserted that this equality would be brought about by a fall in the interest rate raising the level of investment (and indeed, consumption) demand. The historical record, however, shows that this mechanism is ineffective. The dominant mechanism is a fall in the national income, and, since savings are a function of the national income, savings also fall until an unemployment equilibrium is re-established at which planned investment and savings are again equal to one another (but not equal to their previous level). Thus it is precisely because this classically conceived interest rate mechansim is ineffective that positive government action is needed when a lack of demand threatens to cause unemployment.

Summary

§1. The creation of a monetary system is analysed in order to explore the influences affecting the size of the money supply.

§2. The process of creating money by the commercial banks is detailed.

§3. The role of the central bank in economic management is discussed.

§4. The creation of a money commodity results in a divorce of the decision to invest from the decision to save, and so makes possible an under-employment equilibrium due to deficient demand.

§5. The effect of change in the money supply is considered for three cases: constant production, constant prices, and variable production and prices.

§6. It has been suggested that, if a deficiency of demand sets off a business recession, financial mechanisms will have a countervailing effect to the limit of the fall in national production by stimulating investment for consumption demand. The practical importance of these mechanisms is a matter for debate.

§7. The role of the money supply and of the interest rate in the economy are examined. Considering them in turn:

    (a) There is little use in discussing the effects of a change in the money supply without a detailed analysis of the mechanism (notably change in demand for goods) involved in bringing about those effects;

    (b) The rate of interest has historically failed to equate intended investment to the savings available at full employment.

Further reading

J.M. Keynes, *The General Theory of Employment, Interest and Money* (London: Macmillan, 1936).

F.S. Brooman, *Macroeconomics* (London: Allen and Unwin, 1967), ch. 10.

J.M. Culbertson, *Macroeconomic Theory and Stabilization Policy* (New York: McGraw-Hill, 1968).

L.V. Chandler, *The Economics of Money and Banking* (New York: Harper & Row, 1969).

Questions

1. Explain why people may prefer to hold their assets in the form of money rather than other commodities.
2. Explain the phrase 'fractional reserve banking'. How is the ability of the commercial banks to create money limited?
3. Detail the sequence of events in a typical situation in which a commercial bank does create money.

4. Explain (a) two equivalent ways of expressing a state of equilibrium in the commodity market; (b) how it is that, in a period in which the commodity market is not in equilibrium, savings and investment are equal on one set of definitions and unequal using another set of definitions.

11. In a simple economy with no government and no foreign trade, households spend 80 per cent of their income on consumer goods. The level of investment that businessmen seek to undertake has been shown by an investment survey to be holding steady at $500m per quarter. What will the level of savings be when there is equilibrium in the commodity market?

12. Again in a simple economy with no government spending or taxes and no foreign trade, households plan to save 10 per cent of their incomes. The level of intended investment is $1,000m per quarter, and the level of national product in the current quarter is $11,000m. What do you expect to happen?

21. Appraise monetary and fiscal measures as alternative instruments available to control aggregate demand.

22. Explain the simple quantity theory of money and objections to it.

23. Consider the proposition that there are stabilising influences that tend to keep the economy near high levels of employment.

24. Must the money supply be increased in order to allow growth in the value of national product?

25. What is 'the capital market'? Has it served capitalist economies well?

The Price Level

Inflation may be initiated either by excess demand for goods or by higher wage claims by trade unions. The first can be controlled by controlling final demand, but to contain the second may require a rethinking of the role of organised labour.

1. Introduction

Whereas chapter 3 was primarily concerned with analysing how demand affects the national level of employment and production, this chapter analyses the determination of the general level of money wage-rates and prices. Money wage-rates are singled out for attention because the national wage-bill is the dominant component of national income. For simplicity the entire national income is divided into two parts: wages and surplus.[1]

2. The wage-rate

The average money wage-rate throughout the nation may change owing to any of the following six influences.

(a) The proportion of the work force unemployed

In modern industrialised nations, government commitment to a policy of low unemployment has increased the bargaining power of organised labour. Following a line of reasoning that goes back to Marx's 'surplus army of unemployed', theorists have suggested that the lower the proportion of the work force unemployed, the greater is the annual rate of increase in the money wage-rate.

One implication of this postulate is that it would require some positive amount of unemployment to prevent the wage-rate from rising. For example if we imagine the annual rate of growth of the

---

[1] A more ambitious analysis would recognise other factors (e.g. land) and their income.

wage-rate $(\Delta P_n/P_n)$ to be related, as follows:

$$\frac{\Delta P_n}{P_n} = -1.9 + 2\frac{N}{W}$$

where P_n is the average money wage-rate

ΔP_n is the annual increment in wage-rate

to the proportion (N/W) of the work force employed, then unemployment would have to be 5 per cent of the work force for the wage-rate to be constant. (These figures are wholly imaginary.) This is illustrated in figure 5.1.

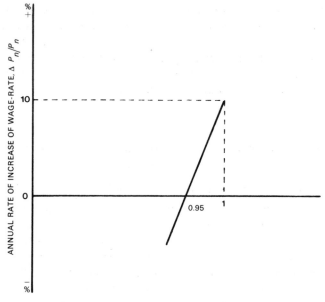

FIGURE 5·1   THE POTENTIAL INFLUENCE OF HIGH LEVELS OF EMPLOYMENT ON THE ANNUAL GROWTH OF THE AVERAGE MONEY WAGE-RATE

PROPORTION OF WORK FORCE IN EMPLOYMENT, N/W

Note: Recent work in this field stems from investigations by Professor A.W. Phillips at the London School of Economics. In reality it is unlikely that such a relation would be a straight line.

(b) *The annual growth rate of average output per worker*

Again, it has been suggested that trade unions use their bargaining power to claim a rate of annual increase in the money wage-rate equal to this growth rate of 'labour productivity' or output per worker.

Such a claim by labour may be additional to the previous one, in which event the relationship could be summarised:

$$\frac{\Delta P_n}{P_n} = -1.9 + 2\frac{N}{W} + \frac{\Delta p}{p}$$

where the last term is the annual growth rate of labour productivity (p).

(c) *The dispersion of the rate of growth of labour productivity among industries*

The effect of the growth of labour productivity on the national average wage-rate depends not only on average productivity but also on its spread among industries.

To illustrate, imagine that there are just two industries, motor vehicles and education (i.e. schools), and that they are roughly equal in size (to keep the arithmetic simple). Now, if labour productivity rises 5 per cent during the year in *both* industries, both unions may demand a 5 per cent wage rise. In reality it is more likely that technological change will cause labour productivity in motor vehicles to rise 10 per cent during the year, while labour productivity in the schools does not rise at all—which is still an *average* rise in national labour productivity of 5 per cent as in the previous example. Now, however, motor vehicle workers may successfully claim a 10 per cent wage-rate rise and, *because of this,* schoolteachers also claim a 10 per cent wage-rate rise. So the rate of growth of the national average wage-rate depends here not only on the average growth of productivity but also on its spread.

The sequence of events outlined here is known variously as 'pattern-setting', 'flow-on' or simply 'emulation'. It is a well-known characteristic of the labour-market.[2]

---

[2] It also shows the naivety of the idea that price rises can be prevented by giving each worker a wage-rate rise equal to the productivity rise in 'his' industry. The worker in the low-gain industry will still want a wage-rise to match the worker in the high-gain industry.

(d) *Rising commodity prices*

The proposition here is that organised labour claims a higher money wage-rate 'because prices and the cost of living have risen'. It should be immediately noted that if prices have risen, then someone is receiving those prices in the form of wages or surplus.[3] The rational questions to ask then are (i) whether there has been a shift in the distribution of income to surplus; and (ii) whether there has been a shift in the distribution of income as between different classes of wage-earners. If the answers to these questions are negative, then such a claim for higher money wage-rates seems a rather empty negotiating gambit.

(e) *Excess demand for goods and services*

We come now to consider not the claims for higher wage-rates by labour but the offer of higher wage-rates by employers.

When excess demand for commodities develops there are two possible basic responses by business: to raise price or raise output. In rural and mining industries the initial response is commonly to raise price because output cannot be increased in the short-run; in manufacturing and service industries the typical response is to seek to raise output, and this is the response that will be assumed to prevail here because it appears to be the dominant response in industrialised nations.

Now, in order to raise output the businessman must typically employ more labour, and if unemployment is low he must bid for labour by offering higher money wage-rates to attract labour from other firms. (These higher wage-rates raise his unit production costs and so, applying a fixed percentage profit mark-up, he then raises the price of his product. This is discussed below.)

The implication of this is that, even if labour were making no wage claims, excess demand for goods would be sufficient to result in rising money wage-rates.

(f) *Other autonomous causes*

This catch-all category is included since the intervention of wage tribunals and of governments may cause wage-rates to change in an otherwise unpredictable way.

---

[3] Or payments for imports in a trading economy.

Summary

The explanation of change in the price level is approached here by first considering change in the average money wage-rate. The reason for this is our belief that the wage-rate exerts a dominant influence on the price level.

The average money wage-rate is affected by many influences, including:
— percentage unemployment
— the size and dispersion of the annual growth rate of output per worker
— the 'cost of living'
— excess demand for goods

3. The price level

The price of a good is by definition equal to the sum of the cost items for each input, where each item is calculated as the input volume (required per unit of output) multiplied by its price and multiplied by the profit mark-up, i.e.:

$$P_i = \sum_j a_{ji} \, P_j (1 + v_i)$$

where P_i price of commodity i
a_{ji} quantity of input j
per unit of output of i
P_j price of input j
v_i profit mark-up

If the sole input is labour, then:

$$P_i = a_{ni}.P_n(1 + v_i)$$

where a_{ni} labour input coefficient
(by definition $a_{ni} \equiv 1/p$
where p is output per worker)
P_n wage-rate

It follows that if the profit mark-up is constant, then the price level rises if the wage-rate rises proportionately more than labour productivity. This simple proposition can be applied to any of the causes of rising wage-rates listed in the previous section.

Consider, for example, an excess demand situation in which the economy is already near full employment and demand for goods begins to rise rapidly—say owing to an investment boom. It is possible that in such a situation the profit mark-up may rise—reflected in a rise in the ratio of surplus to wages—as producers respond to the excess demand by raising prices. However, in industrialised countries, it seems more typical for employers to bid for labour, thus raising the money wage-rate and so unit cost of their product, with an unchanged percentage profit mark-up being applied to this cost so that price rises proportionately. It is assumed here therefore that the profit mark-up is constant[4]—though the argument could readily be extended to analyse predictable change in the mark-up.

Summary

If labour is the sole input:

| price level | = | ratio of wage-rate to labour productivity | × | the profit mark-up |

i.e. $P_i = \dfrac{P_n}{p} \cdot (1 + v_i)$

In summary, we have said that the price level may change if labour productivity, the wage-rate, or the profit mark-up, change. It is easy to explore various combinations of these. No really new principles would be involved in recognising inputs other than labour (e.g. land, imports). However, there is one further matter—the analysis of the *time-path* of rising prices. This is commonly called the inflationary process.

4. The economic system: the inflationary process 🗒

Our starting point is the model of the economic system set out in chapter 3, page 71.[5] To the centre, price formation, block of this model we can add a relationship to portray the manner in which the wage-rate is proximately determined. Since our aim is to analyse the inflationary process of rising prices through time, the model needs to be adapted for this purpose by dating the variables. The most convenient operational way of using the model is to lay out

---

[4] However, it is recognised that time-lags can cause some variation in the ratio.

[5] It may be convenient to rewrite the production function $aX = N$ as $X = p.N$, where $a \equiv 1/p$; i.e. labour productivity (p) is the reciprocal of the labour input coefficient (a).

a sequence table of the kind used in chapter 3. Two modifications to the previous sequence table are needed. First, since we wish to explain price changes, the values in the sequence table will be at current prices and no longer at constant (or deflated) prices. Second, the sequence table should portray not only the relations in the demand block of the model, but also should show the cost account so that the effects of changes in factor costs on the price level can be analysed. (Figure 5.2 sets out the model used in figure 5.3)

FIGURE 5·2 MODEL OF THE ECONOMIC SYSTEM

Resource supplies	:	work force W is known
Technology	:	$X = p.N$
Income distribution*	:	$XP = N.P_n$ (1.33)
Wage-rate**	:	$P_{n_t} = \left[\dfrac{(C.P + I.P)_t}{(C.P + I.P)_{t-1}} \right] P_{n_{t-1}}$
Demand***	:	$C_t.P_t = 0.8\ Y_{t-1}$
		$I_t.P_t = 25\ P_t$

For meaning of symbols refer page 311.
Note: All variables are to be read as carrying the subscript t for the current period, unless otherwise indicated.
* Profit mark-up is one-third on wage costs.
** As a result of employers bidding for labour, the wage-rate rises proportionately to the rise in demand for goods.
*** There is a one period lag in consumer-spending. For simplicity there is no output lag.
Real investment is initially maintained by raising investment spending proportionately to the price level.

From a policy viewpoint it is worthwhile distinguishing two separate *initiating causes of the inflationary process.* The first is *excess demand for goods,* which causes businessmen to bid for labour and so raise the wage-rate, with the result that, after application of a profit mark-up, the price level rises. The second cause is *increased wage claims by labour,*[6] which raises the wage-rate, and so again after application of a profit mark-up the price level rises. These two initiating causes are called 'excess demand' inflation and 'wage-cost' inflation.[7] (In

[6] More generally, any factor may claim a higher money price for its services.
[7] In each case wage-rates rise. So it is a fallacy to deduce from the observation that wage-rates are rising that they are the *cause* of the inflation. To ascertain the cause we need to know whether the *leading* element was a rise in wage claims or a rise in wage-bids (by businessmen) stimulated by excess demand for goods.

reality both may occur simultaneously and so may be difficult to distinguish.) An important question to be asked in each case is whether the inflation tends to slow down. Consider the two causes in turn, taking the simple case in which there is full employment and constant capacity volume of production.

When a rise in investment demand for commodities occurs at full employment, the immediate effect of this excess demand of say 5 per cent is to result in a bidding up of the wage-rate and prices, all by 5 per cent. Since money incomes have risen in this period by 5 per cent, we may assume that consumer demand will rise in the next period by 5 per cent.[8] To summarise, in the first period a rise in demand causes a rise in income and so a further rise in consumer demand in the next period. This establishes the cumulative nature of the process. The next question is whether the cumulative process slows down. This depends on whether *all* elements of demand keep rising proportionately or whether some elements of demand are fixed in money terms and so can be squeezed (in real terms) by rising prices. To illustrate, the first sequence in figure 5.3 assumes that investment demand keeps rising in money terms because business-men wish to maintain their *physical* investment programme. In this case 5 per cent excess demand in one period leads to a 5 per cent excess demand in the next period and the process continues unabated.

However, if the money supply is kept fixed, the need for active money balances by businessmen as the inflation proceeds may begin to drive up the rate of interest or cause the banks to ration overdraft credit. This can slow down the rate of growth of investment in money terms.[9] The second sequence in figure 5.3 illustrates the simple case in which investment in money terms fails to rise at all once the inflation has begun. A comparison of the two sequences shows the slow-down in price increases. It is to be noted, however, that in reality *government action may be needed to bring a sufficient slow-down because so many elements of final demand do tend to rise pro-portionately with rising prices.*

---

[8] Two assumptions are being made here: there is a one-period expenditure lag; and households raise consumer spending proportionately to money income (which has the effect here of defending their real living standards).

[9] Rising prices might also discourage consumer spending by reducing the real value of consumers' money balances.

FIGURE 5·3 INFLATIONARY PROCESS CAUSED BY EXCESS DEMAND FOR GOODS

Quarter	Demand		Wage-rate (index)	Price level (index)	Production costs (incomes)		
	Consumption	Investment			Wages	Profits	TOTAL
base	80	20	1	1	75	25	100
1	80	25	1.05	1.05	78.75	26.25	105
2	84	26.25	1.1025	1.1025	82.69	27.56	110.25
3	88.2	27.56	1.1576	1.1576	86.82	28.94	115.76
4	92.608	28.94	1.2155	1.2155	91.16	30.39	121.55

Quarter	Demand		Wage-rate (index)	Price level (index)	Production costs (incomes)		
	Consumption	Investment			Wages	Profits	TOTAL
base	80	20	1	1	75	25	100
1	80	25	1.05	1.05	78.75	26.25	105
2	84	25	1.09	1.09	81.75	27.25	109
3	87.2	25	1.122	1.122	84.15	28.05	112.2
4	89.76	25	1.1476	1.1476	85.8	28.96	114.76

The *cause* of the inflation is a rise in investment demand. In the upper sequence the new level of investment demand is maintained in physical terms but in the lower sequence it is only maintained in current prices.

The *mechanism* of the inflation is a bidding for labour, which raises wage-rates and so unit costs and commodity prices.

The second initiating cause of inflation, higher wage-claims, also causes a rise in prices. But this is not cumulative in principle, since a 5 per cent rise in money wage-rates results in a 5 per cent rise in profits, prices and the value of supplies, while consumption and investment may also rise 5 per cent. No further change need occur. However, *if wage-contracts include a cost-of-living adjustment (or escalator) clause then the process does become cumulative* because higher wage-rates cause higher prices, which cause higher wage-rates in the next period. Statistically the sequence of events may then look the same as in the first sequence in figure 5.3—the difference being that higher wage-rates are being *claimed* instead of bid. It may be added that, whatever the cause of inflation, increasing monetary stringency may cause rising interest rates and credit rationing and so hold back the level of investment demand (as well as consumer demand financed by borrowing).

Summary

Excess demand for goods is a cause of cumulative price rises. The cumulative process will slow down only if some elements of demand are fixed in monetary terms.

Wage claims in excess of rising labour productivity are a second cause of inflation. They are not cumulative, but will become so if cost-of-living adjustment clauses are introduced. (However, 'pattern setting'—refer page 113—is another sort of cumulative sequence.)

5. Policy

Inflation may constitute an economic policy issue for any of four reasons:

— hyper-inflation
— income distribution
— economic efficiency
— foreign trade

Hyper-inflation is a situation in which price inflation has proceeded so rapidly that there is a mass shift of asset holdings from money (and debentures) into physical goods. This process accelerates the rate of inflation as expectations of continued high price increases effectively bring about that result. The result is a dislocation of the financial system.

Income distribution is an issue if rising prices bear harshly on the poorer section of the community such as pensioners on fixed money incomes.

The effect of inflation on economic efficiency is unclear. On the one hand it is suggested: first that inflation, by reducing the real burden of debt on borrowers, stimulates investment in capital equipment; and second that, since inflation is associated with high levels of employment, businessmen are spurred to make more effective use of scarce resources. On the other hand inflationary excess demand can cause bottlenecks and thus reduce national efficiency.

It is a concern for the effects of inflation on the ability of a nation to pay its way in foreign trade that is the most common policy issue. It is here that the distinction between excess demand and wage-cost inflation is useful. Where excess demand for commodities is the cause of inflation, the excess demand can be eliminated by budgetary or monetary measures. The problem is essentially the converse of eliminating unemployment due to inadequate demand, but with one modification regarding the effectiveness of monetary measures by the central bank. For whereas credit-expansionary measures (such as a cut in the interest rate) may fail to stem a recession if the pessimism of businessmen is such that they cannot be persuaded to borrow for investment, credit-contractionary measures by a determined central bank can undoubtedly stop an inflation caused by excess demand. Thus a sharp rise in interest rates, accompanied by a cut-back in trading bank advances, can be used to reduce investment demand.

Wage-cost inflation poses a less tractable problem. Thus suppose the government aims at say 3 per cent unemployment (if for no other reason than that a higher level will remove it from office at the next election), but that at this level the wage claims of labour are for a 7 per cent annual increase in money wage-rates, although labour productivity is only rising 2 per cent annually, so that costs are rising at 5 per cent annually. Now, if that country is an exporter of manufactured goods and the costs of her competitors are only rising at say $2\frac{1}{2}$ per cent annually, she will gradually be priced out of third country markets. This is essentially the dilemma that faced the United Kingdom at the start of the decade of the 1970s: Any country, whose labour market is such that the excess of the rate of growth of wage-rates over the rate of growth of labour productivity is greater than for other nations, faces an immediate problem of trade solvency. The solution is to encourage the responsible use of the vast power of organised labour, not to try to curb that power by creating mass unemployment.

Summary

The policy issue posed by inflation due to excess demand is essentially the converse of the policy issue posed by unemployment caused by deficient demand. The solution is to control aggregate demand.

However, the control of demand is not a rational solution to inflation caused by wage claims. The problem involves some recasting of social institutions.

Summary

§1. The aim is to analyse the determinants of wages and prices.

§2. The proximate influences affecting the level of the money wage-rate are: unemployment; growth rate of labour productivity; the industrial dispersion of that growth rate; the cost of living; and excess demand for commodities.

§3. The price level is determined by adding to wage-costs a profit mark-up, which is here assumed constant.

§4. Excess demand for goods, and wage claims, are distinguished as initiating causes of inflation. The mechanism of inflation is considered with particular reference to whether the process is cumulative and, if so, whether it decelerates.

§5. The distinction drawn as to the causes of inflation is a necessary one for government to make in framing corrective measures.

Further reading

C.L. Schultze, *National Income Analysis,* ch. 5.

G.C. Harcourt, P.H. Karmel and R.H. Wallace, *Economic Activity* (London: Cambridge University Press, 1967), ch. 14.

D.C. Rowan, *Output, Inflation and Growth.*

Questions

1. Specify the influences affecting the average wage-rate.

2. What are (a) the causes and (b) the mechanism of the inflationary process? Is all inflation cumulative? Comment on the phrase 'inflationary spiral'.

3. If you observe money wage-rates rising, do you conclude that rising prices are *caused* by wage claims?

4. In what respects has this chapter simplified the analysis of inflation?

11. Suppose that the economy is at a full-employment national production of $1,000m. This capacity production is assumed to be constant. The income shares of this national income are determined by a 25 per cent profit mark-up on wage costs. Consumer spending is 0.8 of national income in the preceding period. There are no other time-lags.

     Now, from an initial position of equilibrium, investment spending rises by one-quarter, which initiates an inflationary process. Moreover as the inflation proceeds businessmen seek to maintain this higher physical investment programme.

     Calculate how the price level moves in the first four periods. Comment on the long-run situation.

     Calculate how your results are changed by supposing that once investment is lifted by 25 per cent (i.e. the cause of inflation), it is then maintained constant in money terms, i.e. at current prices.

12. If the volume of output were constant at capacity level, could one use a national income multiplier (at current prices) to deduce the ultimate price rise?

21. Why is inflation an economic policy issue?

22. Do you consider it irrational for a government to seek to control inflation by raising rates of indirect tax which themselves raise the price level?

23. Comment on the expected effect on (a) inflation and on (b) the wage share of the national income, of union claims for higher money wage rates based on:

    (a) capacity to pay
    (b) productivity
    (c) cost of living.

24. Contrast the approach to explaining the price level in this chapter with the argument on p.92 that the price level is proportional to the money supply. Have we really 'explained the price level'?

25. In the modern debate on the control of inflation, assertions such as the following have been made:

   (a) Inflation should be controlled by the central bank controlling the money supply;

   (b) Inflation should be controlled by increasing the money supply steadily by an annual percentage slightly above the rise in the target real gross national product. (To be fair, the proviso is added that a balance of payments deficit should be allowed to decrease the money supply by the amount of that deficit);

   (c) The choice between monetary and fiscal measures to control inflation should be premised on having a tax structure that yields the government a balanced budget at full employment.

   Discuss

26. In the last 25 years central banks have occasionally tried to hold down interest rates while inflation developed. Sometimes the reason for this has been that the pursuit of low interest rates has seemed intrinsically desirable (lower taxes to meet interest on the national debt, lower interest rates for home builders); sometimes it has been because of a fear that if interest rates rose, the accompanying fall in the market price of government securities would cause the public to lose faith in government securities so that as old securities fell due they would not be converted into new securities but would have to be paid off by newly created central bank money.

   Consider this dilemma of a central bank.

PARLOUR GAME FOR PLANNERS

The economy can produce only almonds, beer, cheese and doughnuts. Consumers buy these four goods in the fixed tonnage ratios 1:10:2:2 and the planner's job is to achieve the greatest possible tonnage while maintaining these ratios.

There are three ways (or recipes) for producing both almonds and beer, and four ways of producing both cheese and doughnuts. These recipes require the following amounts of labour:land (measured in men and acres per annum) to produce one ton per year of the good:

almonds	10:1	5:2	1:4	
beer	5:1	3:4	2:9	
cheese	8:1	7:3	5:4	4:7
doughnuts	7:1	5:2	4:3	3:6

The nation's resources are two million men and one million acres.

The planner can *direct* resources (including labour) into any industry, but he may prefer to create a market economy. If he is matched against a team of capitalists, they of course *must* use a market economy.

Suitable rewards (stock options or hero medals) and punishments (bankruptcy or the salt mines) can be incorporated in the game. How can the economy be run at maximum efficiency?

Potential Production

A fundamental choice for any nation is the choice of technology, e.g. whether to use more or less land-intensive methods of production. Given the data on resources, technology and final demand, we can deduce the technology that can yield maximum production.

Example:
The nation has 7 million men and 3 million acres and produces only beer and cheese. A ton of beer can be produced annually by $2\frac{2}{3}$ men and $5\frac{1}{3}$ acres or by a more labour-intensive method using 8 men and $1\frac{1}{3}$ acres. A ton of cheese can be produced annually by 4 men and 8 acres or by a more labour-intensive method using 8 men and 4 acres. Consumers demand beer and cheese in the physical ratio 3:1. What is the potential national product?

1. The nature of technology

For any industrial process two technical characteristics of major importance are the nature of: *scale returns*; and *substitution between productive factors* such as land and labour.

An industrial process in which a doubling of all variable inputs results in a doubling of output is said to have *constant* scale returns. Of course some industries have *increasing* scale returns—for example, in petrochemicals plants, engineers consider that a big plant double the size of a small one will cost only 50 per cent more to build, will use only 15 per cent more labour and will have gains in thermal efficiency.[1] When scale returns increase at this rate the implications for living standards are tremendous. But we will consider here only the common case in which productive processes have constant scale returns.

Where it is possible to substitute factors, factor substitution may be perfect or imperfect.[2] *Perfect substitution* describes a simple

[1] 'The Protean Carbon Atom', *The Economist* (3 October 1970).
[2] When a productive process is characterised by constant scale returns, and when it is also the case that factors are not at all substitutable (i.e. used *in fixed proportions*) then it has become common practice to call the productive process an *activity*. Such an industrial process or activity can then be described by a set of *technical input coefficients*; e.g. to manufacture one ton of cement requires 1.4 tons of limestone, shell and coral, 0.05 tons of gypsum and 0.1 tons of clay materials.

situation in which factors are substitutable for one another at a *constant* rate; e.g. half a gallon of fuel oil may substitute for five pounds of coal as a source of heat.

However, the ultimate factors of production—labour, land, capital equipment—are typically *imperfectly substitutable*. For example in farming, a switch away from labour and into more land-intensive methods to produce an unchanged tonnage of output will be found to require progressively *greater* increases in input of land to replace successive units of labour. This is illustrated in figure 6.1 where five factor-combinations (*A*, *B*, *C*, *D*, *E*,) capable of producing a ton of output are plotted. Starting from *A*, if land and labour were perfectly substitutable the 'equal-output curve' would be the straight line *ABX* along which labour is swopped for land at the constant rate $1:\frac{1}{2}$. In fact the equal-output curve is *ABCDE*; and the wedge-shaped area *XBCDE* protrays how, as the land-labour ratio rises, factor requirements rise owing to imperfect substitution. The argument in the following box shows how imperfect substitution can be described in terms of the concept of *marginal product*: Imperfect substitution describes a constant output situation in which, as the intensity of use of a factor rises, the relative marginal productivity of the factor diminishes.

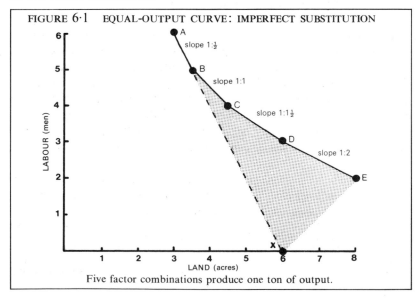

FIGURE 6·1   EQUAL-OUTPUT CURVE: IMPERFECT SUBSTITUTION

Five factor combinations produce one ton of output.

IMPERFECT SUBSITITUTION
a) *Definitions*

Suppose wheat production is under consideration. Use labour as a 'benchmark' factor for comparison. Then:
— *marginal product of labour* is the rise in output when one more labourer is employed;
— *marginal product of land* is the rise in output when one more acre is employed;
— *the relative marginal productivity of land (q)* is the ratio of the marginal product of land to the marginal product of labour;
factor intensity is the land/labour ratio.

Argument

Figure 6·1 portrays a situation in which, as the factor-intensity rises, the marginal product of land falls relatively to the marginal product of labour. (Note that *the slope of any segment* of the curve must measure the ratio of marginal products q). Hence a reduced input of successive units of labour has to be replaced by progressively *greater* increases in the input of land. That is imperfect substitution.

In conclusion, figure 6.1 is redrawn on a smaller scale in figure 6.2 in order to show the nest of equally-spaced parallel equal-output curves for 1, 2, 3, 4 tons of output. Starting from any point in figure 6.2 such as A, we can see that an increase in the input of land, *labour input remaining constant*, carries us to higher output curves in such fashion that (q) the relative marginal productivity of land diminishes progressively. It follows that if an economy had all labour employed, but some land was unemployed, then the endeavour to use all available land by introducing more land-intensive technology would be associated with a diminishing level of (q) the relative marginal productivity of land.

Finally, suppose there are just 3 consumer goods in an imaginary economy, and for each good there are 2 possible methods of production, each characterised by constant scale returns. If we assume that the 3 goods are demanded in a fixed proportions 'basket', it follows that there are eight ($=2^3$) possible ways of producing a basket of these goods. It is easy to show that if we plot all the efficient ways of producing a basket we obtain an array of points precisely as in figure 6.1. (If there are 100 goods and three ways of producing each good, there are 3^{100} ways of producing a basket—but the curved array of figure 6.1 remains). Hence our discussion of figures 6.1 and 6.2 can be thought of as referring to an *entire economy* where consumer goods are demanded in fixed proportions (and of course scale returns are constant).

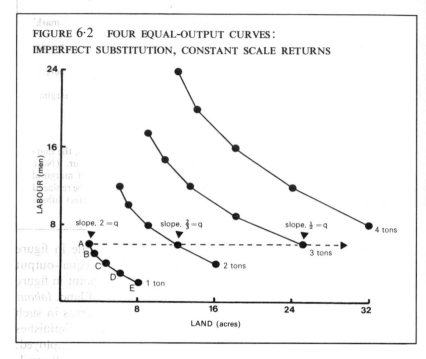

FIGURE 6·2   FOUR EQUAL-OUTPUT CURVES:
IMPERFECT SUBSTITUTION, CONSTANT SCALE RETURNS

2. Potential production

Economic policy is basically concerned with three problems:
  (a)   to use *all* the resources available;
  (b)   to *allocate* the resources in the best manner;
  (c)   to *distribute* the national income among income recipients in some acceptable fashion.
All nations face the solution of these problems—whether the means of production are organised under centrally planned socialism, competitive socialism, private enterprise capitalism or some combination of these.

The *allocation* of resources is often regarded as the classical economic problem. It involves choice between alternatives, such as the choice between:
    different methods of producing a good;

— consumption versus saving;

— guns versus butter;

— foreign trade versus economic self-sufficiency.

Consider for example the problem in the box below, where there is a choice between alternative methods of production, and the task

---

The nation has 7 million men and 3 million acres and produces only beer and cheese. A ton of beer can be produced annually by: $2\frac{2}{3}$ men and $5\frac{1}{3}$ acres; or by a more labour-intensive method using 8 men and $1\frac{1}{3}$ acres. A ton of cheese can be produced annually by 4 men and 8 acres or by a more labour-intensive method using 8 men and 4 acres. Consumers demand beer and cheese in the physical ratio 3:1. What is the potential national product?

---

is to specify the technology that can achieve maximum production. Obviously there must be a solution. The solution in fact is: 0.258 million tons of cheese produced by the second productive process and three times that amount of beer, of which 30 per cent is produced by the first beer-making process and 70 per cent by the second. But it is not the answer that is important—it is the *method*, since a sound method will solve much more complex problems than this simple case. In order to set up a method we now pause to state a most important concept—the concept of cost.

The idea of cost

Imagine that the government is planning a bigger army. For it to achieve this, labour must be diverted from producing food and television sets into producing guns and into expanding the number of regiments. So in physical terms the cost of having a bigger army is the fall in civilian consumption. Indeed the cost of any proposal involving the use of resources is *the loss of production elsewhere in the economy* that necessarily results from transferring resources from their existing use to the new proposed use. So if we propose to produce a ton of beer annually by a process that requires 8 men and $1\frac{1}{3}$ acres, then the cost of that ton of beer is the loss of production elsewhere in the economy. That is, the *cost of a ton of beer* by this process *is the output that 8 men and $1\frac{1}{3}$ acres could have produced in other processes* or industries.

It is intended to measure the cost of production of goods in *marginal product of labour* units, or mp_n units. On this measuring scale the product of one man is 1. Since we don't know the marginal product of land we will call it q. (If q should turn out to be 2 mp_n units, that would mean that the marginal product of an acre of land is twice the marginal product of a labourer). It follows that, on the stated definitions, the cost of a ton of beer by the above process is $(8 + 1\frac{1}{3}q)$, expressed in marginal product of labour units.

3. The central planner

It is of great interest to look at the problem of choice of technology as a central planner views it. For to him it is a *physical* problem of maximising production. To achieve that aim he will rationally seek to choose the method of producing each good which minimises the cost per ton[3]. But he has to overcome the fact that while the cost of producing a ton of beer by a process is $(8 + 1\frac{1}{3}q)$, he does not know the level of q. He overcomes this by assigning the levels 1, 2, 3, 4 ... to q and computing his demand for land at each level. The level of q at which all resources are demanded is the one he picks. Thus his method of solving his problem is essentially *ascertaining his demand schedule for land*, assuming labour is fully employed.

The planner's logic can be looked at in detail with the help of the technical information in the next box. If he begins arbitrarily with $q = 2$, it is seen that he will choose the labour-intensive (i.e. the second)

FIGURE 6.3 TECHNICAL INPUT COEFFICIENTS (a_{ni}, a_{li})

Resources		Products: Processes:	Beer (1)	Beer (2)	Cheese (1)	Cheese (2)
men	a_{ni}		$2\frac{2}{3}$	8	4	8
acres	a_{li}		$5\frac{1}{3}$	$1\frac{1}{3}$	8	4

Calculation
When marginal product of:
    labour is 1 unit
    land is $q = 2$ units
then the cost in mp_n units will be:

	Beer (1)	Beer (2)	Cheese (1)	Cheese (2)
labour cost	$2\frac{2}{3}$	8	4	8
land cost	$10\frac{2}{3}$	$2\frac{2}{3}$	16	8
TOTAL COST	$13\frac{1}{3}$	$10\frac{2}{3}$	20	16

Note: Where q equals 2, the second process is selected for producing each product.

---

[3] 'Cost' is of course used in the sense defined in the preceding section.

process for both goods in order to minimise cost per ton. He can then calculate that his demand for land is 1.75 million acres (see box below). The two figures ($q=2$, $h=1.75$) are the co-ordinates of a point on the planner's demand schedule for land. Plainly there is unused land going to waste since there are 3 million acres available.

Demand for resources $\leq$ *Supply*
   $8(3x)+8x$ $= 7$ million men
   $1\frac{1}{3}(3x)+4x$ $= h$ million acres

where x is cheese tonnage and $3x$ is beer tonnage. Then:

   $24x+8x=32x$ $= 7$ million men
   $4x+4x= 8x$ $= h$ million acres
or $32x : 7 :: 8x : h$
so $h=1.75$

Note: Where the second means of producing each product is selected (which happens when q equals 2), the resources demanded are 7 million men and $1\frac{3}{4}$ million acres.

Looking back at that calculation: if one imagines momentarily that land resources *were* only 1.75 million acres, then the relative marginal product of land would indeed be 2, and the planner would have chosen the best technology; i.e. the technology that *both* minimises unit cost *and* uses all available resources. His only error is that in reality some resources are unused. So he tries a new level of q. (See figure 6.4).

The planner's calculations are now repetitive. The reader can check that if $q=1.1$ then the least-cost method of producing beer is the first land-intensive process, and that as a result total demand for land jumps to 8.75 million acres, which greatly exceeds the 3 million acre supply. The planner thus has 'overshot' and must find the level of q—between 1.1 and 2—at which the demand for all resources equals the supply. It turns out that the critical figure is $q=1.33$, at which both beer processes are competitive,[4] and the demand for land can equal the supply if these two processes are used in the right proportion. That proportion can be calculated as shown in the following box, which yields the solution given earlier.

---

[4] The nation's technology at the two points on figure 6.4 is the same except for a difference in beer processes. It follows that in order to use a quantity of land between 1.75 and 8.75 million acres, both beer processes must be used.

Let x be the cheese tonnage, $3x$ then is beer tonnage, k is the proportion of beer produced by the first process, $(1-k)$ is the proportion produced by the second process:

Factor	Factor requirement	Factor supply
labour	$2\frac{2}{3}(3x)k + 8(3x)(1-k) + 8x =$	7
land	$5\frac{1}{3}(3x)k + 1\frac{1}{3}(3x)(1-k) + 4x =$	3

This gives the result that land and labour are demanded in the same ratio as they are supplied when $k = 10/33$.[5] This then yields an output for cheese (x) of 0.258 million tons.

The above discussion has been wholly in physical terms—and this is valuable because most economic policy issues are ultimately concerned with the options in using physical resources. But it is natural to ask whether the central planner makes the same decisions as individual socialist factory managers in a market economy. This shift from centralised socialism to competitive socialism is discussed in the next chapter.

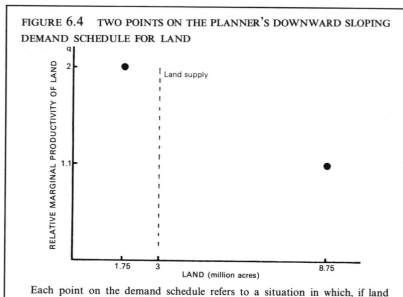

FIGURE 6.4   TWO POINTS ON THE PLANNER'S DOWNWARD SLOPING DEMAND SCHEDULE FOR LAND

Each point on the demand schedule refers to a situation in which, if land supply were equal to that demand, national production is maximised.

[5] The two equations for the demand and supply of factors are two simple simultaneous equations in the two unknowns k and x, and so can be solved by the familiar (though tedious) technique of elimination.

Summary

The choice of technology is a vital one for any economy. For the central planner an operational method of making this choice is to minimise unit cost

$$a_{ni} + q \cdot a_{li}$$

for each good, and shift q until full employment is reached. This will be found to be an analogue of the mechanism of a market economy.

4. The economic system ▤

Since this chapter has examined how the level of potential production is calculated, the argument can be summarised by setting out the first block only of the three-block model—i.e. resources and technology—provided we also specify the three : one proportion of final demand for beer and cheese. The analysis has developed the concept that if we propose to introduce a productive activity, then the production cost of that activity is the loss of output in transferring resources from other activities, and this concept has been used to calculate potential production. This basic idea is valid for any number of commodities, activities and resources.

The analysis of potential production raises two further issues, both of political importance, to be explored in the next chapters:

First, having calculated potential production, how does one go about actually achieving it? This is the problem of how to organise the means of production.

Second, what implication does the calculation of the marginal product of land and labour have for the size of land-rent and the wage-rate in a real economy? This is the problem of income distribution.

Summary

§1. Any specific method of producing a commodity has a 'scale' characteristic and a 'factor substitution' characteristic:

(a) The scale characteristic refers to a situation in which *all* variable inputs are changed in the *same* proportion. Output may then increase in the same proportion or by more or less—situations respectively called constant, increasing and diminishing scale returns.

(b) The factor substitution characteristic refers to a situation in which output is held constant while factor proportions are changed. Factors may be not-substitutable, perfectly substitutable, or imperfectly substitutable.

§2. If consumer goods are demanded in fixed proportions and scale returns are constant, then the technology that will maximise national production from available resources can be found by an approach that calculates the production cost of any proposed activity as the loss of output of other activities from which resources are transferred.

§3. The choice of the technology that maximises national production is a physical choice (assuming a given composition of demand), which a central planner can solve using physical concepts. But his method can be seen to be an analogue of the manner in which a market economy solves the same problem of choice.

Further reading

P.A. Samuelson, *Ecomics,* ch. 27 ('Theory of Production').

R. Dorfman, *The Price System* (Englewood Cliffs, N.J.: Prentice Hall, 1964), ch. 2.

K. Boulding, *Economic Analysis,* 4th ed. (New York: Harper & Row, 1966), I, ch, 25.

Questions

1. Define the marginal product of a factor.
2. What is meant by scale returns? Illustrate diminishing and increasing scale returns.
3. Define imperfect factor substitution. Is factor substitution always imperfect? What is the significance of imperfect substitution?
4. The economy is at full employment. An inventor now announces a new process. Viewing the issue as one of making the best use of the nation's resources, how would you decide whether to use his process?

11. Specify the production function for pig iron.
12. In figure 6.3 suppose that the second activity for producing cheese did not exist. What would be the optimal technology?

13. Suppose in section 3 there were three activities able to produce cheese—the third requiring inputs of 6 men and 7 acres to produce 1 ton under constant scale returns. Under what circumstances would this process be used?

14. Imagine an economy in which there are four goods *A B C D* (almonds, beer, cheese, doughnuts), which can be produced under constant scale returns by several methods of production. The amounts of labour: land (measured in men and acres per annum) needed to produce one ton per year of output by these various processes are:

Product	Process (1)	(2)	(3)	(4)
	Ratio of labour to land			
A (3 processes)	10:1	5:2	1:4	
B (3 processes)	5:1	3:4	2:9	
C (4 processes)	8:1	7:3	5:4	4:7
D (4 processes)	7:1	5:2	4:3	3:6

The nation's resources are two million men and one million acres. Profit mark ups are zero in all four industries.

Consumers demand the four goods *A B C D* in the physical proportions 1:10:2:2.

What is the volume of output of commodity *A* when the economy is operating at maximum production?

21. Comment on the Malthusian notion that as population and work force grow, production grows less rapidly and so living standards are jeopardised.

22. Is the choice of technology really an important economic issue? How does it rank against other economic decisions a nation must make?

23. Would you advise a relatively poor nation seeking to raise its living standards to adopt the highly mechanised methods of production of the wealthy industrialised nations?

24. You are now familiar with three different meanings of the phrase 'the cost of production of a commodity':

    (a) some specified dollar cost;

(b) the cost expressed as listed physical factor inputs (men, acres);

(c) the cost expressed as the loss of production in transferring resources from elsewhere in the economy to produce this good by the specified activity.

Consider the merits of these different meanings. Which meaning would you use in:

(a) discussing the 'cost' of the nation's defence programme;

(b) debating the proposition: 'The burden of the defence programme can be reduced by financing through locally raised loans instead of taxation'?

The Organisation of the Means of Production

A central planning bureau can choose, from among the alternative productive processes available, the technology that will maximise physical production.

But a nation of factory managers—seeking to minimise their own unit costs, free to bid for labour and land, and free to choose their own methods of production—choose technology by using a criterion that is equivalent to the one used by the planners.

Thus, instead of the choice of technology being made by a central authority, these decisions can be decentralised among individual business managers using a financial criterion of minimum unit cost, and bidding for the services of productive factors in the market.

1. Competitive socialism

One may readily imagine that the centrally planned economy of the preceding chapter is changed to a competitive socialist economy in which factory managers can choose their own methods of production and hire their own factors of production. It can be assumed that a watchful central government will ensure that the entire labour force available to work is in fact in employment.

Types of economic systems

Economies may be classified according to whether the means of production are owned by the State or by individuals. Economies may also be classified according to whether the use of resources is decided by a central authority or by individual managers of factories and farms who hire labour and rent land from workers and landowners offering their services in the factor market. The names given to economies thus classed are:

	Resources are State owned	Resource use is decided by individual managers
Centralised socialism	yes	no; by central authority
Competitive socialism	yes	yes
Capitalism	no	yes

Under central planning, (q) the ratio of the marginal product of land to the marginal product of labour played the role of land-rent: the higher q, the less the demand for land. Planners call q the 'shadow' land-rent. Now, under competitive socialism there is an actual land-rent which, expressed in wage-units—i.e. as a multiple of the dollar wage-rate—will be found to equal $q = 1\frac{1}{3}$ in the previous example. This will be illustrated below in a simulation of the market on page 140.

But even if land-rent under competitive socialism does settle at the *same* level as q under central planning, will the individual socialist factory managers choose the same technology as under central planning? To answer this, compare the two groups of decision makers.

Symbols

a_{ni} labour input per ton of output i
a_{li} land input per ton of output i
P_n wage-rate
P_l land-rent
mp_n marginal product of labour
mp_l marginal product of land

The central planner aims at minimising $(a_{ni} + q.a_{li})$ his unit production cost, for each good. Individual competing managers who are constrained to be efficient will aim at minimising $(P_n.a_{ni} + P_l.a_{li})$, the unit dollar cost of the quantity of the good they produce; or, what is the same thing, they aim at minimising $(a_{ni} + a_{li}.P_l/P_n)$, the unit cost measured in wage-units. Now, if individual managers do in fact minimise their unit production cost, it must be true that the ratio of the factor's marginal product to the price of the factor's services is the same figure for each factor,[1] i.e.:

$$\frac{mp_l}{P_l} = \frac{mp_n}{P_n}$$

so that:

$$\frac{P_l}{P_n} = \frac{mp_l}{mp_n} \equiv q$$

---

[1] In other words a dollar spent on labour must yield the same 'pay-off' in output as a dollar spent on land. If this were not true then unit cost can be reduced by switching to the factor with the higher pay-off.

It follows that the individual manager's criterion for choice of technology is to minimise $(a_{ni} + q.a_{li})$, which is the same criterion used by the planning agency. One can conclude that provided the same information is available, provided the same incentives exist to use the information, and provided both groups are rational—then the individual managers will choose the same technology and achieve the same potential production as the central planners.

Thus we have seen how a factor market can serve as an alternative to physical planning of resources, as a way of organising the means of production and of choosing technology. It is a small step further to imagine that the means of production are *privately* owned—especially in a world where the manner of operation of giant corporations would give no clue to an interplanetary visitor whether they were owned by the State or by individual 'capitalists'.

Life is of course rather more complex than portrayed here. Thus nations that are centrally planned do face problems of information and incentives in making and executing decisions regarding resource administration. It is no less true that market economies display cases of gross excess capacity and monopoly.

2. Simulating the market

Our analysis has shown that individual managers (who measure costs in dollars or roubles) can choose the same technology as the central planner (who uses the physical concept of cost, page 129). Our reasoning can be confirmed by running through the beer and cheese example for a market economy as in figure 7.1, which shows that, assuming the wage-rate to be $100, then at a land-rent greater/less than $133\frac{1}{3}$, there will be a deficient/excess demand for land, so that land-rent will fall/rise. At the equilibrium rent of $133\frac{1}{3}$, individual managers choose the optimal technology.

3. Conclusion

Consider now in a modern political context the issues involved in deciding whether to administer resources by central directive or by the market.

The most extreme form of central economic planning would have three elements:

(a) physical direction of resources so that, for example, labour would have no choice as to how or where it was employed;

FIGURE 7·1 RESOURCE ALLOCATION BY THE MARKET (WAGE-RATE = $100).

If land-rent is bid to	then managers' choice of least cost activity is		So, at full employment of labour, there is excess or deficit demand for land; so rent will rise ⬆ or fall ⬇
$	for beer	for cheese	
0	(1)	(1)	⬆
110	(1)	(2)	⬆
$133\frac{1}{3}$	(1) & (2)	(2)	—
150	(2)	(2)	⬇

Sample calculation for second line

At wage-rate $100, rent $110, unit production costs are:
(1) for beer ($2\frac{2}{3}$ men × 100 + $5\frac{1}{3}$ acres × 110 =) $853
(2)   (8 .... + $1\frac{1}{3}$ .... =) 946

(1) for cheese (4 men × 100 + 8 acres × 110 =) $1280
(2)   (8 .... + 4 .... =) 1240

Hence activities chosen in the second line are beer (1), cheese (2), being the cheaper alternatives.

Thus if x is cheese tonnage, $3x$ is beer tonnage, total factor needs are:

labour required = $2\frac{2}{3}(3x)$ + $8x$ = $16x$
land required   = $5\frac{1}{3}(3x)$ + $4x$ = $20x$

i.e. land/labour are demanded in the proportion 20:16, which exceeds the supply ratio 3:7. So rent rises (towards $133\frac{1}{3}$, at which the cost of production of beer for *both* activities

(1) $2\frac{2}{3} \times 100 + 5\frac{1}{3} \times 133\frac{1}{3} = \$977.7$
(2) 8............ + $1\frac{1}{3}$............ = $977.7
equals $977.7)

(b) central governmental decision as to what to produce (especially the allocation of resources between producing consumer goods, capital equipment and military hardware) and how to produce it (e.g. by labour-intensive or capital-intensive processes);

(c) paying the factors of production, including labour, with some quota of foods and other consumer goods.

The first and third of these imply the absence of a factor market and a consumer-goods market respectively—and, save in time of national emergency, they would be criticised as detracting from civil liberty. It is the second that represents the hard core of central economic planning and it is to this that we now turn.

The notable problem in centralised decision-making is that it requires a vast amount of information. Moreover while all administrative systems need incentives, it is especially difficult to devise incentives that will ensure that a head office clerk keeps in touch with changing demand in outlying centres. There is reason to doubt whether a central decision-making authority can ever have the up-to-date, comprehensive accurate information on all aspects of resources, technology and final demand that is necessary for efficient resource administration. However, central decision-making may work well in a primitive economy where the problems are simpler, or in a national emergency where a few physical goals are given national priority.

While the market appears superior to central planning with respect to information, the market faces other dangers as a means of administering resources, notably the creation of excess capacity through wasteful competition, and obversely the restriction of output through monopolistic practices. Moreover experience shows that the market is not always efficient. To give some examples, in recent years some nations have experienced wasteful increase in the number of petrol retailing outlets, and there has been excess world production of sugar; the opposite situation is illustrated by the diamond monopoly. On the score of efficiency, the capital market in private enterprise economies has historically failed to ensure that the volume of intended investment equals the supply of savings at maximum national production.[2] Again, if the same factor is bought at different prices in different industries, national production may be below maximum. Finally, the market system of resource allocation works inefficiently when the costs to the producer differ from the true costs to the nation, as illustrated by pollution of the environment by industrial wastes.

Thus there is no dogma that one method of resource administration is necessarily better than the other. If in practice economic planners have shown an increasing interest in using the market, it is even more true that market economies operate within a basic framework of government directives. Thus the search for maximum production has produced a hybrid form of resource administration.

[2] This is discussed in chapters 3 and 4 above.

For issues as diverse as limiting wheat production or increasing military recruitment, it is a matter for rational enquiry whether the resources are best allocated by central decision (acreage quotas, military conscription) or by the market (fall in wheat prices, rise in army pay).

In conclusion it should be pointed out that the market method of administration is consistent both with private ownership and with State ownership of the means of production. The former is called *capitalism* and the latter *competitive socialism*. It is conceivable that under competitive socialism the decentralisation of decision-making to the managers of nationalised industries could go so far as to give managers complete autonomy subject to the control of profit mark-ups and of bank finance. At that point socialism and capitalism may differ no longer in the physical organisation of the means of production but only in the distribution of the national dividend. Both of course are to be clearly distinguished from central economic planning or *centralised socialism*.

Summary

§1. In a centrally planned society the sort of calculation in the preceding chapter could be performed and resources directed accordingly. But in a market economy (whether corporations are privately or publicly owned), technology is chosen instead by business managers selecting minimum unit-cost methods of production and bidding for factors in the market.

§2. Managers are assumed to minimise unit cost. By setting up an imaginary process of bidding we find that with labour fully employed at a wage-rate of $100, the price of land will be bid to $133.3 and that the managers will choose the processes that maximise physical production. When a manager costs alternative activities at existing factor prices, this costing can be interpreted in physical terms as loss of output from existing activities. For example, if a ton of steel currently produced at a cost of $1,000 could be produced by a new process at a cost of $950, then this means that the cost per ton of the new process is 0.95 tons loss of production due to factors transferred from the old process.

§3. The defects of both central planning and the market, as alternative methods of resource administration, are examined.

Further reading

R.W. Campbell, *Soviet Economic Power* (Boston: Houghton Miflin, 1967).

A. Bergson, *The Economics of Soviet Planning* (New Haven, Conn.: Yale University Press, 1964).

G. Grossman, *Economic Systems* (Englewood Cliffs, N.J.: Prentice Hall, 1967).

Questions

1. Explain how a factory manager's aim of minimising unit costs affects his choice of the ratio of factor inputs.
2. Explain how a manager's cost calculations can be interpreted in physical terms.
3. Suppose the present process for producing glass cost $500 a ton and a new proposed method will cost $400 a ton. What does this imply, expressed in terms of the nation's physical production?
4. The concept of 'cost' on page 129 is known as 'opportunity cost' or 'option cost'. Explain it in your own words.

11. In the beer-cheese example, calculate the consequences of land-rent being held at $150 per acre by a cartel. Is maximum output produced from those resources that are employed in industry?
12. In chapter 6 suppose there is a third beer-making process requiring $5\frac{2}{3}$ men and $3\frac{1}{3}$ acres to produce one ton of beer. Comment.

21. Compare capitalism, competitive socialism and centralised socialism as means of administering resources.
22. Explore the idea that whenever a decision has to be made concerning the use of physical resources, it may be implemented by physical directive or by the market. Examples may be drawn from farm quotas, import quotas, rent controls, military conscription.
23. Is there an 'invisible hand' that ensures that individuals pursuing their own self-interest will also serve the interests of society?

8

The Distribution of Income

For the example set out at the head of chapter 6, if the profit mark-up is 25 per cent in all industries we deduce the shares of the national income: wages 51 per cent, land-rent 29 per cent and profit 20 per cent.

However, the government can alter these shares by taxation.

1. Determinants of distribution

The distribution of the national product depends predominantly on:
- — the prices paid to owners of productive factors (labour, land);
- — the distribution of ownership of the means of production;
- — the degree of competition as reflected in the price-setting behaviour of firms;
- — the effects of foreign trade;
- — government intervention by taxation and other means.

Consider these in turn:

It has already been shown that in a market economy, the effect of industry managers aiming at minimum unit cost is that the ratio of factor prices in an industry tends to equal the ratio of their marginal products in that industry. Thus if land suddenly becomes plentiful (e.g. owing to some inexpensive discovery whereby trace elements boost the fertility of barren land), then as land-rent falls relatively to the wage-rate, land will be used in processes where its marginal product is lower. Conversely in some populous countries, work force growth brings lower labour marginal productivity and the wage-rate falls relatively to land-rent. None of this means that a factor is necessarily paid the value of its marginal product, for this depends on the degree of competition in industry.

The degree of competition in an industry is reflected in the price behaviour of the factory managers in the industry. Managers seeking maximum profit will aim at setting a price on their firm's product that rewards them for their initiative, efficiency and risk-taking. However, their ability to set a price higher than production cost will depend on their ability to limit entry into that industry.[1] Thus, in Australia for example, the steel and brewery managers have a long record of success in limiting entry into their industries. In practice, entry into most industries seems to be neither wholly free nor wholly barred but rather characterised by various restrictions (e.g. assuring raw material supplies, obtaining large blocks of finance, establishing distribution outlets). The degree to which entry is restricted is reflected in the profit mark-up on paid-out operating costs, whereby the price of the product is set. Such profit mark-ups tend to become firmly established (until some change disrupts them). If a manager applies a 25 per cent profit mark-up on costs, it follows that each factor is paid 80 per cent (i.e. $1/1.25$) of the value of its marginal product. In this chapter the *specification* of such profit mark-ups enables us to by-pass the classification of market forms

Number of firms	:	single, few, many
Product	:	branded, unbranded
Behaviour	:	collusion, leadership, independent
Entry	:	open, closed

that seeks to describe situations and procedures resulting in profit mark-ups of different size. It is in order to achieve a simple approach to income distribution that no attempt is made here to *explain* how firms set prices that imply different profit mark-ups. Such explanation is an important part of economic theory, which can be regarded as a natural extension of this analysis.

For the economy as a whole, the fact that individual firms use established profit mark-ups is reflected in a fairly stable ratio of profits to wages. Fluctuations in the profit/wage ratio for the economy may be merely the result of time-lags in the price-setting process, rather than a change in the competitive climate. Thus competition for labour in a boom may cause wage-rates to rise ahead of prices, with a consequent temporary shift in income distribution from profits to wages.

[1] In principle it is possible to set price so high that it actually reduces profits. But this possibility is only likely to cause concern to a few monopolists. *This upper limit* to a price (which is rational in the seller's view) is set by equating marginal revenue to marginal cost.

Where a nation sells one or two primary products on the world market, income distribution in the nation can change markedly as a result of fluctuations in the world market price of its exports. This is important for exporters of grains, natural fibres and non-ferrous metals since unit production costs at home may change slowly while the export price in foreign currency may rise or fall rapidly.

Since income distribution depends on the distribution of asset ownership, it is notable that it is possible to change the ownership of industry without adverse effect on its actual operation. The emergence of giant corporations whose ownership may be State, private or mixed is responsible for this.[2] A class of managers has emerged in both socialist and capitalist economies capable of operating these corporations. In both sorts of economy, incentive schemes have been developed to reward successful management (including high salaries, stock options and bonuses). However, in rural industry the separation of ownership and operation has proven much less successful and this represents a continuing problem in socialist nations.

Modern governments intervene in income distribution in a dramatic way by levying taxation, which may be as much as one-quarter of the national income, and by redistributing part of those revenues in a variety of subsidies and income supplements. Government also affects income distribution by manipulating interest rates and exchange rates, by the use of import tariffs, exchange controls and import quotas and by other direct intervention such as prohibiting specific exports and controlling capital flows. Measures with longer-term impact on income distribution include inheritance taxation, which breaks up large asset holdings; and subsidies which increase effective educational opportunity (e.g. government grants to universities).

2. Distribution in Demos

Assume that the arithmetic example in the previous chapter related to the imaginary market economy of Demos; there the unit of value was chosen as a wage-rate of $100. It was concluded that beer would be produced by both methods of production, that cheese would be produced by the second (labour-intensive) process and that land-rent

[2] Steel in England, tobacco in France, railways in Australia are publicly owned. In some other nations these industries are privately owned. The efficiency with which they are operated does not obviously depend on their ownership.

would be bid to $133\frac{1}{3}$ per acre. If we now suppose that all industry managers apply a 25 per cent profit mark-up to costs, then we may calculate that the price of *beer* is $1,222.2 a ton and the

Calculation

$$XP = \left[N.P_n + L.P_l \right] (1+v)$$

i.e. $P = \left[\dfrac{N}{X}.P_n + \dfrac{L}{X}.P_l \right] (1+v)$

$$= \left[(2\tfrac{2}{3} \times 100) + (5\tfrac{1}{3} \times 133\tfrac{1}{3}) \right] 1.25$$

$$= \$1,222.2$$

price of *cheese* is $1,666.7 a ton. Profit incomes are 20 per cent of the national income, the remaining 80 per cent being divided between wages and rent. This division can be calculated readily since 7 million men each receive an annual wage of $100 and the owners of 3 million acres receive an annual rent of $133\frac{1}{3}$ per acre. Hence the national income is divided: 51 per cent wages; 29 per cent land-rent and 20 per cent profit.

3. The economic system ☐

How may we give a general answer to the question: what determines the distribution of income between wages, land-rent and profits? The answer is in two parts.

First, if the profit mark-up levied on paid-out costs is a proportion (v), then the profit share is $v/(1+v)$. For example, if the monopoly power of industrialists is such that they can levy a profit mark-up (v) of 25 per cent, then the profit share is $(25/125=)$ 20 per cent of incomes. Likewise if industry is owned by the State then a profit mark-up is indistinguishable from an indirect tax. Thus a purchase tax of 25 per cent added to the wage and rent costs would give the State a one-fifth share of national income.

Second, the level of land-rent (relatively to the wage-rate) depends on the demand and supply of land, as illustrated in figure 8.1. It is seen there that if land-rent were set too high, demand would be less than supply (and conversely). The argument behind the demand schedule for land is: given full employment of labour and a specific wage-rate ($100), then for any arbitrarily chosen land-rent (say

$200) managers will choose the specific industrial processes that minimise unit cost for the desired output. If it then turns out that the demand for land is less than the supply, land-rent will fall. The downward slope of the demand schedule reflects the diminishing marginal productivity of increasingly land-intensive processes. Thus if the supply of land were somehow to be miraculously increased, the land-rent would have to fall in order to persuade industrialists to absorb that land into more land-intensive processes, which are characterised by a lower marginal productivity for land.

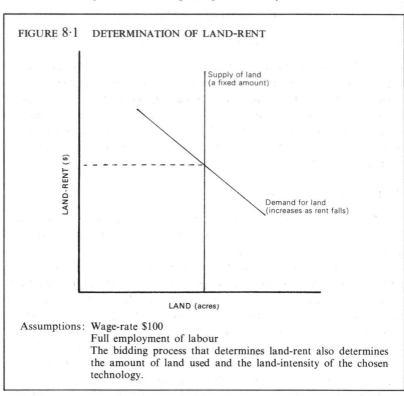

FIGURE 8·1   DETERMINATION OF LAND-RENT

Supply of land
(a fixed amount)

LAND-RENT ($)

Demand for land
(increases as rent falls)

LAND (acres)

Assumptions: Wage-rate $100
Full employment of labour
The bidding process that determines land-rent also determines the amount of land used and the land-intensity of the chosen technology.

Finally, let us turn from the discussion of the relative wage-share and profit-share to the absolute size of the return to the individual factor: What determines the wage-rate? If we begin with the simple case in which the profit mark-up is zero, then the wage-rate will equal the value of the marginal product of labour because employers would bid the wage-rate to this level. For example if the value of the marginal product of labour exceeded the wage-rate, the business-man could profitably bid for more labour in order to expand his output. This argument still holds even when there is a positive profit mark-up, provided we value the marginal product by using the firm's internal 'accounting price' which is *prior* to the profit mark-up. However, if there is a positive profit mark-up v and we choose to value the marginal product using the ordinary *market* price, then we must state that the wage will equal a proportion $1/(1+v)$ of the value of the marginal product of labour.

> *Example:* In the case of Demos above, a 25 per cent profit mark-up would lead us to expect that the wage is 80 per cent of the value of the marginal product of labour. This is confirmed as follows:
> The marginal product of labour in brewing is 9/88 tons.[3] The price of beer is $1,222.2 a ton. Hence the value of the marginal product of labour is $125. A proportion of 80 per cent of $125 is $100, which is indeed the wage-rate.
> A similar calculation can be carried out for land, whose marginal product in brewing is 12/88 tons.

4. The determination of factor prices*

In this chapter the ratio of wage-rate to land-rent has been determined by *factor-substitution*, i.e. by the fact that the final product can be produced by alternative productive processes having different ratios of factor inputs. Now, even if such factor-substitution were non-existent, the ratio of wage-rate to land-rent could be determined by *consumer-substitution*, i.e. by the fact that consumers respond to change in relative commodity prices by substituting the cheaper commodity for the dearer, it being understood that these commodities have *different* ratios of factor inputs.

[3] From the first two columns of figure 6.3 it will be seen that while $2\frac{2}{3}$ men and $5\frac{1}{3}$ acres produce 1 ton of beer, it is also true that (multiplying the second column by 4) 32 men and $5\frac{1}{3}$ acres produce *four* tons of beer. By subtraction it follows that, starting with the first process, the employment of $29\frac{1}{3}$ more men increases output by 3 tons. Taking the ratio of these last two figures, we find the marginal product of one man is $9/88 = 0.102272$ tons.

The marginal product of land is obtained by symmetrical reasoning.

* This section can be omitted on a first reading.

A very simple illustration is an economy with resources of 7 million men and 3 million acres producing two goods, beer and cheese, there being only one method of producing beer (requiring inputs of 8 men and $1\frac{1}{3}$ acres per ton) and one method of producing cheese (requiring 8 men and 4 acres per ton). (Observe that cheese production is land-intensive compared with beer). We deduce that full employment of all resources implies that 0.1875 million tons of beer (X_b) and 0.6875 million tons of cheese (X_c) are produced and it will now be assumed that those are the supplies annually available. (Observe that the ratio of tonnages is 3.675).

Calculation
$$8X_b + 8X_c = 7 \text{ million men}$$
$$1\tfrac{1}{3}X_b + 4X_c = 3 \text{ million acres}$$
$$\therefore X_b = 0.1875 \text{ million tons}$$
$$X_c = 0.6875 \text{ million tons}$$

Now introduce consumer tastes and suppose that consumers wish to spend their income on beer and cheese in the proportions 1 : 7.35. Then we deduce that the ratio of the land-rent (P_l) to the wage-rate (P_n) will be 6.

Calculation[4]
$$\frac{X_b P_b}{X_c P_c} = \frac{1}{7.35}$$

$$X_b = 0.1875; \; X_c = 0.6875$$
$$P_b = 8P_n + 1\tfrac{1}{3}P_l; \; P_c = 8P_n + 4P_l$$
$$\therefore P_l = 6P_n$$

[4] The working for this calculation in greater detail is as follows:

$$\frac{X_b P_b}{X_c P_c} = \frac{1}{7.35}$$

Where:

X_b output of beer in tons $= 0.1875$
X_c output of cheese in tons $= 0.6875$
$0.1875 : 0.6875 :: 1 : 3.675$
P_b price of beer $= 8P_n + 1\tfrac{1}{3}P_l$
P_c price of cheese $= 8P_n + 4P_l$
P_l price of land, or land-rent
P_n price of labour, or wage-rate

Therefore:

$$\frac{0.1875(8P_n + 1\tfrac{1}{3}P_l)}{0.6875(8P_n + 4P_l)} = \frac{1}{7.35}$$

or $\quad \dfrac{8P_n + 1\tfrac{1}{3}P_l}{3.675(8P_n + 4P_l)} = \dfrac{1}{7.35}$

or $\quad 7.35(8P_n + 1\tfrac{1}{3}P_l) = 3.675(8P_n + 4P_l)$
or $\quad 2(8P_n + 1\tfrac{1}{3}P_l) = 8P_n + 4P_l$
$$(16 - 8)P_n = (4 - 2\tfrac{2}{3})P_l$$
$$6\,P_n = P_l$$

However, if tastes change so that consumers want to spend their incomes on beer and cheese in the proportions 1 : 5.5125 then this relative fall in demand for the land-intensive good cheese will result in the ratio of the land-rent to the wage-rate falling to 2.

Summary

The ratio of factor prices—and so the distribution of incomes—is affected by both factor substitution and consumer substitution. Wherever the composition of goods entering final demand is physically predetermined, this 'locks in' the consumer-substitution effect in the sense that some other physical composition of final demand would result in a different set of factor prices.

5. Profits

The aim of this section is to discuss first the concept of profit and second the concept of fixed profit mark-up.

If the total costs are divided between wages, land-rent, materials and profit, then it follows that

Value of output ...	Wages	
	Land-rent	operating costs
	Materials	
	Profit	
100%	TOTAL COSTS 100%	

profit includes the following elements: managerial wage, interest on capital, depreciation provision, and surplus attributable to some monopolistic restriction on entry. In this book the analysis will be simplified in two ways. First, the managers' wages will be included in total wages and not in profits; second, unless it is critical to the argument we will tacitly assume that interest and depreciation are a constant proportion of the wage-bill because this then enables us to attribute changes in the profit/wage ratio as between firms to differences in the degree of monopoly. Plainly, before one can do this in reality, one must first calculate how much of the difference in the profit/wage ratio between firms and industries is attributable to differences in the ratio of interest-and-depreciation to wages.

The postulate of a *fixed proportionate profit mark-up* on operating costs has clearly been of great use in the discussion. For it not only gives a simple explanation of how prices are fixed, it also explains the distribution of the national income between profits and other incomes. But is it realistic? The empirical answer to this is that it is supported both by the evidence of price-setting behaviour of individual firms in manufacturing and service industries, and by the relative constancy of the over-all profit/wage ratio in those industries collectively. Nonetheless various objections may be raised to the fixed profit mark-up postulate and it is the purpose of this section to discuss them.

First some minor points should be clarified. One is that profit mark-ups certainly change when some basic change occurs in the degree of competition in an industry; e.g. profit mark-ups may fall sharply when discount-retailers move in. Another point is that while profit mark-ups are assumed to be on all operating costs, *materials* as well as wages, since all materials costs can be decomposed into incomes paid by industry to productive factors, it is valid when considering all industries collectively to speak of profits as a mark-up on factor-costs such as wages and land-rent.

However, it may be objected that the businessman regards profits (excluding managerial salaries) as a return on the value of capital in the enterprise; i.e. he regards profits as covering depreciation, interest, risk and any further return attributable to monopoly. This is of course true and so is the implication that the businessman is really aiming at some desired rate of return on capital. Nonetheless his standard approach to price-setting is to apply a normal profit mark-up on operating costs, which is intended to achieve the desired return on capital. In reality this procedure is made inevitable by the existence of fixed or *overhead costs,* the effect of which is that the businessman has to aim at some level of 'capacity output' at which, if achieved, his price-setting procedure will cover both overhead costs and the desired rate of return on capital.

A final objection is whether the fixed profit mark-up postulate is applicable to farmers. Like any other rational manager, the farmer will aim at some desired rate of return on capital. But he can commonly only expect to achieve this over decades rather than years. For in the short run the farmer makes business decisions in a state of acute uncertainty: his costs vary with the weather; his production period is so long (6 months for wheat, 3 years for beef, 25 years for softwood) that, by the time his output is ready for sale, demand may have changed; and he does not know what crop other competing farmers will produce. While these short-run issues are important, they will not be discussed here. The record shows that farmers, like other businessmen, do switch from unprofitable crops to new crops that are expected to yield a desired return on capital. Moreover it does happen that a typical government approach to solving farmers' problems is to use some implicit concept of a normal profit mark-up in determining home prices.

6. A view of distribution

- (a) Different wages for skilled labour
- (b) How distribution changes.

Different wages for skilled labour

Market supply and demand schedules (such as in figure 8.1) for productive factors can also be used as a conceptual device in discussing the differences in wage-rates (or salaries) for different occupations and skills. In previous discussion (for example in figure 8.1) it has been assumed that the supply of any factor or resource was fixed and freely available at any price—hence the representation of the factor supply by a vertical line in figure 8.1. Now, however, we must recognise that the supply of such resources as skilled or specialised labour is not fixed but depends on such influences as the price offered for the services of the factor, i.e. on the 'wage differential' or *margin* for skill that is offered. The factor supply schedule may then no longer be a vertical straight line, but rather an upward sloping line as in figure 8.2. Though it is difficult to obtain statistical information on such factor supply schedules, their usefulness in clarifying ideas may be illustrated by the following comments concerning the manner in which wage differentials are determined:

- (a) The supply of different skills is not fixed. By increasing the wage-differential for nurses the supply of that skill can be increased (figure 8.2).
- (b) The supply of skills can also be increased without changing differentials, by increasing educational opportunity or altering community attitudes, e.g. to manual labour. Thus the supply of nurses may be increased merely by knowledge of the demand, or may be increased by training scholarships (figure 8.3).

(c) Over relevant salary ranges the size of the differential for skill may not affect the choice of technology; e.g. the staffing of hospitals may not be affected by wide change in nurses' differentials (figure 8.4) because over a vertical range the demand for nurses' services is unresponsive to price.

(d) As is the case in some commodity markets, there are substantial time-lags in producing a supply of skilled labour. During the lag those already possessing scarce skills may receive special wage differentials.

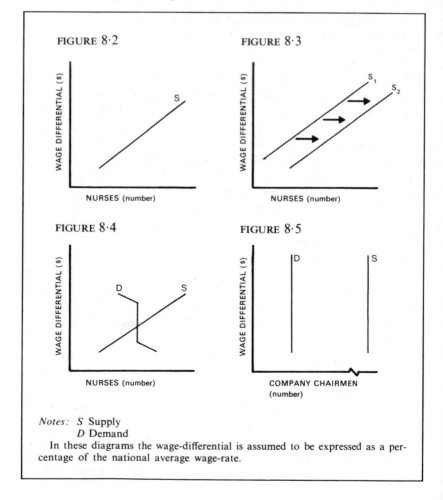

FIGURE 8·2

FIGURE 8·3

FIGURE 8·4

FIGURE 8·5

Notes: S Supply
D Demand

In these diagrams the wage-differential is assumed to be expressed as a percentage of the national average wage-rate.

(e)   The size of some differentials (e.g. those of company chairmen in figure 8.5) may not be determined by the market in any meaningful sense but rather by institutional or hierarchical attitudes.

Summing up, the mechanism by which relative wage differentials are determined may also involve change in the supply of skilled factors and change in technology. *Where there are no such effects on factor supply and technology, a change in relative wage-differentials in essence redistributes an unchanged social product among members of the community.* Thus a tax on rents received by landowners (who have no choice but to use the land or leave it idle) can alter income distribution without any other effects.

How distribution changes

It remains for us to consider how income distribution reacts to change. The first of two examples to be discussed is the response of income distribution to technological change. In an economy in which profit mark-ups were being held unchanged (reflecting a certain state of competition), technological change resulting in lower unit costs would be followed by falling prices. In sum, the fruits of increased productivity are passed on by the fixed profit mark-up on falling unit costs. In many economies, however, trade union demands for higher money wage-rates are based on increased productivity—in which event the fruits may be passed on by higher money wage-rates at constant commodity prices—thus giving the accolade of success to trade union negotiators.

The second example is concerned with the case of a nation whose exports are dominated by a few primary products (rural or mineral). A rise in the world price of such primary exports both increases the surplus of exports over imports and increases the profits of exporters. A government wishing to redistribute some of these profits to the community at large may do so:

— by taxation;
— by internal inflation, which raises the wage costs to the exporter;
— by currency appreciation, which reduces the exporters' income expressed in local currency.

The whole issue takes a more acute form when the prices of a nation's primary exports fall sufficiently to cause hardship in the rural community—for then the question is one of redistributing income in the opposite direction by subsidy, deflation or currency depreciation. Some of these measures are discussed in later chapters.

The discussion in this chapter has indicated a variety of ways in which the government may intervene to change the distribution of the national income. But apart from the use of inheritance taxes aimed (as in the United Kingdom) at modifying the distribution of property, government intervention has typically been motivated by the twin aims of raising revenue wherever it is most readily taxable, and achieving social welfare programmes in health, education and pensions. Thus over the past decades, income tax rates have been raised, commodity taxes on beer, tobacco, petrol (where demand is relatively unresponsive to price rises) have been raised, while welfare subsidies and benefits for health, unemployment, old age have been increased. Thus a huge official tax-spending apparatus has grown, much of which is devoted to giving back to the same persons the income it has taxed from them. In view of the disincentive effects of high taxation rates, it is surprising that more attention has not been given to options such as a national superannuation scheme operating outside the taxation system. As with other aims of economic policy, the government should seek to aid the needy and the underprivileged by measures consistent with the largest possible national product.

Summary

§1. Income distribution depends on relative factor supplies, the degree of competition, the price of exports, asset ownership and on government action.

§2. The distribution of income between wages and profits is calculated from a knowledge of profit mark-ups.

§3. The demand schedule for land is ascertained. From a knowledge of the wage-rate, land-rent and profit mark-up, the complete distribution of income can then be calculated (51 per cent wages, 29 per cent land-rent, 20 per cent profit).

§4. Relative factor prices are determined both by factor-substitution and consumer-substitution.

§5. The concept of profit and of a constant profit mark-up is re-examined.

§6. Influences affecting income distribution are reviewed.

Further reading

P.A. Samuelson, *Economics*, part IV.

L. Tarshis, *Modern Economics* (Boston: Houghton Miflin, 1967), section V.

R G Lipsey, *Positive Economics* (London: Weidenfeld and Nicolson, 1966), book I, part IV.

Questions

1. How would you describe a situation in which all profit mark-ups in industry were equal? Is it the inequality of profit mark-ups or their size that suggests a lack of competition?

2. Explain how population growth can affect income distribution between wage-earners and the owners of land.

3. Analyse the major influences affecting the distribution of national income among members of the community.

11. If all industries applied a profit mark-up of 50 per cent, what conclusions do you draw as to the share of profits in the national income?

12. In section 2 calculate the price of beer produced by the second brewing activity. Calculate the value of the marginal product of land and explain its relation to the land-rent of $133.3.

13. The following relation between profits V_t in the current quarter and the wage-bill (W) of industry in the current and two preceding quarters was obtained in an actual statistical enquiry:

$$V_t = -0.73W_t + 0.58W_{t-1} + 0.77W_{t-2}$$

(This simplified form of the relation only applies to the situation in which employment and physical output is constant.) What conclusions would you draw?

14. Refer back to chapter 6 question 14 for which you are now able to calculate commodity prices and the wage share. Look

at your answer to that question and observe which commodity is relatively labour intensive.

Now you are told that the composition of demand changes from 1:10:2:2 to 10:1:2:2. This represents a switch in demand *away* from the labour-intensive product. Can you explain how this means that there will be a switch to *more* labour-intensive methods of production throughout the economy? Do your calculations confirm this?

21. Compare the effects of a tax on land-rents and a tax on wage incomes.
22. How are the fruits of new scientific discoveries and improved technology distributed in the form of higher real incomes among members of the community?
23. Suppose a sudden fall in world farm prices causes a major fall in farmers' incomes. What measures are available to redistribute the national income in order to relieve the farm community?
24. Explain the effect of a switch in consumer tastes to land-intensive goods.

Pricing Policy

In both central planned and competitive market economies the question
arises: What criterion for setting the level of individual commodity prices is in
the national interest? Maximum profit? Maximum value added? Maximum
output? Minimum price?

1. Markets and prices

In most modern economies it is assumed that individual consumers
should be free to choose what consumer goods they want—rather
than be allocated goods by a central commissariat. So long as this
judgment is accepted then the allocation of resources to producing
one consumer good rather than another is not an issue of government policy.[1] However, the goods consumers buy depend on their
relative prices, and the question of what these relative prices are
to be *is* a policy issue.

What price-setting procedure by factory managers is in the national
interest? Should managers aim at maximising profit, or maximising
value produced, or simply selling at the lowest possible price? The
question is important both in framing a regulatory policy in a private
enterprise economy and in giving instructions to managers of nationalised industry in a socialised economy.

This issue will be tackled in three steps. First its relationship to
the material in previous chapters is briefly explored. Secondly a
foundation for solving the problem is laid in section 2. Finally a
solution is set out in section 3.

Up to this point it has been assumed for simplicity that consumer
goods are demanded in fixed proportions. Now, however, we will
recognise that those proportions depend on relative commodity
prices. Thus a new cheaper process for producing a commodity will

[1] This does not absolve government from responsibility in such matters as narcotics,
pollution, advertising, child welfare.

alter its price and so affect the demand for that good compared with other goods—with a consequent shift in resources between industries. This raises two policy issues. First, *do the commodity markets work efficiently* in the sense that, in response to such a change in the composition of demand, resources are transferred readily between industries, without either unnecessary fluctuations in production or creation of excess capacity? Second, *are the prices set by producers consistent with national welfare?* Consider now the first question before proceeding to the second question in the next section.

Most commodity markets appear to work efficiently, but this is not always so. Thus there is evidence of wasteful competition when:

— petrol stations proliferate along the highways, with substantial unused capacity;
— large numbers of farmers switch over to producing a temporarily high-priced product (wheat, sugar, pigs) whose price then slumps because of over-production;
— a few powerful competing petrochemical producers create substantial excess capacity in a bid to capture a larger share of the market.

Such examples[2] suggest that: the *number* of firms in an industry is not a guide to the efficiency of the market as a resource allocation mechanism; excess capacity or excess production are sufficiently frequent to warrant a greater measure of government sponsored information and guidance to industry.

The market also works badly when collusive practices prevent new firms and new technology entering an industry in response to demand, or when a cartel restricts output to force up prices. These monopolistic practices are at the extreme end of the spectrum of business behaviour, and require government intervention. The question to which we now turn is the more general one: What price-setting procedure by factory managers is in the national interest?

2. Economic welfare

It is possible that the commodity markets work efficiently in the sense that there is no excess capacity or over-production, and that

[2] On farm response ('cobweb') refer Samuelson, *Economics,* ch. 20. On petrochemicals refer *The Economist,* 3 October, 1970.

the national product is maximised in the sense that to produce more of one good means that less of another must be produced. Nonetheless there may also be a sense in which the goods being produced are not those that people most want, and in that event economic welfare could be increased by transferring resources from the production of one commodity to another.

To illustrate a situation where economic welfare could be increased we will initially consider a socialised economy in which all profits are paid to the State. The purpose of this is that it enables us to set to one side the effects of any change in income distribution on welfare, and consider only the effects of resource allocation on welfare.

Economic welfare refers to the material satisfaction that a community gains from its use of resources. Such welfare is affected by:
  (a) the volume of resources employed in industry. (This may operate both ways; e.g. welfare might be *increased* by shortening the number of hours in the working week, or by refusing to permit land to be used by factories that pollute the environment.)
  (b) the distribution of the national product between rich and poor;
  (c) the commodity composition of the national product.
This chapter has the limited aim of explaining the third aspect. In reality all three aspects have a major effect on economic welfare.

Now, in all economies, private enterprise and socialist, factory managers apply a profit mark-up to paid-out costs. There are a variety of reasons for this:

— to reward owners of capital for initiative, efficiency and risk-taking;
— to accumulate finance for plant expansion;
— to help finance the government administrative process (in which case the profit mark-up is indistinguishable from an indirect tax).

Imagine there is a standard (say 20 per cent) profit mark-up on all commodities in the economy, but that one industry manager decides to double his mark-up (to 40 per cent), conceivably in a well-meaning attempt to increase profits for the State.[3] Now, there is no effect

---

[3] We assume his market researchers have found that such a price rise will result in a mere 5 per cent drop in sales volume, so that his profits will indeed rise under constant unit costs.

on income distribution since all profits are paid to the State, but there will be a reallocation of resources from this industry to others as consumers are induced by the relative price change to switch demand to competing products. This resource reallocation involves a loss of economic welfare. The following paragraphs successively explain this and show how to measure the loss.

If we are prepared to take a simple approach, then the necessary conditions for consumers to attain maximum welfare are three.[4] First, consumers are to allocate their spending so that an extra dollar spent on any commodity would yield the same increment in satisfaction, i.e. the same *marginal utility*. This condition can be stated:

$$\frac{\text{marginal utility}_a}{\text{price}_a} = \frac{\text{marginal utility}_b}{\text{price}_b} = \ldots$$

for all goods $a, b, c, \ldots$

If this condition were not satisfied, it is seen that welfare could be increased by consumers switching their expenditure to the commodity with a relatively high marginal utility. As more of that commodity were consumed its marginal utility would fall until finally the equi-marginal condition were satisfied. With some qualifications it is not unreasonable to assume that consumers do seek to act in a way that satisfies this condition.[5]

The second condition is that commodity prices are proportional to their marginal cost, i.e. the addition to total cost involved in producing another unit of the commodity. This condition can be stated:

$$\frac{\text{price}_a}{\text{marginal cost}_a} = \frac{\text{price}_b}{\text{marginal cost}_b} = \ldots$$

for all goods $a, b, c, \ldots$

In the simple case of constant scale returns and divisible factor inputs, this second condition would be satisfied by a standard percentage

---

[4] The following argument implicitly makes a number of simplifying assumptions: that ownership of resources is predetermined; that effects on income distribution are ignored; that problems of interpersonal comparison of utility can be ignored; that there are no intermediate goods; that there has not been some prior intervention creating a second-best situation.

[5] For a discussion of qualifications refer G.J. Stigler, *The Theory of Price* (New York: The Macmillan Company, 1969).

profit mark-up on the constant marginal cost of production, e.g. 20 per cent mark-up on all commodities.

The third condition is that the firms are constrained to operate efficiently so that any specified volume of output is produced at minimum unit cost. This of course implies that the firms satisfy the equi-marginal productivity condition, in which the ratio of a factor's marginal product to that factor's price is the same for all factors used by the firm.

Taken together the significance of these three conditions is clear enough. The last condition means that national production[6] cannot be increased from the available resources by altering the ratio of factor inputs to any industry. The first two conditions taken together imply that

$$\frac{\text{marginal utility}_a}{\text{marginal cost}_a} = \frac{\text{marginal utility}_b}{\text{marginal cost}_b} = \dots$$

for all goods $a, b, c, \dots$

the marginal pay-off to unit marginal cost is the same for all commodities. Hence consumer welfare cannot be increased by moving resources from producing one good to another so as to alter the ratio of consumer-good 'inputs' to households.

It follows that any industry manager who is able to raise his profit mark-up—for example to 40 per cent compared with a standard 20 per cent—is reducing economic welfare because the marginal utility pay-off to unit cost for that good is abnormally high, relatively to other goods.[7] It is to be emphasised that we are here speaking of *a loss of welfare due to producing an inappropriate collection of consumer goods—this is an issue distinct from either productive efficiency or equity in income distribution*. The nature of the issue can be further clarified by attempting to measure the loss of welfare, to which we now turn.

To illustrate, imagine that just two goods, milk and honey, are produced in an imaginary economy in which consumers are assumed

[6] For any chosen set of consumer-good proportions, i.e. any chosen commodity basket.

[7] Conversely a zealous manager, confronted by a highly price-responsive demand for his output, can maximise his value added by cutting his profit mark-up below the national norm and expanding sales. But he is not promoting national economic welfare since the marginal utility pay-off to unit cost would be abnormally low.

to exercise their freedom of choice between goods so as to satisfy the equi-marginal utility condition. For simplicity, land is a free good, labour is the sole scarce resource and initially the ratio of the price of each good to its marginal cost is the same. Specifically, we choose physical units of output such that it takes 2 man-weeks to produce one unit of each good, the wage-rate is $1 per week, profit mark-up is zero and each good is priced at $2 per unit. Suppose this initial position is disrupted by honey-producers (but not milk producers) levying a 50 per cent profit mark-up[8] so that the price of honey rises to $3. Suppose that the volume of honey sold, previously 50 units, now falls to 33 units. Then the loss of welfare to consumers can be measured as $8.5 as follows:

The rise in the price of honey pressures consumers to alter their composition of demand to one that is not optimal, in the sense that the satisfaction yielded by a marginal unit of resources (labour) is unequal as between commodities. The resource transfer involves both a gain and a loss. The gain is that 17 units more milk are produced valued at the constant price of $2, i.e. a gain of $34. The loss is that 17 fewer units of honey are produced valued at between the old $2 price and the new $3 price. Assuming a straight line demand schedule we may value at the average $2.5 (since in the first equilibrium consumers valued the marginal unit at $2, and in the second equilibrium at $3). So the loss is $17 \times \$2.5$, i.e. $42.5. Hence the net loss is (loss $42.5 - gain $34=) $8.5.

In summary, our reasoning has been that when a consumer buys (n) units at the existing price, his willingness to buy neither more nor less than this enables us to deduce that the price is an index of the marginal utility he gains from the nth unit. Using commodity price as an index of marginal utility, we can proceed further to designate a common ratio of price to marginal cost for all commodities as a necessary condition for maximising economic welfare. For if that ratio is different as between commodities, then there is a welfare loss as compared with the situation where the ratio is the same for all goods. The size of the welfare loss has been calculated in this constant scale returns example as the fall in the volume of production *times* half the rise in the price of the commodity. This loss could also be expressed as a proportion of national income.

[8] The profit is paid to the State for redistribution to the community.

Summary

For consumers to obtain maximum welfare from a given collection of resources, it is necessary that:
— the equi-marginal utility condition be satisfied;
— there be a standard profit mark-up on all goods;
— unit production costs be minimised.
(This statement assumes a variety of simplifications including no consideration of the effect of income distribution on welfare.)
If profit mark-ups are unequal there is a measurable loss of welfare.

The foregoing discussion has been set out in the simplest terms. Nonetheless it does express a basic idea, namely that *unequal* profit mark-ups can cause consumer goods to be produced in proportions that do not yield maximum welfare. Since relatively high profit mark-ups are often called 'monopolistic', it is worth noting that monopoly[9] is also criticised on quite different grounds, namely: either that monopolists are technically inefficient (which is by no means necessarily true); or that monopoly results in an undesirable income distribution (a view to which most non-monopolists would subscribe).[10]

3. Price policy

A price policy is now formulated that will both serve as a basis for the regulation of private enterprise and for instructions to the managers of nationalised industry. The policy is based on the premise that in order to achieve maximum economic welfare:

(a) restrictive practices should be banned;
(b) firms must be constrained to produce any specified level of output at minimum cost;

[9] The etymology of the word 'monopoly' is misleading. The essence of monopoly does not reside in there being a *single* (or a few) producers but in the exercise of some *restriction* whether on output, entry or technology.
[10] In order to obtain general agreement that a more equal income distribution represents a gain in welfare, we must assume:
   (a) that the marginal satisfaction of extra income diminishes as income rises;
   (b) that the marginal satisfactions of different individuals can be equated;
   (c) that income redistribution does not have too adverse an effect on incentives to produce, save and invest.

(c)   the purchasers of a commodity pay the full cost;[11]

(d)   the ratio of the price of a good to its marginal cost shall be the same for all goods. Hence if consumers have a marginal utility/price ratio that is common to all commodities, no marginal switching between goods can increase welfare.

Assuming constant scale returns and divisible inputs, the *guidelines* for industry managers would be two:

(a)   *for any chosen level of output, minimise production cost;*

(b)   *in assessing the expected volume of demand, use a selling price obtained by applying to marginal cost the uniform profit mark-up that is standard for all industry.*[12]

In the case already discussed the existence of constant scale returns and divisible inputs implies that marginal cost is constant and equal to average cost. Consider now how the guidelines are modified if there are major indivisibilities relative to the scale of industry output. For example, in transport and communications systems there are major indivisibilities in the form of constructing a railway line or a radio network or a telephone system. Does the existence of large overheads in such cases as these modify our guidelines?

Guideline (b) requires modification because, in order to ensure both that consumers *pay full cost* and that the price is set proportionately to *marginal cost,* a price must be charged that has fixed and variable components matching the fixed and variable costs. Thus the price has two parts: an amount paid for *access* to purchase, and a price per unit for each unit purchased. Telephone charges can illustrate this sort of price: the fixed part of the price covering overhead costs and the variable part of the price covering marginal costs. (The price both for access and for the product includes the uniform profit mark-up.)

[11] If this requirement were not met, then either of two things would be true:

(a)   there is no price at which revenue will cover cost, so the users of the commodity do not place as high a value on this use of resources as some alternative use.

(b)   there is some price at which revenue will cover cost but the users of the commodity do not have to pay it, and so they are being subsidised. It is assumed here that it is not the function of industry price policy to provide an income subsidy to the users of some particular good. (This is a value judgment, which has the effect here of avoiding discussion of income distribution.)

[12] There may be risk-loadings in some industry.

Summary

The guideline price policy is:
(a) for any chosen level of output, minimise production cost;
(b) in assessing expected demand volume, use a selling price based on applying the standard profit mark-up to marginal cost. However, where there are major indivisibilities, charge a two-part tariff, i.e. an 'access' price to cover overhead costs and a 'usage' price to cover variable costs.

The assumption of constant scale returns materially simplified the foregoing discussion. In a mining industry subject to increasing unit costs, the marginal cost pricing guideline could yield high profits because much of the tonnage is produced at a cost substantially below marginal cost. This does not destroy the guideline. For it is typically extractive industries that are subject to rising unit costs and their profits can be taxed by suitable royalty payments to the government. This is an appropriate point at which to repeat that the foregoing discussion has not considered income distribution—and there may be situations in which the above guideline conflicts with economic policy on income distribution.

4. The economic system ⊟

Consider an economy in which there are only two industries producing goods b and w respectively. A work force of 100 men is the only scarce resource; returns to scale are constant and quantity units are chosen for arithmetical convenience such that 1 man-year's labour is required to produce one physical unit of either commodity. National income is wholly spent on consumer goods but demand for each commodity responds to a change in relative price. From an initial situation in which there is a common profit mark-up of 100 per cent on wage-costs, the mark-up on good b is raised to 200 per cent. This causes both a change in income distribution and a shift in resources between the industries. We wish to estimate the loss of economic welfare due to this resource shift. The information is detailed in figure 9.1.

One can readily calculate that in the initial situation the national income is $200 and that, of this, $42 is spent on 21 quantity units of b and $158 on 79 quantity units of w, the price of each commodity being $2.

However, when the price of commodity b is raised to $3, while the price of w remains unchanged at $2, the quantity of b bought falls from 21 to 14.76 quantity units, and the quantity of w bought

FIGURE 9·1   MODEL: RESOURCE TRANSFER FOLLOWING HIGHER PROFIT MARK-UP.

Work force Labour input coefficients	: :	100 men $a_{nb} = 1$; $a_{nw} = 1$
Cost account Profit mark-up	: :	in each industry, value of output equals wage plus profits in each industry the mark-up on wage-costs is initially 100 per cent; later it is raised to 200 per cent in industry b. Let the wage-rate be $1.
Consumer demand	:	$C_w P_w = 0.8Y - 2P_w/P_b$ $C_b P_b = 0.2Y + 2P_w/P_b$

rises from 79 to 85.24 quantity units.[13]   When we apply the argument of the previous section we see that the 6.24 fall in volume of b, times one-half the price rise due to the non-uniform profit mark-up (i.e. $0.5), results in a welfare loss of $3.12. This loss is approximately $1\frac{1}{2}$ per cent of the initial national income.

In conclusion, the topic of this chapter may be put in perspective as follows. The loss of welfare we have explored can be expected

[13] The following steps are involved. The national income Y can be stated as follows:

$$Y = 2x_{nw} + 3(100 - x_{nw}) = 300 - x_{nw}$$

where x_{nw} is labour employed in producing w. Hence (remembering that $P_w = 2$, $P_b = 3$) the demand functions are:

$$C_w P_w = 2C_w = 0.8(300 - x_{nw}) - 2(\tfrac{2}{3})$$
$$C_b P_b = 3C_w = 0.2(300 - x_{nw}) + 2(\tfrac{2}{3})$$

The solution can now be obtained by writing:
   (a) In equilibrium, output of w equals demand for w:

$$X_w = C_w = 0.4(300 - a_{nw}X_w) - \tfrac{2}{3}$$

   (b) Labour is fully employed

$$100 = a_{nw}X_w + a_{nb}X_b$$

where a_{nw} is the labour input coefficient in producing w, and X_w is the volume of output.

to be quantitatively small in many situations because it applies only to the fact that output of some commodity has been expanded beyond the optimal at the expense of some other commodity—in the above example production of *w* is 6.24 units too great, and of *b* 6.24 units too small, the source of loss being the *difference* in the value placed by consumers on this *marginal* production. Hence as an issue of national policy this will usually rank below capital formation, full employment, productive efficiency and perhaps even below income distribution. Nonetheless it is an issue of substance for a socialist economy to have rational guidelines for its managers, and it is scarcely less important for a capitalist economy to have a rational basis for regulation of private enterprise.

Summary

§1. The aim is to examine what criterion for setting the prices of individual commodities is in the national interest.

§2. A necessary condition for maximising economic welfare with respect to resource allocation is a common ratio of price to marginal cost for all commodities.

§3. Guidelines for pricing are set out: minimise unit cost for the saleable scale of output, and apply a uniform profit mark-up. If there are major cost indivisibilities, the guidelines are modified by charging a two-part price.

§4. The loss caused by imposing a higher profit mark-up on one commodity equals, in the simplest case, one-half the price rise times the fall in output of that commodity. This loss is calculated on the assumption of continuous full employment, and can be expressed as a proportion of national income.

Further reading

H. Kohler, *Scarcity Challenged 1968*, 1st ed. (New York: Holt, Rinehart & Winston, 1969), ch. 15.

G.B. Richardson, *Economic Theory* (London: Hutchinson, 1966), ch. 2.

K. Lancaster, *Modern Microeconomics* (Chicago: Rand McNally, 1969), ch. 10.

Questions

1. What is meant by 'inefficiency' of a market? Illustrate.
2. Distinguish market inefficiency from the idea of a price policy that maximises consumer welfare.
3. Explain the meaning of marginal utility. Explain the 'equi-marginal utility' condition.

11. Explain the rule of thumb for calculating welfare loss when percentage profit mark-ups are unequal.
12. In the example in section 4 the introduction of a higher profit mark-up on one good raises the national income from $200 to $214.76. Yet the community's welfare (ignoring distributional effects) is stated to be *lower* in the latter situation. How do you explain this?
13. A group of firms combines in a monopolistic cartel and raises the price of their product from $100 to $120 a ton, which cuts back sales from one million to 0.9 million tons. What is the loss of welfare to the community?

21. Comment on the following attempt to debunk the example in section 4:
    'Consumers are initially buying 21 units of *b* and 79 units of *w*. The higher price does not *force* the community to alter these figures—since if they didn't they would receive a national income of $221, which is sufficient to buy the same quantities at the new price. So there is no community loss of welfare, other than that due to redistribution of income in favour of the owners of industry *b*.'
22. Explain the idea of a two-part tariff. Give an illustration.
23. 'If it is good enough for the government to aim at maximum national income, it is good enough for the manager of an industry to aim at maximum contribution to the national income; i.e. he should aim at maximising *value produced* in this industry.' Comment.
24. 'Producers should aim at maximum profit.' Comment.

Resource Allocation

> When a government subsidises an industry it causes a reallocation of resources, involving a calculable loss of economic welfare. This analysis of subsidies illustrates a general approach to examining government intervention in resource use.

1. Introduction

There are various counts on which a central government may choose to influence the allocation of resources.

First, we have seen that if the government of a fully employed economy wishes to embark on a programme of raising living standards by increasing the amount of equipment per worker, then it must bring about a reallocation of resources in the form of a transfer of productive factors from consumer-goods industry to the industries producing equipment. Irrespective of whether the financial measures used to raise the nation's savings-income ratio are a rise in tax rates or a rise in the interest rate, they must succeed in releasing resources from the consumer-goods industry if the policy aim is to be achieved. Similar comment applies to a government that plans a sustained immigration programme, such as that operated by the Australian government since the second world war. In this case, high tax rates have been maintained in order to hold down consumer demand.

Second, if large-scale unemployment develops owing to deficiency of demand, the central government can apply its own priorities for resource use in deciding what areas of demand to stimulate.

Third, there are various types of communal use of resources where decision by the government is either essential or has become traditional. Examples are defence, law and order, geophysical surveys, cartography, urban planning, development of virgin lands, environmental control, education and health services. For many of these types of resource use there is no normal market criterion by which the government's efficiency of resource use may be appraised—thus it is difficult to appraise in advance the relative efficiency of alternative untried weapons systems, just as it is difficult to appraise the efficiency of alternative educational systems. For some of these activities, however, commercial criteria are applicable—for example it would be unwise to develop virgin lands without an analysis of the market for the produce and an over-all calculation of the costs and benefits of the project.

Fourth, it is apparent from the previous chapter that efforts by the government to control restrictive trade practices and other impediments to entry into an industry will also affect resource allocation.

Fifth, it is worth emphasising that there is a considerable area of initiative open to the central government in promoting research and training both in universities, technical colleges and research institutes, and in private industry. In an industrial era in which the most important resource is knowledge, the opportunities for government to make an effective contribution to welfare are considerable.

Sixth, the government may also choose, for a variety of reasons, to influence resource allocation by subsidy to specific industries. Such subsidy may be motivated by considerations of national defence, industrial decentralisation or by political lobbying. Whatever the motive there will be a cost to the nation in as much as there is a loss of economic welfare in diverting resources to an industry that would not otherwise survive in the competition for resources. A rational government will wish to know the resource-transfer cost of any specific policy objective and it is the aim of this chapter to show how that cost can be calculated.

2. An industry subsidy

Consider the example in section 4 of the previous chapter in which the economy has a work force of 100 men; the units of quantity are such that the labour input coefficients into each of the two industries are unity; the profit mark-up is 100 per cent on wage-costs; but the consumer-demand functions are here altered to the form:

$$C_w = 0.4Y_d - 20(P_w - k)/P_b$$

$$C_b = (Y_d - C_w P_w)/P_b$$

in which C designates quantity demanded, P price at factor-cost, k is the commodity subsidy and Y_d is disposable income defined as national income at factor cost minus all taxes and plus all subsidies.[1] The wage-rate is designated as $1. Initially there are no taxes or subsidies.

We can readily calculate that, when there are no subsidies, full-employment disposable income is $200 and the price of each good is $2. By substituting these figures into the consumer-demand functions we deduce that the output of w is 60 physical units and the output of b is 40 physical units, and the two industries are employing the entire labour force.

Now suppose that the government plans to introduce an income-tax-financed subsidy on w in order to raise that industry's output to 70 units [2] We can regard the subsidy of $$k$ per unit of w purchased as a reduction in the market price of any given amount of w sold. In other words producers maintain their 100 per cent profit mark-up unchanged but, by then cutting their price by k, they pass on the subsidy as a cash benefit (or negative tax) to consumers. The level of disposable income is unchanged at $200 since

$$Y_d = \text{wages} + \text{profits} - \text{income tax} + \text{subsidies}$$

income tax revenues collected equal the subsidy payments to purchasers of w.

It is easy to calculate that a $1 subsidy per unit of output of w will raise the quantity demanded to 70 units, thus causing 10 per cent of the labour force to transfer from industry b. The calculation of the effect of the subsidy on economic welfare is as follows: There is a loss of production of 10 units of b, valued at $20. There is a gain in production of 10 units of w, valued at $15—i.e. valued at a price of $1.5, which is the average of the value placed on the marginal unit in the old situation ($2) and the new situation ($1). Hence there is a net loss of welfare of $5, equal to 2.5 per cent of the national income.

[1] The particular form of the demand functions is chosen for convenience so that the first function gives a straight line relation between C_w and P_w, and the two functions show total consumer spending equal to disposable income.

[2] The motivation may be that this was the old output and that though tastes have changed to those portrayed by the above demand functions, nonetheless some producers do not wish to move out of the industry and they do not wish to cut their profit mark-up. But whatever the motivation, our concern here is with calculating the cost.

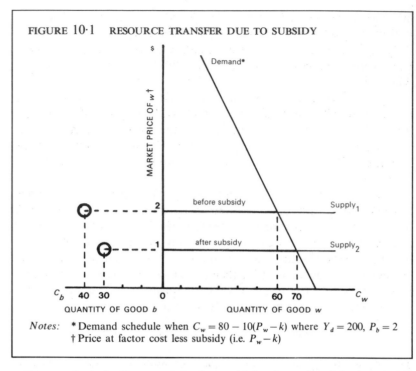

FIGURE 10·1   RESOURCE TRANSFER DUE TO SUBSIDY

Notes: * Demand schedule when $C_w = 80 - 10(P_w - k)$ where $Y_d = 200$, $P_b = 2$
† Price at factor cost less subsidy (i.e. $P_w - k$)

The analysis is illustrated in figure 10.1 where the right-hand side shows the demand schedule for w as well as the supply schedules (constructed directly from the cost account) showing the price at which the producer supplies any specified level of output. The left-hand side shows a plotting of the calculated volume of (production and) consumption of b, both before and after the subsidy on w is introduced.[3] The diagram has the sole function of portraying the resource transfer caused by changing the subsidy k. For this purpose the physical units of measurement chosen are the amounts producible by one unit of resource—so that the length of the horizontal line summing outputs remains constant. *The introduction of such a dis-*

---

[3] The co-ordinates of the points on the left-hand side are given by:

$$k \cdot C_b = 5(P_w - k)^2 - (40 - 5k)(P_w - k) - 40k + 100$$

The reader should be warned that P_w is not itself an independent variable in this diagram but is determined as equal to $a_{nw} \cdot P_n(1 + v_w)$, and if this expression were changed then Y_d would also change. The only autonomous variable in the diagram is k.

criminatory subsidy (or a discriminatory tax) is essentially analogous to a discriminatory profit mark-up, so that the argument is analogous to that of the preceding chapter. Hence the welfare loss is measured as one-half the price rise times the change in volume of output, i.e. $0.5(1) \times (10) = \$5$. As in the previous chapter, it is to be emphasised that this argument is based on a number of simplifying assumptions and takes no account of any change in income distribution that may occur. The argument simply demonstrates the feasibility of measuring the welfare loss when relative market prices do not reflect resource costs because of unequal profit mark-ups, taxes or, as in this case, subsidies.[4]

There are three further comments to be made on the situation illustrated by this example.

The first is that no attention has yet been paid to any loss of economic welfare due to the *method of financing the subsidy*—all we have been concerned with so far has been the welfare loss due to resource transfer. If the subsidy is financed by income tax, then there is a further welfare loss due to altering the marginal returns to work and leisure. If the subsidy were financed by a tax on the other commodity, then this tax would also involve a welfare loss, which can be calculated by the method used above.

The second matter is to check whether there is any *change in income distribution*. In a sense there is no net change in income distribution in this particular example: for producers of *w* are assumed to pass on the subsidy to consumers, while, for households as a group, their income tax payment of $70 is offset by the $1 fall in price of the 70 units of *w* that they buy. *Individual* taxpayers may not concur if their tastes do not conform to the national average, and of course the income tax formula will not have equal impact on each individual.

A third comment is that the above example has assumed that *'competitive conditions' remain unchanged*. In fact the introduction of a subsidy on a good is sometimes the occasion for manoeuvring as traditional 'normal' profit mark-ups are discarded and purchaser and seller vie for the larger share of the subsidy. It is to be emphasised that this manoeuvring goes on irrespective of the government's intentions. Thus in the above example the government may have

---

[4] If an industry is polluting the environment, the *failure* of the government to make the industry meet the cost of eliminating the pollution can be treated as the equivalent of a subsidy.

intended that the *purchaser* would benefit in the sense that the price of w would fall from \$2 to \$1. But it is possible (to take the extreme case) that the existing producers of w might revise their normal profit mark-up from 100 per cent up to 200 per cent and so hold the price unchanged at \$2 while reaping the entire subsidy. In terms of the cost account, the difference in the two situations would look as follows: The cost account at market price is:

$$\text{market price} = P_w, \quad \text{price at factor cost } less \text{ subsidy per unit}$$
$$= a_{nw}.P_n.(1+v_w) \qquad -k$$

In the initial situation before subsidy this gives a price of \$2 and after subsidy a market price of \$1. But if the producers are powerful enough to hold the market price at \$2 *after* the introduction of the subsidy, then by simple substitution this implies that v_w is raised to 200 per cent. This involves a significant income redistribution. Income redistribution also occurs in real-life situations in which a subsidy is provided to increasing-cost industries, ostensibly to help the marginal (i.e. high-cost) producer; but it is not uncommon for low-cost producers to receive the bulk of subsidy payments.

Summary

A subsidy (whether positive or negative) on a commodity causes a change in the composition of production accompanied by a loss of economic welfare.

For since market prices are no longer proportional to resource costs (i.e. marginal cost), the ratio of marginal utility to marginal cost will no longer be the same for all goods.

The reasoning parallels the argument of the preceding chapter where unequal profit rates were the source of the loss of welfare. This loss of welfare is measurable in the same fashion. However, there may be separate effects on welfare through change in income distribution.

Finally, it will be observed that the welfare loss due to a subsidy (or a tax, which is a negative subsidy) will be greater the more responsive quantity demanded is to changes in price. In an extreme situation in which quantity demanded is completely unresponsive to a change in market price, the subsidy has no effect on resource allocation and so causes no welfare loss—although there may be changes in income distribution. It is interesting to speculate that in a poor society the demand for foodstuffs and shelter could prove to be relatively unresponsive to change in commodity price ratios, but that, as the society grows wealthier, the wider array of choice results in demand being increasingly price responsive—and so increasingly vulnerable to the sort of welfare loss explored here caused by differential subsidies.

3. The economic system ⊟

The model used above may be summarised in figure 10.2 in order to emphasise once again that we are concerned with resource transfers between industries and hence with the entire economic system. This emphasis on resource transfer takes the analysis of the physical system one step further.

It should be added that, in an industry in which unit costs are rising or falling, a tax or subsidy (k) on a commodity will normally cause market price to change by a *different* amount. Thus if unit costs are rising as output expands, then a tax on a commodity will normally cause the market price to rise by an amount that is less than the tax rise—since the price rise will cut back the volume demanded and thus reduce the before-tax supply price.

This chapter has emphasised the nature of the costs of unequal rates of taxes and subsidies. These costs of course still exist when the taxes and subsidies are on internationally traded commodities and it is in the area of international trade that this sort of analysis has major application.

FIGURE 10·2   MODEL: RESOURCE TRANSFER FOLLOWING SUBSIDY

Work force	:	100 men
Technology	:	labour input coefficients in both industries b and w are unity
Profit mark-up	:	100 per cent in both industries
Cost account includes provision for subsidy (k)		
Market price	:	$[a_{nw}P_n(1+v_w)] - k$
Final demand	:	$C_w = 0.4Y_d - 20(P_w - k)/P_b$ $C_b = (Y_d - C_wP_w)/P_b$

4. Resource transfer diagrams*

Figure 10.1 establishes the basis of a common method of analysis in which the right-hand side of that diagram is used to analyse the

*This section may be omitted on a first reading.

effects of some event on the allocation of resources and hence on the output of this industry. As commonly drawn the diagram would appear simply as a set of demand and supply schedules in figure 10.3. The argument would then be summarised: the introduction of the subsidy, shifting the supply schedule from S_1 to S_2, raises output from A to B. It is to be emphasised that such argument assumes first that other commodity prices are constant, and second that disposable national income is constant.

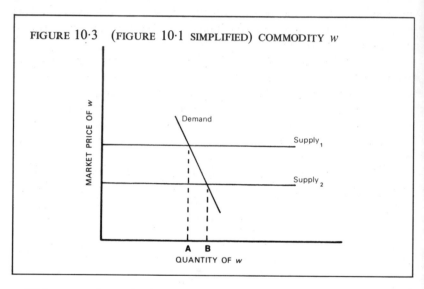

FIGURE 10·3   (FIGURE 10·1 SIMPLIFIED) COMMODITY w

This type of supply-demand diagram can also be of great help in sorting out the effect on the volume of an industry's output of such events as a change in consumer tastes (shifts demand schedule), a change in technology or in the degree of competition (shifts supply schedule). The diagrammatic approach is the more attractive because both the supply and demand schedules can be drawn at any angle from vertical to horizontal and because both can be drawn straight or curved. But it should be repeated that such diagrams are based on the assumption that other prices and incomes are constant. This includes the implicit assumption that a fall in output of w reflects a *resource transfer* in which the output of other industries has risen. For if this assumption were not true then national income must have changed.

In summary, commodity 'demand-and-supply' diagrams like figure 10.3 conceal a potential ambiguity. For when we observe in figure 10.3 that the output of w has risen from A to B then it could be that this was associated with either:

(a) no change in output of other goods (and so disposable national income rises); or

(b) a resource transfer involving a fall in output of other goods (with no change in disposable national income).

In case (a) the analysis would not be valid because national income has changed. The whole problem of course is overcome by using figure 10.1, which specifies that a resource transfer is being analysed.

Having introduced demand and supply diagrams for individual goods, it is appropriate for us to point out that the *responsiveness* of demand (or of supply) to a change in price is commonly measured as the ratio of the percentage change in quantity demanded to the percentage change in price. This ratio is called *the price elasticity of demand* [5]

$$\frac{\text{price elasticity of}}{\text{demand for a good}} = \frac{\%\ \text{change in quantity demanded}}{\%\ \text{change in price}}$$

and its frequent use is due to the fact that, being a ratio of percentages, it is independent of the units of measurement originally used. Useful examples of this concept are shown in figure 10.4 where, if expenditure (measured by the area of the rectangle under the curve) is constant, it follows that a 0.05 per cent price rise causes a 0.05 per cent fall in quantity demanded, so that the price elasticity of demand (ε) is unity.

Valuable as the concept of elasticity is as a measure of the responsiveness of demand to price, it will be apparent that this elasticity is unlikely to be constant. For example if technological change caused the price of butter to fall it is possible that the elasticity observed might first be high, but if the price continued to fall the community would approach satiety and the elasticity observed would be low.

---

[5] A more precise definition of elasticity is given in the supplement (p. 262). The important qualification is that the absolute increment in price must be quite small so that we have the elasticity at a point (i.e. at a specific price, not over a price range).

FIGURE 10·4 ELASTICITY OF DEMAND (ε)FOR GOOD w

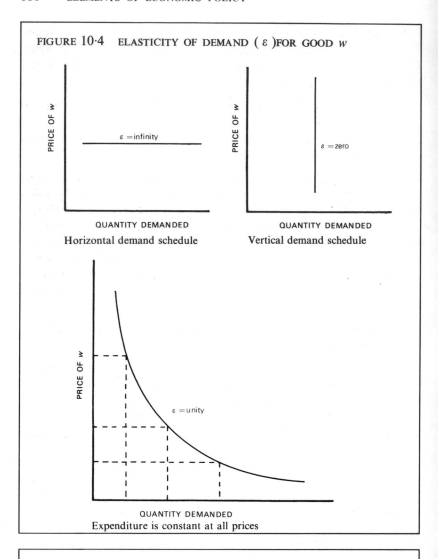

Horizontal demand schedule

Vertical demand schedule

Expenditure is constant at all prices

Summary

'Supply and demand' diagrams are essentially resource-transfer diagrams.

A demand (or supply) schedule portrays responsiveness to price. It may be convenient to measure this responsiveness as an elasticity (or ratio of percentages). But the elasticity itself need not be constant.

In summary whenever one variable is functionally dependent on another—demand dependent on price, crop yield dependent on rainfall—the responsiveness may be measured as a ratio of percentages, i.e. as an elasticity. But the elasticity itself can be expected to vary with the level of the determining variable.

Summary

§1. The government's concern with resource allocation arises out of such issues as living standards, unemployment, communal consumption ('collective goods'), restrictive practices, research and training. The government may also subsidise individual industries—which is the topic examined here.

§2. Assuming continuous full employment, we calculate the loss of welfare caused by a subsidy reallocating resources. In the simplest case this loss equals one-half the market price fall (due to the subsidy) times the rise in output, and this can be expressed as a proportion of national income.

A complete analysis, however, must also explore: the effects of the method of financing the subsidy; income distribution change; any changes in competitive conditions.

§3. This sort of analysis establishes a basis for examining the effects of tariffs and subsidies on internationally traded goods.

§4. Care is needed in using resource-transfer diagrams to ensure that they are relevant to the issue.

Further reading

P.A. Samuelson, *Economics*, part III.

R.H. Leftwich, *Introduction to Economic Thinking* (New York: Holt, Rinehart & Winston, 1969), part 2.

R.G. Lipsey, *Positive Economics*, book I, part I.

Questions

1. Discuss the nature of government intervention in resource allocation.
2. Outline a situation in which you envisage that government intervention in a *specific* industry may be needed.

3. Outline a situation in which you envisage that government intervention in industry *at large* may be needed.

11. Could figure 10.1 be used to explore the effects of a new invention that halved the amount of labour needed to produce a unit of w? What could the effect be? (There is no subsidy).

12. What is the price elasticity of supply in figure 10.3?

13. In figure 10.2 suppose there is a change in tastes so that the coefficient 0.4 now changes to 0.3. Calculate the effect on the output of w when there is no subsidy.

   Write out the new and old demand schedules for w showing consumption depending on price.

14. An island nation devotes 100 acres of land and 80 men to producing exports. There are three potential export industries—oats, barley and wheat—selling on the world market at constant prices (in U.S. dollars) of 30, 45 and 15 per ton respectively. The land : labour factor input requirements per ton are—oats 2:2, barley 2:4, wheat $2:\frac{1}{2}$. What are the maximum possible foreign exchange earnings from exports?

   What is the effect of a barley subsidy of \$US15 per ton that raises the return to the barley exporter to \$US60 though the return to the island nation is unchanged at \$US45? (Hint: Think of the three crops as 3 activities capable of 'producing' a unit of foreign exchange).

21. Outline a situation in which, in order to achieve a specific aim, the government is willing to sacrifice a measurable amount of economic welfare.

22. Explain how some measures can be regarded as equivalent to subsidies and hence involve a measurable welfare loss.

23. How may the argument that a subsidy causes a welfare loss have to be modified if public and private costs and benefits already diverge?

24. Consider how the argument concerning the effects of subsidies can be applied to unequal rates of indirect tax on commodities.

25. Can the reasoning in this chapter be used to analyse the effect of income tax in causing a reallocation of man-hours between work and leisure?

Technological Change

> Better technology may cause an industry to use fewer resources; thus government action is needed to prevent technological unemployment. Farm industry illustrates the problem of social adaptation to technological change.

1. The problem

Technological change is a basic characteristic of modern economies. The problem of creating conditions that encourage the creation of new scientific and technical knowledge is an elusive task—though one necessary condition seems to be a well-endowed and innovating educational system.

The adoption of new technical knowledge in industry affects the welfare of the community in three ways:

(a) Living standards are raised by making more effective use of society's physical resources.

(b) The welfare of workers in the industry is affected in as much as there may be more or less of: noise, repetitive work, manual labour, nervous tension, toxic conditions, danger to life.

(c) The environment may be affected—not only by noise, or by pollution of the atmosphere or waterways by toxic chemicals, but also in such matters as global temperature and carbon dioxide concentration.

We are concerned here with the first, though the importance of the other two is obvious.

Imagine that the nature of technological change were such that the productivity of the factors employed in each industry grew at the same rate. Imagine also that, as the nation's production potential grew, the community's demand for all goods grew in the same proportion. If the assumptions set out in the last two sentences were true, then all industries would grow at the same rate—the only mild complication would be that the community might choose to take out some of its improved welfare in the form of leisure rather than physical goods. But in reality life is not like that—neither of the assumptions is valid.

In recent decades high rates of technical change have been concentrated in some agricultural and manufacturing industries—the productivity of factors in these industries has grown at markedly higher rates than in other industries. On the other hand as the nation's production potential per head has grown, people have wanted to spend a relatively large proportion of their incomes on some manufactured goods and on services—so that the proportion of expenditure on these goods has risen and on other goods has fallen. A crude indicator[1] of the changes implied is the fall in the proportion of the work force engaged in agriculture in nations such as the United States and Australia.

In summary the development of an improved technology in an industry does not carry the corollary that that industry's greater productive capacity will be demanded by consumers. On the contrary *consumers may want to take out the fruits of better technology by releasing resources from that industry to produce other goods or services.* This must have been a source of social conflict ever since the human race first emerged from the status of a simple hunter to an agrarian way of life. The conflict continues as people in an industry resist the impact of technical change that, while advantageous to society, is harmful to themselves because it creates excess capacity in their industry and threatens their established way of life. It seems clear that in order to prevent technological change creating unemployment, the government must both (a) maintain aggregate demand, and (b) provide job retraining, income supplement and capital grants, so that resources may transfer smoothly between industries. Society, which seeks to benefit from technological change, may well be held to have

Summary

Consumers may want to take out the fruits of improved technology in industry *A* by consuming more of the products of industry *B*—thus necessitating transfer of resources.

Government action is required to:

(a) maintain aggregate demand

(b) assist resource transfers by retraining and finance.

[1] 'Crude' because of exports, imports, and inputs (e.g. fertiliser) from other industries.

a responsibility towards those who are adversely affected by such change.

2. Case study: farm policy

The above argument can be illustrated by many industries, but by none more clearly than farming. A modern nation can feed its population with no more than five per cent of its work force in farming. Technological change in rural industry has steadily reduced the proportion of the work force engaged in farming. Recent years have seen the emergence of something in the nature of a farm crisis as farmers have resisted adaptation to this technological change. The political power of farmers in nations like France, Italy, Germany, Britain and the United States has resulted in policies of increasing agricultural protectionism in those nations so that traditional exporters of rural products (e.g. in the Southern Hemisphere) find their export markets contracting as their own productive capacity increases. The issue plainly warrants closer examination.

Imagine that an industry is initially at equilibrium with supply and demand equal at the prevailing price level. However, during the ensuing years the industry's ability to supply goods grows faster than the demand for such goods. This may arise either because it is technically innovative or because the community approaches a satiety phase in demand, or for both reasons. Some adjustment process is needed. Light can be thrown on the adjustment process by restating the problem in the form: the supply schedule is shifting to the right faster than the demand schedule (see figure 11.1). The implication of this manner of presentation is that the adjustment process can proceed via the price mechanism. Consider the possibilities.

In figure 11.1 the initial position is at B, the intersection of the demand and supply schedules labelled D_1, S_1. Now the supply schedule moves to position S_2, which is much to the right of the new position of the demand schedule, D_2. If it were the case that supply simply grew as if the price were going to remain unchanged at A, then supply would grow to D; but then there would have to be a price fall to F in order to clear the market, and at that price producers would make a considerable loss.

The second possibility is that the price mechanism works in such a manner as to reduce the price to G, and output changes to K—

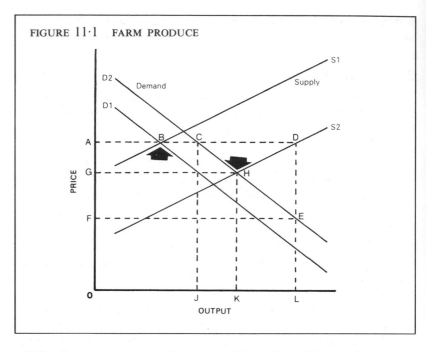

FIGURE 11·1   FARM PRODUCE

which of course corresponds to a position of equilibrium at *H* where demand equals supply. *It is when political moves are made to avoid the operation of this mechanism that difficulties develop.*

Thus a third possibility is that producers use political power to: first, prevent a cut-back in production from *L* to *K* because this would mean some producers moving out of the industry; and second, prevent a cut in the price from *A* because this would reduce the living standards of producers. Such political demands are of course normal, legitimate, in conflict with the rest of the community, and often successful. Since at the price *A* the volume demanded is only *AC*, it is necessary for the government to buy the amount *CD* in order to meet such political demands. The purchase is financed by taxation, and the amount *CD* may then either be destroyed, given away or sold at low price on the world market.

If the output *CD* is destroyed, then there is a national loss of welfare (due to resource misallocation) measured by the amount of other goods that could have been produced by the resources used to produce *CD*. There is also an income redistribution in as much as, for example, the producers who would have been prepared to supply a volume OK at price G receive the higher price A.

A fourth possibility is that the government may give a subsidy DE per ton of output. This can be represented by a parallel shift downwards of S_2 by the vertical amount DE to intersect D_2 at E. The total value of the subsidy in dollars is the rectangle $AFED$ and is met by taxation. Thus the market price to the consumer is reduced to F. In these circumstances the loss of welfare (due to reallocating resources from position II) directly associated with the subsidy may be estimated as equal to one-half the price difference FG times the increase in output KL. There is also an income redistribution because all producers—low-cost as well as high-cost producers—receive the subsidy.[2]

The sort of 'farm policies' just outlined are plainly open to critical comment on two grounds: first, they involve a loss of economic welfare by endeavouring to neutralise the fruits of improving technology; secondly, their tax-subsidy measures become increasingly untenable because technological change is a continuing cumulative process. It seems clear that a rational solution is a generous phased programme of farm reconstruction including income while retraining and capital payments for farms purchased by the government.

The farm policies of many European nations, though comprehensible in political terms, have a somewhat Micawberish aspect. How much more, however, is this true of the Australian government's farm policy up to 1970 of subsidising wheat for export. By not spreading the total subsidy among the alternative crops (coarse grains, wool, mutton) that those same farmers could have produced for export, the government stimulated an enormous expansion of wheat. By also being a party to the International Grains Agreement, which sought to place a minimum world price on wheat, the Australian government succeeded in making much of that subsidised wheat unsaleable.

---

[2] In essence the 'third possibility' indicates the approach of the European Economic Community up to 1970; the 'fourth possibility' indicates the United Kingdom approach up to 1970. The two approaches are not simply equivalent: if demand is highly price-inelastic, the subsidy may simply not work; but the government can always destroy crops.

Summary

When improvements in agricultural technology cause productive capacity to outstrip demand, the imbalance can be corrected by transferring resources out of farming, and allowing farm prices to fall. The attempt to prevent such resource transfer involves either farm subsidies or government purchase of crops.

Summary

§1. Improved technology in an industry may result in a drop in resources used in that industry. Farm industry is a notable example.

§2. In such a situation, the industry concerned may use political means to prevent transfers of resources out of the industry. Examples of such political means are farm support prices and farm subsidies. Such response denies society some of the fruits of improved technology.

Further reading

C. Ferguson and J. Kreps, *Principles of Economics* (New York: Holt, Rinehart & Winston, 1965), ch. 29.

P.A. Samuelson, *Economics*, ch. 21.

R.T. Gill, *Economics and the Public Interest*, p. 60.

Questions

1. Explain how unemployment may arise owing to improvement in technology.

2. Imagine that technical efficiency in each industry increased at the same annual rate. Would you expect any reallocation of resources between industries?

3. Explain two ways in which a government can provide financial help to an industry sufficiently politically powerful to resist technological improvement that would reduce the resources employed in the industry.

11. The probability of technological unemployment is greater if the income elasticity of demand for the industry's product is:

    (a) greater than one;
    (b) less than one.

    Which is correct?

12. The problem of adjustment to improved technology is greater in the farm sector than other industry because the price elasticities of both demand and supply are low. Do you agree?

13. The potato industry sells 100 million pounds at 8 cents a pound one year; the following year a bumper crop of 130 million pounds can only be sold at 6 cents a pound. Comment.

21. How important is the problem of technological unemployment? Is it any different in kind as a result of automation and 'computer-operated plants'?

22. What is 'the farm problem' in western industrialised nations? How would you solve it? Does it differ from the problem of adapting to changing technology that may occur in any industry?

23. Industrial research is usually aimed at technological change affecting only the first of the three matters listed at the start of this chapter. Consider a broader approach.

Part III—Trade

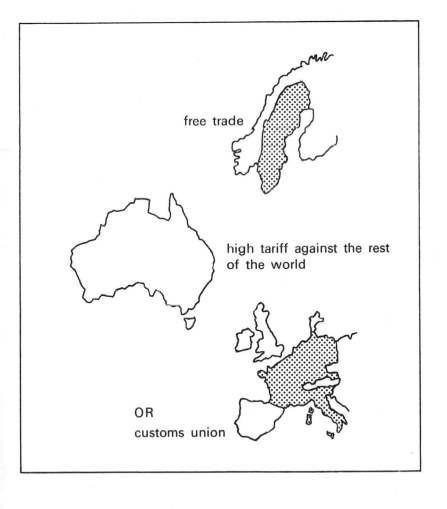

free trade

high tariff against the rest of the world

OR
customs union

Foreign Trade

> The gain from trade lies in the nation's ability to shift resources into the production for export of those goods in which it has *relative* superiority. But if the nation is equally superior in the efficiency with which it produces all goods, there may be no trade.

1. The origins of trade

Nations trade for three reasons.

(a) They obtain imported commodities that they could not produce themselves in the desired quantity. This motive to trade applies to a great deal of world trade in raw materials (metallic ores, grains, natural fibres, tropical products).

(b) They obtain imported commodities at a *lower cost in real resources* than by producing the goods themselves. Thus New Zealand may be capable of producing large electric generators and yet find that fewer resources are used if those generators are imported from Japan or Italy in exchange for exported mutton.

(c) A few nations are so deficient in material resources relatively to their population that the motive for trade is almost literally survival;[1] e.g. Hong Kong. They need to import raw materials, process them and re-export them in order to be able to pay for imports for their own final use. A nation such as the United States, with plentiful natural resources of arable land and minerals, does not have this motive for trading.

The gains from trade may be substantial. Cuba, with its tropic region suited to sugar; Australia, with its dry flat hinterland suited to wheat and wool; Bolivia, with its tin deposits: such countries have a capacity for high volume production of these products, from which they cannot adequately benefit without foreign trade. A major contraction of world trade would see a significant fall in living

---

[1] Assuming emigration is impossible.

standards as those countries switched their labour out of export industries into import-competing industry.

Having specified the motives to trade, and having noted that the gains from trade may indeed be substantial, we now consider more closely the sources of these gains from trade.

We may begin by pointing out that if two nations are not trading but their *relative* home prices differ, then there is an opportunity for profitable trade by each importing what is to them the relatively cheaper good. Thus in the example in section 2 below, before trade the home price of sugar is five times that of wheat, but overseas the world price of sugar is eight times that of wheat—hence it will be profitable to export sugar in exchange for wheat. But what determines these relative price differences? The answer is that a good may be relatively cheap at home:

— because of high-grade natural resources (mineral deposits, fertile soil, climate, rivers);
— because there is a plentiful supply of some productive factor (land or labour);
— because the nation has been first in developing an advanced technology (the United Kingdom around 1800, later overtaken by Europe and then by the United States);
— or because mass production has brought economies of scale.

It is to be noted that these influences are themselves subject to change —new mineral deposits are discovered (Australia, Brazil), and new nations join the race for technological supremacy (Japan)—and so trade patterns change as a result.

In the historical development of ideas about trade, two of the causes of trade just listed were analysed at length, and they are briefly summarised in the next two paragraphs.

Early in the nineteenth century David Ricardo suggested that differences in technology offered a major opportunity for trade. The following example illustrates his argument. Consider two imaginary countries: 'Queensland' and 'Victoria'. Suppose Queensland, with a work force of 4,500 men, has the following technology: sugar production requires 0.5 men per ton annually; wheat production requires 0.1 per ton. Victoria on the other hand, with a work force of 5,000 men, has the technology: sugar production requires 2.0 men per ton annually; wheat production requires 0.15 men per ton.[2] From this information, two conclusions may be intuitively deduced:

RESOURCES AND ANNUAL LABOUR INPUT COEFFICIENTS

Queensland	Victoria

4,500 men
0.5 men per ton of sugar
0.1 men per ton of wheat
[∴ 1 ton sugar 'costs'
    5 tons of wheat]
	5,000 men
	2.0 men per ton of sugar
	0.15 men per ton of wheat
	[∴ 1 ton sugar 'costs'
	    13.3 tons of wheat]

At a world sugar price of 10 tons of wheat, Queensland will import 10 tons of wheat for 1 ton of sugar exported; since 10 tons of wheat produced at home cost 2 tons of sugar (in transferred resources).	

Queensland will have a higher living standard because of her superior technology; secondly, because there are *relative* differences in technology between the two regions, the collective output of the two regions could be raised by each specialising in the production of the commodity in which its relative advantage is greatest (or relative disadvantage least). The heart of the matter is that Queensland can produce an extra ton of sugar at a cost of 5 tons of wheat, while Victoria can produce an extra 5 tons of wheat at a cost of $[(5 \times 0.15)/2.0 =]$ 0.375 tons of sugar—so the resource transfers yield a gain from trade of 0.625 tons of sugar the benefit of which is shared between the countries.[3]

EFFECT OF RESOURCE TRANSFER ON PRODUCTION TONNAGE

	Queensland	Victoria
Sugar	+ 1	− 0.375
Wheat	− 5	+ 5

[2] Land is plentiful in both countries and labour cannot emigrate.
[3] Observe how this argument fails if the Victorian labour input coefficient for wheat is not 0.15 but 0.4.

It can readily be calculated: that if there is to be trade, the price of a ton of sugar will be between the two home pre-trade figures 5 and 13.3 tons of wheat; and that, at an assumed world sugar price of say 10 tons of wheat, there is a gain to Queensland from importing wheat because 10 tons of wheat produced at home cost 2 tons of home-produced sugar (in terms of transferred resources). If each region can satisfy total demand for a traded good, Queensland will concentrate on sugar production and import her wheat.

In the 1930s Bertil Ohlin pointed out that differences in the relative supply of productive factors opened another major opportunity for trade. Consider the following information given on two countries *A* and *B*.

	Nation A	Nation B
Work force, million	1	4
Pastoral land, million acres	3	4

If both regions have the same technical knowledge and methods of production, which region would we expect to import wheat and which region to import manufactures? If there were no trade, land-rents would be relatively low (compared with the wage-rate) in *A*. So land-intensive products would be relatively cheap in *A*. Wheat is such a good, and we would therefore expect *A* to export wheat.[4]

---

[4] If country *A*, in which land is plentiful, is able through foreign trade to switch into expanding production of a land-intensive good, it follows that she will use *less* land-intensive methods of production. (The reason is that switching from producing labour-intensive goods to land-intensive goods requires that land-intensity be reduced for all goods, since full employment of all resources is assumed throughout.) These less land-intensive methods will be characterised by a *higher* marginal productivity of land (since diminishing marginal productivity of all factors is assumed). This higher marginal productivity is the source of the physical gain from trade in the Ohlin case.

Summary: Two nation trade

Viewing foreign trade as a business proposition: each nation can profitably trade by importing the goods that are *relatively* cheap overseas.

Example: Before trade the ratio of the price of sugar to wheat is 5 in Queensland and 13·3 in Victoria. So Victoria will import sugar; Queensland will import wheat.

The *source* of differences in relative prices between nations lies in resource distribution, population density, technology; other influences include education and size.

To summarise: Ricardo pointed out that the home price of a good (sugar) could be relatively cheap because of relatively better technology, and Ohlin pointed out that the home price of a good (wheat) could be relatively cheap because it had a high content of a relatively plentiful factor (e.g. land). In either case trade can be profitable. Ricardo was perhaps the first to make clear that even a nation with all-round technical superiority can gain from trade by concentrating on producing for export those goods in which her *comparative* advantage is greatest (e.g. Queensland concentrating on sugar in the above example). However, it should be emphasised that Ricardo and Ohlin, great as was their contribution, were concerned with only two of the causes of trade. We cannot afford in practice to ignore other causes—including distribution of mineral deposits, climate and economies of scale, all of which cause relative prices to differ as between nations.

The next section sets out a worked example. This shows that, when relative prices at home are different from those abroad, we may obtain one commodity at less cost in real resources by importing it in exchange for something else than by producing it ourselves.[5] The gain from trade is calculated.

2. The economic system: the gains from trade ⊟

Consider the imaginary economy Queensland in which the sole scarce resource is a work force of 4,500 men; and there are only two industries—sugar, requiring 0.5 men per annual ton of output; and wheat requiring 0.1 men per annual ton of output. The profit mark-up is 100 per cent in each industry. Suppose for simplicity

[5] If monopolistic activity causes profit mark-ups to be unequal, this statement requires qualification inasmuch as price is no longer proportional to marginal cost.

that households spend half their income on each good. This information is summarised in figure 12.1. Then if we set the wage-rate at \$1,000 and compute all prices with reference to this, we can readily deduce that the price of sugar is \$1,000 per ton and the price of wheat is \$200 per ton. Moreover the full-employment annual national income is \$9m and annual consumption is 4,500 tons of sugar and 22,500 tons of wheat.

Imagine that Queensland, hitherto cut off from world trade, now explores the potential gains from trade. When she looks at world

FIGURE 12·1   QUEENSLAND

Work force	:	4,500 men
Labour inputs	:	0.5 men per ton of sugar
	:	0.1 men per ton of wheat
Profit mark-up is 100 per cent in both industries		
$C_s P_s = 0.5 Y$ $C_w P_w = 0.5 Y$		

prices (expressed in her own currency at the prevailing exchange rate) of wheat and sugar, she might find any of four logical possibilities:[6]

World prices of sugar and wheat are:

(a) both below home prices;
(b) both above home prices;
(c) both equal to home prices;
(d) one cheaper, the other dearer, at home relatively to world prices.

Queensland's exchange rate will depreciate in the first case, in the second case appreciate, until the third or fourth case is reached; and in the third case no trade will occur. The fourth is thus the interesting case. Suppose that the world price of sugar is \$1,200 per ton and the world price of wheat is \$150 per ton—the figures are chosen arbitrarily. Then it is apparent that Queensland can gain by: ceasing wheat production entirely; setting her entire labour

[6] Transport costs are assumed zero in order to avoid discussing both f.o.b. and c.i.f. prices at this stage. F.o.b. or 'free on board' designates the price at point of export; c.i.f. or 'cost, insurance and freight' is the price at point of import.

force to produce 9,000 tons of sugar, consume 4,500 tons of this and export the remaining 4,500 tons for $5.4m of foreign exchange, which will buy 36,000 tons of wheat. This is a gain from trade of 13,500 tons of wheat. In fact there will be a shift in the pattern of consumer spending in Queensland because of the change in prices—but the gains from trade will remain.

It may be added that, if Queensland wheat producers successfully obtain say a 50 per cent tariff on imported wheat (say because it is produced by 'cheap foreign labour'), then Queensland will not trade, for other nations will be unable to earn Queensland currency to pay for Queensland sugar. So any sectoral advantage to Queensland wheat producers is set against the collective loss to all Queensland consumers.

The above example has been deliberately simplified by assuming constant scale returns and that rising sugar exports will not depress the world sugar price. In reality the volume of a nation's exports may be limited by:

(a) physical limits in export industry's capacity to produce;
(b) diminishing scale returns (or rising unit costs) in export industry that gradually erode the advantage to another country of obtaining a good by import instead of by home production;
(c) diminishing value returns, where a rise in one's export volume depresses world price.

But, within these limits, the gains from trade are real.

3. The balance of payments

The international transactions of a country over the year are recorded in a statement called 'the balance of payments', illustrated in figure 12.2. It will be observed that the balance of payments is here divided into two parts—'current' and 'capital'—and that each is balanced by entering a residual. It is these residuals that are of special interest.

The imaginary balance of payments in figure 12.2 is seen to portray a capital-importing nation (see interest and dividend payments, 2.5), which uses foreign ships to transport its imports and exports (see freight, insurance costs, 2). The net position on all its current transactions is a balance of current payments deficit of 4.7 per cent of

FIGURE 12·2   THE BALANCE OF PAYMENTS

CURRENT ACCOUNT				
Receipts		Payments		
Exports of merchandise f.o.b.[a]	14.7	Imports of merchandise f.o.b.[a]	15.1	
		Freight, insurance	2.0	
Interest, dividends	0.4	Interest, dividends	2.5	
Tourism	1.3	Tourism, aid to foreign nations	1.5	
Balance of current payments (deficit)	4.7[b]			
	$\overline{21.1}$		$\overline{21.1}$	
CAPITAL ACCOUNT				
Receipts		Payments		
Capital inflow	4.8	Balance of current payments (deficit)	4.7	
		Rise in international monetary reserves and foreign assets	0.1[b]	
	$\overline{4.8}$		$\overline{4.8}$	

Notes: a Free on board (at point of loading).
        b Residual.
    Figures are expressed as a percentage of GNP instead of in home currency as is customary.

gross national product. This is the most critical figure in the whole account for it represents an excess of foreign exchange payable over foreign exchange earnings and it must be financed in some way. In this case it is more than financed by an inflow of foreign capital, there being a rise in foreign exchange reserves of 0.1.

It is a dominant aim of short-term economic management by the government to keep the balance of current payments (i.e. the current account residual in figure 12.2) within manageable limits—i.e. the deficit or surplus should not be too large. Typical influences that can have a strong effect on the size of this residual are:

— a boom that results in rising spending on imports—a situation that can develop rapidly if either demand for commodities rises rapidly, or trade unions claim large wage increases in excess of rising labour productivity;
— a similar boom in foreign nations, on the other hand, will boost our export earnings;
— protective policies of other nations;
— changes in technology and tastes as between nations.

The means by which a government seeks to manage the size of the balance of current payments are discussed in chapter 13.

This is a convenient point at which to mention the concept of *the net terms of trade*, defined as the ratio of the nation's export price index (P_e) to the import price index (P_m). Thus for a nation exporting primary produce such as cocoa, copper or wool on a fluctuating world market, one way to explore influences affecting her balance of current payments is to watch trends in the overseas purchasing power of her exports. This is calculated by mutiplying the volume of her exports (X_e) by the net terms of trade, or equivalently by dividing the value of

$$ X_e \cdot \left\{ \frac{P_e}{P_m} \right\} = \frac{(X_e \cdot P_e)}{P_m} $$

exports ($X_e.P_e$) by the import price index.

4. The exchange rate and the finance of trade

The finance of a nation's trade consists essentially in earning foreign currencies by export, and using these foreign currencies to pay for imports. The manufacturer or farmer or importing agent who exports or imports may never handle any foreign currency, however, since his commercial banker typically handles this; i.e. the banker pays the exporter in home currency for his foreign exchange, and then sells this foreign exchange to the importer in exchange for home currency. This normal financial process presumes two things: access to *a store of foreign exchange* (since, in any period, payments may exceed receipts of foreign exchange), and an *exchange rate* at which foreign currencies are exchanged. Consider these two matters in turn.

A nation may have access to a *store of foreign exchange* either by accumulating foreign assets or by borrowing overseas. Assets may be accumulated overseas by exporting more than the nation imports or, more accurately, by having a balance of current payments surplus. Borrowing overseas may be done in a variety of ways—by raising a long-term loan, by establishing a short-term line of credit, or by having 'drawing rights' with an international agency such as the International Monetary Fund (I.M.F.). The most advanced development in this respect has been the non-repayable Special

Drawing Rights (S.D.R.) created and administered by the I.M.F.
in order to sustain the growth of foreign assets needed to finance
the growth of world trade.[7]

The *exchange rate* between two currencies is the amount of one
currency that will purchase the other—for example one Australian
dollar may exchange for 14 Bolivian pesos. Two questions are now
considered concerning the exchange rate between currencies: What
determines a change in the exchange rate? What social function
does the existence of more than one currency perform? We now
consider these.

The hypothesis has been advanced that one may explain *changes*
in the rate of exchange by examining changes in the *internal* purchasing
power of the currencies in their respective countries. This intuitively
appealing hypothesis is called the *purchasing power parity theory,*
and is illustrated in figure 12.3. This hypothesis was used to explain
the observation in the early twentieth century that when a nation

FIGURE 12·3   PURCHASING POWER PARITY THEORY

Call 1970 the *base year* in which the rate of exchange R^* is 14 Bolivian pesos
for one Australian dollar; and in each nation A and B a price index is constructed
for all goods satisfying home demand and equated to 100 for that year.

Suppose that by 1990 the price index in A doubles to 200 while the price index
in B is constant.

Then the purchasing power parity hypothesis asserts that since the *internal*
purchasing power of the $\$A$ falls to one-half that of the peso, then the *external*
purchasing power (i.e. the 1990 exchange rate R) will also fall by one-half, to
seven pesos.

Summary

$$R = R^* \times \frac{B's \text{ price index}}{A's \text{ price index}}$$

where R, R^* are the rates at which $B's$ currency exchanges for $A's$ currency,
R^* being the base year rate.

---

[7] The creation of S.D.R. constitutes a move away from the situation in the first
half of this century when a group of nations would form a financial bloc (e.g. the sterling
area) in which the 'satellite' members would acquire foreign exchange reserves in the
form of the 'centre' country's currency either by a balance of current payments surplus
with the centre or by borrowing from the centre (i.e. capital flow), for financing trade
between members of the bloc.

experienced a major internal inflation, its exchange rate fell on the foreign exchange markets. The mechanism of this currency devaluation is that, as internal prices rise: nationals are prepared to pay more for imports and so force a devaluation of the currency; while at the same time the price of the nation's exports expressed in foreign currency has to be reduced if foreigners are to be persuaded to buy them.

However, there are two objections to the purchasing power parity theory—one technical and the other general. The technical objection is that the theory implicitly assumes that the prices of all goods change in the same proportion, whereas, if the prices of home-consumed goods for example rose much more than the prices of exports, then it does not follow that 'internal' and 'external' purchasing power will change in the *same* proportion. The second and more important objection is that the purchasing power theory discusses only monetary influences and ignores 'real' influences on the exchange rate. In reality there may be no inflation and yet a change in the exchange rate may occur because of international changes in tastes or technology or indeed simply because national product grows.[8] Moreover government intervention (by tariffs, subsidies and quotas) can prevent a devaluation, which might otherwise occur, and a capital inflow may have the same effect. We must conclude that while the purchasing power parity theory is valuable in explaining the link between inflation and devaluation, it fails to give a general explanation of exchange rate changes.

Since the purchasing power parity hypothesis fails to provide a general explanation of *changes* in exchange rates, it follows that a more ambitious version of the hypothesis, which asserts that the *absolute* level of the exchange rate equals the ratio of internal purchasing power of the currencies, is also not valid. For even if this absolute postulate chanced to be true at some initial date, it could then be invalidated by any 'real' or non-monetary influence on the exchange rate.

Finally, *what social function does the existence of more than one currency serve?* One answer is that the existence of separate currencies for regions, between which productive factors are immobile, provides a relatively simple way of re-establishing trade equilibrium by

[8] Some nations display a characteristic tendency to spend a rising proportion of their growing GNP per capita on imports—which may force them to devalue.

currency devaluation. For example suppose that there is a shift in Austrian tastes from Bulgarian to home-produced goods—creating unemployment in Bulgaria and increased demand in Austria. The situation cannot be remedied by migration of workers if we assume that labour is immobile. But it may be remedied by devaluing the bulgar relatively to the Austrian schilling. In summary, the existence of different currencies enables a shift of the entire structure of factor prices in one country as compared with another.

A second reason for having different currencies lies in the different internal economic policies that different governments pursue. Thus a government pursuing a rigorous anti-inflation policy compared with other nations may develop a continuing balance of current payments surplus, which it may choose to eliminate by appreciating its exchange rate. Thus having a separate currency gives a government greater independence in its internal economic policy. This is well illustrated by the past historical situation in which a large number of nations pegged the price of gold in terms of their own currencies. This creation of a gold standard bloc of pegged currencies in effect created a single uniform currency, and the endeavour to maintain the pegged rate limited the freedom of a nation to pursue an independent internal economic policy (as discussed in the following chapter).

Summary

§1. Nations trade to obtain unprocurable goods, to obtain goods at lower real cost, or to survive.

The existence of relative price differences indicates opportunity for gainful trade. Such relative price differences may be due to relative differences in technology, factor supplies or resource endowment.

§2. It can be shown how to calculate the gains from trade.

§3. The nation's international transactions are set out in the balance of payments. The critical figures in this are the balance of current payments and (if it is a deficit) the way in which it is financed.

§4. The finance of trade presupposes access to reserves of foreign currency, obtained either by an export surplus or by borrowing or special drawing rights (S.D.R.).

The purchasing power parity theory is useful in explaining

the impact of inflation on the exchange rate but is unable to provide a general explanation of changes in the exchange rate.

The existence of many currencies performs a social function where factors are regionally immobile or where governments seek to pursue independent internal economic policies.

Further reading

R.T. Gill, *Economics and the Public Interest,* ch. 13.

P.B. Kenen, *International Economics* (Englewood Cliffs, N.J.: Prentice Hall, 1964).

P.T. Ellsworth, *The International Economy,* 4th ed. (London: Macmillan, 1964).

Questions

1. What are the motives to trade?
2. Does a difference in relative home prices in two different nations indicate that trade would be profitable? What are the possible causes of such differences in relative home prices? Use the concept of resource transfers to illustrate the source of the physical gain from trade.
3. Define balance of payments, balance of current payments, net terms of trade.

11. In the paragraph (page 192) summarising David Ricardo's theory of foreign trade, examine the consequences of varying the example by replacing the Victorian labour input coefficient for wheat of 0.15 by 0.4.
12. Obtain the most recent official balance of payments statement. Express all the major categories as percentages of the national product for the year. Consider what this conveys concerning the national economy.
13. If export prices fall this year 20 per cent on last year while import prices rise 20 per cent, what is the change in the net terms of trade?

21. If you flew from New York to Stockholm and changed your US dollars for kronor at the ruling exchange rate, would you

expect the cost of living to be the same as back home?

22. What do you think of the idea of replacing the large number of existing currencies by a single international currency?

23. Use the concept of opportunity cost (or option cost) to explain how it is that trade is caused by a nation's comparative and not its absolute advantage or superiority in production.

24. Imagine that nation A is technically superior to B in producing all goods but its superiority is least in producing clocks. Appraise the complaint of clock-makers in A that they are being put out of business by imports of clocks produced in B by 'cheap foreign labour'.

The Balance of Payments

Imagine that the nation could eliminate its deficit in current trade either by introducing a 35 per cent uniform import tariff or by devaluing the exchange rate by 20 per cent. Then the *difference* between these two approaches is equivalent to the effect on resource allocation and income distribution of a combination of a 12 per cent import tariff and a 17 per cent export tax.

1. Balance of payments equilibrium

We have seen that the most important single figure in the balance of payments is the balance of current payments. This is the difference between a country's receipts of foreign exchange from sale of exports and tourism and other sources over the country's payments of foreign exchange for imports and other current purposes. Thus if earnings are less than receipts of foreign exchange the nation is said to have a balance of current payments deficit. In the converse case it is said to have a balance of current payments surplus; while a zero balance of current payments is regarded as a state of trade equilibrium (in the absence of planned capital flows). In summary then, a balance of current payments deficit, since it measures the amount by which our imports of goods and services exceed our exports of goods and services, can be regarded as a measure of the extent to which the nation is using the resources of other nations. (This statement can be accepted as a general proposition on the understanding that remittances of profits and dividends overseas are treated as a payment for the import of capital services.)

A nation faced with a balance of current payments deficit may react in any one of three ways:

(a) By using up foreign exchange reserves, borrowing abroad or selling overseas assets. In modern times the foreign exchange reserves that a nation may accumulate for precisely this purpose have been supplemented by drawing rights on the International Monetary Fund. It is worth noting in this context that, since the establishment of the International Monetary Fund at the end of the Second World War, it has not only revised drawing rights upwards from time to time as world trade has expanded but has provided drawing rights under three categories: firstly, drawing rights as initially introduced; secondly, 'compensatory drawing rights' introduced primarily to assist the exporters of primary produce; and thirdly, more recently, special drawing rights (or 'paper gold').

(b) The nation may reduce the level of imports by such means as quantitative import restrictions, an increase in tariffs, or by deflating the national income. The nature of these three techniques is briefly this: Whereas import quotas operate by denying the members of the nation access to the imports they wish to buy, tariffs operate by pricing imports out of the home market, while the third technique of credit deflation works both by reducing the spendable incomes of nationals and also by reducing home prices compared with the prices of imports. Thus the last technique operates both through a fall in real national income and a *relative* rise in the price of imports. The restriction of imports is discussed further in section 2.

(c) The nation may devalue her exchange rate compared with the currencies of other trading nations. The effect of this is discussed below in section 3.

2. Restricting the level of imports

If a nation is confronted with a temporary balance of payments deficit, then this situation may be met by using up accumulated reserves of foreign exchange or drawing rights on the International Monetary Fund. However, if the deficit continues, it is plainly necessary for the government to take some measure designed to eliminate the deficit. Since in the short run it is often difficult to stimulate the level of exports at the desired speed, there is a considerable temptation for nations to use one or other of the methods available for restricting imports. But it should be pointed out here that the use of these measures is controlled to a degree by international agreement. Thus members of the International Monetary Fund are supposed to refrain from using import quotas (i.e. quantitative import restrictions); while signatory nations to the General Agreement on Tariffs and Trade are supposed to refrain from unilateral increases in tariffs. On the other hand in a world where so many governments are committed to a policy of high employment, nations are reluctant to embark on a programme of deflation if this is avoidable. Thus we have an indication of the difficulties confronting a nation proposing to restrict imports in order to eliminate a balance of current payments deficit.

For a nation with a continuing balance of payments deficit, which is unable to increase its exports in the short run, a cut-back in imports is unavoidable if it is to meet its obligation in international trade. Hence it is necessary to compare the effects of the alternative measures available.

Tariffs and quotas on imports both reduce the volume of imports. Their notable common feature is that they solve a balance of payments deficit by restricting the volume of trade (i.e. cutting imports, not raising exports); so that if all nations relied on such measures whenever a deficit appeared, the volume of world trade would be progressively reduced. Another curious feature they have in common is that if tariffs or quotas are used to discriminate against what the government regards as 'non-essential' imports, then their effect is to promote home production of these 'non-essentials' behind the protective barrier of the tariff or quota.[1] However, import quotas (also called 'quantitative import restrictions') have two distinctive features of their own. The first is that the restriction of imports allows the importing agent to charge a higher price and so collect a monopolist's profit—under the tariff alternative, this profit accrues to the government as customs revenue. The second is that the general introduction of quotas requires the establishment of a large government bureaucracy to administer the programme, and this suggests that quotas are an expensive device, especially for short-term use on a wide range of imports. By comparison, since all governments have a Customs Department, an increase in the level of tariffs in the form of a primage duty or tariff surcharge is an administratively flexible device, which can be introduced at short notice. This suggests that international agreements that presently treat import restrictions as preferable to tariff surcharge for short-term use are misconceived and should be reviewed.

The third method of reducing imports is by deflating the national

---

[1] This protective effect can be nullified by a high sales tax on home production of such goods.

income, i.e. by inducing a recession.[2] This method has a long history for it was characteristic, for example, of such international financial arrangements as the gold bullion standard of the 1920s and the

FIGURE 13·1 THE GOLD BULLION STANDARD (1920s)

> Fall in exports implies b/cp* deficit, which is financed by gold outflow.
>
> ⬇
>
> The gold outflow reduced the cash base of the banks, which then contracted bank advances. This banking mechanism could be re-enforced or replaced by conscious government deflationary measures.
>
> ⬇
>
> The consequent fall in investment and other spending caused a fall in both real (production and) income and in the price level.
>
> ⬇
>
> Both these 'real' and 'price' changes reduced demand for imports and so reduced the b/cp deficit. While exports might rise owing to lower home prices, the final equilibrium is likely to be one of unemployment and lower imports to match the lower exports.

Notes: * b/cp: balance of current payments.

If money wage-rates were to fall sharply in response to rising unemployment then the deflation could largely take the form of falling prices. Since in practice money wage-rates do not fall readily, the deflation is likely to involve a substantial 'real' fall in production and income.

sterling exchange standard of the 1930s. The essential nature of such financial arrangements was as follows: The central bank of each member nation pegged the price of its currency in terms of gold (or sterling, in the second case) and thus established a stable exchange rate system. Then, when one member A experienced a fall in exports, it would finance the consequent balance of current payments deficit by paying this amount in gold (or sterling). This fall in reserves of gold or sterling also represented a fall in the cash base of the commercial banks. (Recall that the banking system holds the nation's foreign exchange reserves and these reserves are treated as cash, since they can be sold to the central bank for cash.) Thus the banks would restrict lending and a recession could ensue. If this banking mechanism were slow or ineffective, governments could take action by raising tax rates and interest rates and *directing* that bank lending be restricted in order to accelerate the deflation. The deflation or recession involves both a fall in employment, produc-

---

[2] In principle an alternative method of deflating would be a nation-wide cut in all money wage-rates. Attempts to do this have usually run into such political and administrative difficulties as to make the method ineffective.

tion and real national income, and secondly a fall in home wage-rates and prices relatively to imports. Thus the fall in real spendable income and the relative rise in import prices both reduce the volume of imports and move the nation back towards balance of payments equilibrium. Unfortunately while this is equilibrium in the sense that the balance of current payments deficit has been removed, it is also a recession characterised by unemployment of labour. (See summary in figure 13.1.)

Summary

A balance of current payments deficit can be met by:
(a) using up foreign assets, or increased borrowing—measures that are only temporary because they do not remove the cause of the deficit;
(b) cutting back imports by tariffs, quotas or deflation;
(c) devaluation of the exchange rate.
(Other possible measures—wage-cuts, export subsidies—have less general significance.)
The use of deflation has a long history. The mechanism is that a reduction in home demand (by reduced bank credit or higher tax rates) causes both a fall in real disposable income and a fall in home prices relatively to import prices. Both these effects reduce demand for imports

The next section is devoted to the remaining alternative measure, devaluation or depreciation of the exchange rate.

3. Devaluation

For the past forty years there has been considerable reluctance among nations to devalue their exchange rate—partly for reasons of prestige and partly because a government that fails to devalue speedily and decisively attracts the unwelcome attention of speculators, and so may be best advised not to devalue at all. There are signs that attitudes are changing in this matter, so devaluation warrants careful attention as a means of correcting a continuing foreign payments deficit.

Perhaps the most critical point to emphasise in discussing the effects of devaluation is this: While devaluation in itself simply alters the price of exports and imports (expressed in local currency, which we will call dollars ($A) Australian), these price changes induce changes in spending that affect the national income and so cause spending on imports to change. In other words in addition to the 'price effects' of devaluation we get a feedback or 'income effect' on imports. In many nations, and for example in Australia, all these feedbacks tend to worsen the foreign payments deficit so they must not be ignored.

Our discussion will now proceed on this pattern: Since the foreign payments deficit is being financed by a run-down of foreign exchange reserves, the aim of devaluation is to eliminate this run-down. So *the effect of devaluation on the level of foreign exchange reserves is analysed in the sequence of table 13.2* (which shows the results for Australia):

FIGURE 13·2   EFFECT OF EXCHANGE DEVALUATION ON
FOREIGN EXCHANGE RESERVES: AUSTRALIA

via	foreign exchange reserves rise (+) or fall (−)
Exports	
price effect	+
income effect	−
Imports	
price effect	+
income effect	−

If Australia were to devalue, in the short run there might not be any significant rise in the volume of her exports. But in the long run, after export industry had had time to adjust, the volume of exports would certainly rise. It does not necessarily follow from this that her earnings of foreign exchange would rise since in order to sell a bigger volume of exports she would probably have to reduce her export prices expressed in foreign currency. However, such practical investigations as have been made support the contention that her earnings of foreign exchange *would* rise in the long run.[3] Consequently a plus sign is entered in the table.

However, consider now the 'income effects' that result from the fact that Australian exporters have higher incomes (in $A). Exporters will spend more and this will spread through the community (through the national income multiplier effect) causing a general rise in national

[3] F.B. Horner, 'Elasticity of demand for exports of a single country', *Review of Economics and Statistics*, 1952, p. 326. I.A. McDougall, 'A Note on Tariffs, the Terms of Trade and the Distribution of the National Income', *Journal of Political Economy*, 1962, p. 393.

income. This rise in national income can be divided into two parts: a rise in income *at constant prices* and a rise in the *general price level*. Both aspects cause imports to rise: the first because when income at constant prices rises, people tend to spend more on all goods including imports; the second because a rise in Australian prices makes imports more attractive on a price basis. So we can lump both effects together in the table and put a minus sign to show that foreign exchange reserves fall.

Turning now to imports, we see that the price effect of devaluation is very simple if we assume for a small nation such as Australia that the price of imports in foreign currency is unchanged. For the effect of devaluation is to raise the price in Australian dollars (precisely as if a tariff had been put on the imports) so she buys a smaller tonnage of imports. Since the price in foreign currency is unchanged, it follows that her foreign exchange spending on

> *Example:* The initial exchange rate is $A1:14 pesos at which Australia imports 100 tons of tin at a price of 14 thousand pesos per ton; *total cost:* 1,400 thousand pesos.
>
> The new exchange rate is $A2:14 pesos, which means that the Australian dollar price of the import has doubled and so she cuts back imports to say 30 tons. At the constant price of 14 thousand pesos per ton, *total cost* is 420 thousand pesos.

imports falls. So in the third line of table 13.2 we insert a plus sign to show that foreign exchange reserves rise.

Consider now the income effect of devaluation via imports. The fact that the volume of imports has fallen does not allow us to draw any conclusion at all as to whether spending on imports *measured in Australian dollars* has fallen, risen or remained unchanged. Thus on this point also empirical evidence is needed. Available Australian evidence indicates that the rise

> *Example:* If Australian imports consisted solely of whisky then it is possible that devaluation would cause the gallonage imported to fall very slightly. Thus the purchase of a barely unchanged gallonage would take a larger share of Australians' income (in $A), leaving them less to spend on home-produced goods. Thus the effect on the internal economy would be deflationary. In reality the effect goes in the opposite direction, partly because

demand is responsive to price and partly because devaluation enables home distillers to grasp a larger share of the home market.

in the Australian dollar price of imports caused by devaluation causes the level of spending on imports to fall, measured in $A.[4] What happens in fact is that there is a switch in the stream of spending from imports to home-produced substitutes. This raises incomes and employment in Australian import-competing industry. Thus workers in the industry will spend more and this will spread through the community (the income multiplier effect) causing a general rise in national income. This rise will comprise both a rise in income at constant prices and a rise in the general price level—and both aspects cause imports to rise (as previously noted). Observe moreover that the rise in the general price level may result in the trade unions successfully demanding a higher level of money wage-rates owing to the rise in the cost of living. In turn this rise in money wage-rates will result in a further rise in money incomes and in home prices (when profit mark-ups are applied to the higher wage costs), so that the volume of imports tends to rise again. In summary the income effect—in both its real (or constant price) and price level (or inflationary) aspects—causes rising imports. Thus in the last line of table 13.2 we insert a minus sign to show that foreign exchange reserves fall.

Summing up, it has been essential to use a specific nation (Australia) as a case study because it may be that for some nations the sign in the first row of table 13.2 is zero or negative, and the sign in the fourth row may be zero or positive. On the available evidence the *price effects* of an Australian devaluation would succeed in the aim of preventing the run-down of foreign exchange reserves. *But these favourable effects may be more than offset by income effects.* The importance of the income effects is basically that devaluation is inflationary (or expansionary) in its internal effects on the Australian economy. It is inflationary because exporters have a bigger income to spend and it is inflationary because Australian consumers switch their spending from imports to home-produced substitutes. This might not matter if there were only a rise in national income at constant prices. But if a general inflationary rise in the internal price

[4] Refer B. Cameron, *Production, Employment and Prices* (Melbourne: Cheshire, 1967), page 47.

level develops owing to trade union claims or competition for scarce resources, then devaluation may fail in its objective.[5] Thus a government that proposes to devalue must be prepared to use such measures as a rise in the rate of income tax to prevent income effects resulting in an unacceptable rise in imports.

Summary

In most nations devaluation will reduce foreign exchange spent on imports (because import prices in home currency immediately rise). Also in most nations devaluation gives export industries a cost advantage, which enables them to obtain a larger share of world export markets and so increase earnings of foreign exchange. But even if these price effects do make a successful contribution to reducing the balance of payments deficit, they are only part of the story.

For in many nations devaluation is internally inflationary—both because exporters have larger incomes to spend and because the higher import prices may cause a switch in consumer demand to home-produced goods. If an inflation does develop, then it worsens the balance of current payments deficit —because of rising incomes spent on imports, rising home prices, and trade union pressure for rising money wage-rates due to an increase in the cost of living.

If devaluation is to be successful it must be coupled with measures to contain inflation.

4. Comparing feasible measures

The argument so far has done no more than establish the feasibility of a number of alternative methods of eliminating a balance of current payments deficit. A useful analogy may be drawn with the aim of achieving high employment (in a non-trading economy) for which budgetary or monetary measures by the central bank are feasible alternative means.

In each case, having established the existence of feasible alternative measures, the next task is to compare them. Before doing this we may observe that implicit in this approach is a set of priorities in national economic policy aims. Thus when *full employment was set as the primary aim* in a non-trading economy, the comparison of budgetary and monetary measures was made on the criteria of (a) efficiency and (b) the *secondary* aim of how to use the unemployed resources (e.g. to produce beer, battleships or blast furnaces).

---

[5] In a food-importing nation such as England, devaluation obviously raises the cost of living of trade union members. The fact remains that it is the aim of devaluation to obtain a competitive advantage in export markets and this cannot be achieved if wage claims are too high.

FIGURE 13·3   AN APPROACH TO ECONOMIC POLICY

Single prime aim	Eliminate unemployment (due to deficient demand)
Alternative feasible measures	Monetary: interest rate 　　　　　　bank credit Fiscal　　: tax rates 　　　　　　government spending
Criteria of choice between measures	(a)　efficiency (e.g. time-lags) (b)　secondary aims 　　(i)　resource allocation 　　(ii)　income distribution
Single prime aim	Meet a balance of current payments deficit
Alternative feasible measures	Foreign exchange reserves used Deflation Import tariff Import quotas Devaluation
Criteria of choice between measures	(a)　efficiency (b)　secondary aims 　　(i)　resource allocation 　　(ii)　income distribution

Note: If both the above prime aims are pursued simultaneously, then there are two prime aims; and in analysing alternative *feasible* measures, it is essential to ensure that such measures are consistent with the simultaneous pursuit of both prime aims. This is discussed in the following chapter.

Applying the same logic (refer figure 13.3), the *primary aim is now to eliminate a balance of current payments deficit.* We may interpolate that another primary aim is to maintain full employment without inflation, and it will be assumed here that fiscal or monetary measures are used to prevent aggregate demand being too small or too large—the precise details of this being postponed to the next chapter. The alternative feasible measures for eliminating the foreign payments deficit are then compared on the criteria of (a) efficiency and (b) *secondary* aims concerning the size and distribution of real national income.[6]

Some simplification is legitimate at this point in order not to blur the logical form of the analysis. First of all it is now assumed that

[6] Alternatively our approach can be described as seeking to maximise national income (or welfare) subject to specified constraints, viz. full employment and a zero balance of current payments.

the balance of payments deficit to be eliminated is not due to inflationary excess demand, and further, since our primary aims include full employment, it follows that *deflation* is an inappropriate measure. Moreover having already drawn a comparison between import quotas and tariffs we will now regard them as rather crudely equivalent and make no further reference to quotas. Thus we are left with *two feasible alternative measures for eliminating a continuing balance of current payments deficit: devaluation or import tariff.* It will be assumed that the import tariff is at a uniform percentage rate on the c.i.f. value of all imports—the case of non-uniform rates being discussed in a later chapter. Now that we have thus narrowed the alternative measures to devaluation or a uniform tariff, there is some point in narrowing the number of effects to be analysed. For a uniform tariff or devaluation may have effects on:

(a) the *distribution of national income* as between productive factors engaged in the export, import-competing and other industries;

(b) the *size of the real national income*, through the following distinguishable causes:

   (i) shifting of resources as between industries;

   (ii) promoting skill, knowledge and inventiveness, i.e. increasing human resources. This 'infant economy' argument for tariffs (attributed to Friedrich List) on manufactured imports into an underdeveloped nation regards the tariff as enabling the nation to overtake the advanced science and technology of the industrialised nations;

   (iii) shifting the net terms of trade either up or down;

   (iv) increasing or reducing the use of increasing scale returns (i.e. 'economies of scale').

Although this list is not exhaustive we will initially simplify by *supposing that only effects* (a) *and* (b(i)) *occur*. This should not be taken to imply that the other effects are unimportant, but that to prevent the analysis being swamped with detail, discussion of them is postponed.

Since we are now ready to proceed, it may be interpolated that when the effects of a government measure such as an import tariff are analysed, the politically relevant context is not a casual comparison of the effects of a tariff compared with 'no tariff'. The politically relevant context is one in which the assumed primary policy aims are first specified, and the effects of the tariff are compared with alternative means of achieving those aims. In this case the alternative means are devaluation of the exchange rate and a uniform import tariff. To clarify the nature of these alternatives we should point out that devaluation is in essence a *combination* of a uniform x per cent *ad valorem* import tariff with a uniform *ad valorem* x per cent export subsidy. What we then have to do is to

Example: If Australia devalues her exchange rate on Bolivia from:

$A1 : 13·5 pesos

to

$A1·35 : 13·5 pesos (i.e. $A1: 10 pesos)

then Australian exporters receive a 35 per cent rise in receipts expressed in her own currency (similar in effect to a 35 per cent export subsidy); and Australian importers have to pay 35 per cent more to buy the same imports (similar in effect to a 35 per cent import tariff).

work through the resource allocation and distribution effects of the two alternatives (since it is postulated that both measures are capable of achieving balance of payments equilibrium and that the level of home final demand will be varied to ensure full employment without inflation.)

5. Devaluation versus a uniform tariff

Devaluation of say 35 per cent—having the effect of a combination of import tariff and export subsidy—'saves' foreign exchange by assisting import-competing industry, and 'earns' foreign exchange by assisting export industry. The alternative of only using say a 50 per cent uniform tariff has the result that up to $1.5 of home resources are used to produce import-competing goods to *save* a dollar's worth of foreign exchange; however, only up to $1 of resources are put into the export industry to *earn* a dollar's worth of foreign exchange: hence the balance of payments deficit can be reduced *at less cost in resources,* by moving some resources from import-competing to export industry by means of devaluation.

For example in figure 13.4 the vertical dotted line designates a situation in which the exchange rate is over-valued (so that exports

FIGURE 13·4   THE MARGINAL COST OF FOREIGN EXCHANGE

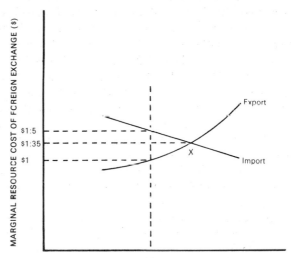

FOREIGN EXCHANGE: EARNINGS AND PAYMENTS (francs)

The use of home resources valued in dollars, to earn foreign exchange measured in francs.

Notes

The vertical axis measures the home resources required either to earn an extra unit of foreign exchange (by expanding exports) or to save a unit of foreign exchange (through replacing imports by home production). The horizontal axis measures the value of exports or imports in foreign exchange.

The export curve shows that as a rising volume of exports earns more foreign exchange (horizontal axis), the marginal cost rises (vertical axis), due either to rising unit costs of exports or to falling world price as export volume rises.

The import curve shows that as rising import volume increases payments of foreign exchange (horizontal axis), the marginal cost falls (vertical axis). This is because the rise in import volume is matched by a fall in home production of import-competing goods—and since the low-cost section of this import-competing industry will survive, it follows that the marginal cost of saving foreign exchange by producing import-competing goods will fall.

In the diagram any vertical line specifies a state of balanced trade with an equal value of exports and imports. The vertical dotted line represents an overvalued currency supported by substantial import tariffs. The optimal position is the intersection of the two schedules.

The above analysis assumes the schedules are 'well behaved'. Serious complications emerge: if the price elasticity of demand for exports is less than unity (the export schedule reverses its slope); or if the world price of imports depends on the volume demanded (the import schedule may reverse its slope).

are lower than at *X*), and a balance of current payments deficit is prevented by a uniform tariff (which holds down imports). If the exchange rate is $1 for 10 francs and for convenience we call 10 francs a 'unit of foreign exchange', then the vertical dotted line plainly does not represent the best use of resources. For by moving a batch of resources out of import-competing industry and into export industry, there is a movement to the right along both schedules with a net saving of resources equal to the vertical distance between the schedules. The nation could of course move from the vertical dotted line by: reducing the tariff from 50 per cent to 35 per cent and introducing a uniform export subsidy of 35 per cent. But this is precisely equivalent to devaluation.

However, devaluation and the tariff affect not only resource use but also *income distribution*. For example suppose that the vertical dotted line in figure 13.4 represents a situation in which export crops are 100 million tons. Now production costs on the farm may rise with rising output as shown in figure 13.5. So that if the 50 per cent tariff is eliminated and replaced by 35 per cent devaluation, there may be a rise in exports to 140 million tons. This implies a substantial rise in profits of low-cost producers of exports (figure 13.5, shaded area), so that incomes are significantly redistributed as between export farmers and the workers in import-competing industry now subject to greater competition from imports.

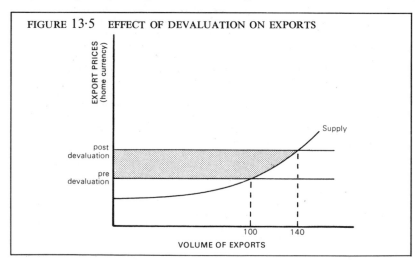

FIGURE 13·5   EFFECT OF DEVALUATION ON EXPORTS

One way of reviewing the argument is to use our imaginary example in which the balance of payments deficit can be eliminated *either* by a 50 per cent uniform import tariff or a 35 per cent devaluation. If the 35 per cent devaluation were accompanied by a 26 per cent export tax and an 11 per cent tariff on imports, then the combined effect of such a 35-26-11 package would be identical with the effect of the 50 per cent tariff.[7] So the effects of a 50 per cent uniform tariff relatively to those of a 35 per cent devaluation are the effects of a 26 per cent export tax and an 11 per cent tariff (refer figure 13.6). This is a salutary way of starting to think about *the size of the comparative effects on resource allocation and income distribution.*

FIGURE 13·6   COMPARISON OF DEVALUATION AND A UNIFORM TARIFF

Let exporters' incomes in home currency be designated by the index 100; let the landed market price of imports in home currency also be designated by index 100.

Then a 35 per cent devaluation say of the Swedish kronor (using imaginary figures)

    from kr 10   : $1
    to   kr 13.5 : $1

would overnight raise Swedish exporters' incomes (in kronor) to index 135. A 26 per cent export tax on this would reduce exporters' incomes back to index 100 (since $0.26 \times 135 = 35$).

At the same time the 35 per cent devaluation would overnight raise the price index of imports from 100 to 135. The addition of an 11 per cent tariff would raise the import price index to 150 (since $0.11 \times 135 = 15$).

Thus the net effect of the 35-26-11 package is to leave exporters' incomes unchanged and to raise the landed market price of imports by 50 per cent. This could have been achieved equivalently by a uniform 50 per cent tariff.

Hence the difference between a 35 per cent devaluation and a uniform 50 per cent tariff lies in the 26-11 part of the package.

The discussion can be carried a stage further if we assume that rural and mining industries commonly experience rising unit costs as output expands while manufacturing industry commonly experiences constant or falling unit costs as output expands. Thus for a nation that is an exporter of agricultural foodstuffs or mining produce, the use of a tariff on her imports of manufactures redistributes the national income from rural exporters to urban workers. The reverse applies in a nation that is an importer of foodstuffs—

[7] $0.26 = 35/135;$ $0.11 = (50-35)/135.$

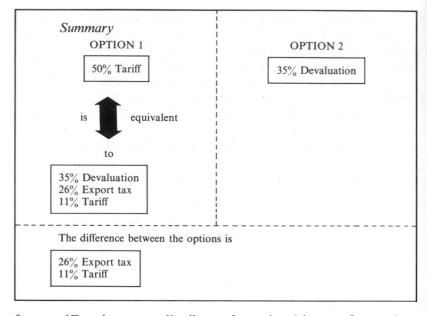

Summary

OPTION 1 | OPTION 2

50% Tariff | 35% Devaluation

is   ⬍   equivalent

to

35% Devaluation
26% Export tax
11% Tariff

The difference between the options is

26% Export tax
11% Tariff

for a tariff on imports redistributes the national income from urban workers (who pay higher prices for food) to home farmers.

The calculation of the size of the effects of the alternative measures on the size and distribution of real national income can be tackled in actual situations.[8] All we need do here is to summarise the issues. First, the *resource reallocation loss* due to the tariff arises from the fact that, while devaluation protects some import-competing industry, a uniform tariff protects an expansion of the import-competing sector. It seems unlikely that this *expansion* would involve as much as one-tenth of the nation's resources shifting from export industry to import-competing industry; and it seems unlikely that the *average* loss per unit of resources so reallocated would be as much as 25 per cent. Such imaginative figuring suggests that an upper limit to the resource allocation loss caused by a uniform tariff would be 2.5 per cent of real national income—but it must be stressed that this represents only an attempt to suggest the order of magnitude of loss.[9]

[8] A theoretical treatment based on chapter 9 is too complex to pursue here.
[9] The situation is very different if *non-uniform* tariffs are used to protect firms against their own inefficiency. See chapter 15.

At the same time the use of a tariff may cause quite a significant *redistribution of income*. If such income redistribution is a government policy aim, the further question naturally arises whether such redistribution can be achieved by some alternative measure (e.g. a land-tax) that reduces the loss of real national income due to resource reallocation. This could be tackled, say for an agricultural exporting nation, by rewriting the original problem as follows: compare a uniform tariff with a combination of devaluation and land-tax, both options being designed to balance foreign trade and to achieve the same distribution of national income.

This chapter has analysed government intervention to balance foreign trade. It would be easy to assume that this implies a *need* for government intervention in order to balance trade. However, in all save extreme cases, payments equilibrium would be achieved without such intervention. The truth is that governments intervene in order to achieve payments equilibrium by measures that are consistent with other policy aims. Thus Britain's final departure from the gold standard in 1931 was not because the system could not work, but because making it work involved mass unemployment. Similarly Australia's use of a high tariff wall is intended to redistribute the national income from the farming and mining export industries. However, the oft-expressed distinction between government intervention in trade for 'balance of payments reasons' and for other motives is a harmless fiction that allows a convenient arrangement of subject matter over this and the two following chapters.

Summary

§1. Faced with a balance of current payments deficit a nation may react by: using up foreign exchange reserves, restricting imports by tariff or quota, deflating, or devaluing.

§2. Using up exchange reserves can only be a temporary expedient; while both tariffs and quotas are biased towards a contraction of world trade. Deflation is unpalatable if there is already some unemployment since it will worsen the domestic situation.

§3. The effects of devaluation operate through both 'real income' and 'price' effects on both the import and export side. No simple generalisation is possible save to emphasise that while the impact effect of devaluation may appear to favour the balance of current payments by changing relative prices, nonetheless there is strong reason to expect that the devaluation will cause an internal price inflation. If fiscal or monetary measures are not taken to counter this, then the devaluation in the long run may fail to eliminate the balance of current payments deficit.

§4. A method of analysing measures capable of achieving a specified policy objective is set out and illustrated.

§5. Having listed potentially feasible alternative measures for eliminating a balance of current payments deficit, the next step is to decide between them. To illustrate this procedure we choose devaluation and a uniform tariff as the alternative measures. It is found that they differ significantly in their effects on both resource allocation and income distribution.

Further reading

P.A. Samuelson, *Economics*.
P.T. Ellsworth, *The International Economy*.

Questions

1. Explain the meaning of: devaluation, deflation, drawing rights, gold standard.
2. What are the similarities and differences between import tariffs and import quotas?
3. Explain how deflation can eliminate a balance of current payments deficit.
4. Distinguish the several ways in which devaluation affects the size of a balance of current payments deficit.

11. Explain the arithmetic in the example immediately following the title of this chapter.
12. Explain the effect of moving along the schedules in figure 13.4.

21. What danger points would you investigate to see if devaluation would eliminate the payments deficit of a specific nation?
22. If you were asked to analyse the effects of a tariff, is it acceptable to examine a given situation that is changed solely by the introduction of the tariff (i.e. would you compare a tariff with no-tariff?)?

23. Could the effect of an import tariff on home production be equivalently achieved by a subsidy on import-competing industry?
24. Do you accept the view that governments do not intervene to correct balance of payments disequilibria but to ensure that such disequilibria are not eliminated by means that have politically unacceptable side effects?

Full Employment
in a Trading Economy

The pursuit of economic policy requires that we look at the *total* situation. The existence of unemployment due to deficient demand does not necessarily imply that the income tax rate should be reduced or bank credit or public works increased. For if there is not only unemployment but also a foreign payments deficit, such measures will increase the deficit.

1. The effect of changes in demand

In chapter 3 the effect of changes in demand was discussed for a non-trading economy. In now extending that analysis to a trading economy, we need the following simple modifications.

First, when a sustained autonomous change in demand occurs it must be divided into two parts: the demand for home-produced goods and demand for imports. It is only the first part that directly sets in train a national income multiplier effect in the home country.

Second, the national income multiplier is the reciprocal of unity minus the marginal propensity to

$$\text{multiplier} = \frac{1}{1 - mpc_{hp\ ex\ ni}}$$

consume *home-produced* goods out of national income ($mpc_{hp\ ex\ ni}$). The reason is that, at each stage of the multiplier process, the part of the rise in consumption that is spent on consumer-imports is a 'leakage'; i.e. only the part that is spent on home-produced consumer goods keeps the multiplier process going. Thus it is the marginal propensity to consume *home-produced* goods out of national income that determines the ratio of the size of successive income increments in the multiplier sequence, and hence determines the value of the multiplier.

A third point now arises, namely that the multiplier process not only results in a rise in national income but also in a rise in imports. Hence a public works programme for example not only reduces unemployment but also results in a rise in imports (even if only of consumer goods) and so increases the balance of current payments deficit.

The argument so far has assumed that the income multiplier process leaves the level of exports unaffected. This may not be correct for two reasons. First, in a situation in which the economy is already near full employment capacity production, an autonomous rise in home demand may divert supplies from the export market to the home market—with an adverse effect on the balance of current payments. Secondly, an autonomous rise in home demand causes a rise in imports—but, since these are the exports of another nation, this may stimulate prosperity in the second nation, which then buys more imports, some of which are our exports. This repercussion then re-enforces the multiplier process in a manner comparable to a higher marginal propensity to consume; i.e. the size of the multiplier is given by:

$$\frac{1}{1-(mpc_{np\ ex\ m}+h)}$$

where h is some positive figure.

In a simple case where the rest of the world is treated as a single nation, it can be shown that

$$h=\frac{m.m'}{1-c'}$$

where m is 'our' marginal propensity to import, m' is 'their' marginal propensity to import and c' is 'their' marginal propensity to consume their own home produced goods out of their national income.[1] If $m=m'=0.1$, and $c'=0.5$, we obtain a rather small value of h, so that in this case the earlier multiplier formula which assumed exports to be constant (i.e. $h=0$) is a reasonable approximation (though an underestimate) to the true size of the national income multiplier.

[1] Refer F. Machlup, *Foreign Trade and the National Income Multiplier* (Philadelphia: Blakiston Co., 1943).

2. The effects of government measures

It is now possible to make two important generalisations about government measures that affect demand. In order to show the significance of these generalisations we consider a situation in which there is a state of high employment (say 97 per cent employed) but a substantial balance of current payments deficit. The government may (by devaluation or subsidies) stimulate export demand and this will both raise employment and reduce the balance of current payments deficit. Or the government may (by devaluation, tariffs, or import quotas) reduce the share of imports in the home market; e.g. a quota or a tariff on all imports aims at inducing a switch in the stream of expenditure from imports to home-produced goods. If successful this will reduce imports and will raise employment in home import-competing industries.

The first generalisation is that almost any measure a government takes will affect *both* the level of employment and the balance of current payments. For example a cut in income tax rates will stimulate spending and thus cause a rise in both employment and imports; while the introduction of import quotas (or an equivalent rise in tariffs) can cause a switch in demand which reduces imports and stimulates employment.

The second generalisation is that all measures can be classified into two groups because of the asymmetry of their effects. Thus a rise in the rate of income tax, by reducing after-tax income, reduces over-all spending on both home-produced goods (employment then falls) and on imports (the balance of current payments improves). Briefly:

income tax rate ↑ *:   employment* ↓ *imports* ↓

All of the common fiscal and monetary measures are members of this group.

By contrast a reduction in permitted quotas of imports reduces foreign exchange spending on imports (the balance of current payments improves) and causes a switch in the stream of spending from the unavailable imports to home-produced substitutes (employment rises). Briefly:

import quotas ↓ *:   employment* ↑ *imports* ↓

Tariffs and devaluation are measures that are members of this 'demand-switching' group.

The corollary of this analysis is that the government should at any time take such measures as will move it towards its policy objectives. For example if there is unemployment and a balance of payments deficit, a cut in the income tax rate is a wrong move; but an import quota, import tariff or devaluation is likely to move the economy towards both objectives. This is one of the most important guidelines in short-term economic management. Moreover it provides a firm guide for the *sequence* of government action. Consider the following example:

Our imaginary nation is experiencing unemployment due to demand deficiency and a serious balance of current payments deficit. (Historical analysis may show a fall in exports due to foreign recession.) The appropriate initial action is import quotas, tariffs or devaluation. The observed result of this may be a relatively rapid movement towards balance of current payments surplus while unemployment, though declining, persists—in which case the proper subsequent action is a cut in the income tax rate or increased bank credit. However, if the observed result of the initial measure is relatively rapid movement to over-full employment (i.e. high ratio of vacant jobs/unemployed) while the balance of current payments deficit, though

Summary

1. Fiscal and monetary measures affect *total* spending and so have similar effects on employment and imports. Devaluation and tariffs *transfer* spending and so have opposite effects on employment and imports.

2. A government pursuing two policy aims must ensure that a measure designed to achieve one aim does not prevent the second aim being reached. For example suppose the government aims at achieving both high employment without inflation, and balance of payments equilibrium; consider the action in the following situations:

	Situation	Feasible measures	Not feasible
(a)	Unemployment Foreign payments deficit	Devaluation or tariff	Cut in tax rates (would raise imports)
(b)	Excess demand inflation Foreign payments deficit	Raise tax rates or interest rates	Devaluation (would increase inflation)

This analysis is consistent with the approach in chapter 13 section 4.

declining, persists—the proper subsequent action is a rise in the income tax rate.

3. The economic system ▤

The extension of the analysis of chapter 3 to include foreign trade involves the introduction of the volume of exports E, the volume of imports M and some assumption such as that the volume of imports is a fixed proportion (m) of national production; i.e. the share of imports in market supplies is constant. Hence home production is a proportion $1/(1+m)$ of supplies, while imports are a proportion $m/(1+m)$ of total supplies. The demand block of the system is set out in figure 14.1.

FIGURE 14·1   DEMAND BLOCK: FOREIGN TRADE

$C = a + c(1-t)X$
$M = mX$
$X + M = C + I + G + E$ in market equilibrium

I, G, E are known constants.

Exploring the properties of this system, we find it has the solution:

$$X = \frac{a+I+G+E}{1+m} \cdot \frac{1}{1 - \left[\dfrac{c(1-t)}{1+m}\right]} \tag{1}$$

This result is more easily interpreted if we apply it to the case of a sustained autonomous rise in investment (ΔI), in which event the rise in national product is given by:

$$\Delta X = \frac{\Delta I}{1+m} \cdot \frac{1}{1 - \left[\dfrac{c(1-t)}{1+m}\right]} \tag{2}$$

In this expression the term in square brackets is the marginal propensity to consume home-produced goods out of national income—and by writing out the consumption function for home-produced goods out of national income:

$$\frac{C}{1+m} = \frac{a}{1+m} + \frac{c(1-t)}{1+m}X$$

we see that this is the slope of that function. The division of ΔI by $(1+m)$ in equation (2) reflects the fact that only the part of the rise in investment that is a demand for home-produced goods will have a multiplier effect on national income in this model.

A sustained autonomous rise in export demand ΔE will likewise cause a rise in national product (using equation (1)):

$$\Delta X = \frac{\Delta E}{1+m} \cdot \frac{1}{1 - \left[\dfrac{c(1-t)}{1+m}\right]} \tag{3}$$

and hence a rise in imports[2] since $\Delta M = m.\Delta X$:

$$\Delta M = \frac{\Delta E}{1+m} \cdot \frac{m}{1 - \left[\dfrac{c(1-t)}{1+m}\right]} \tag{4}$$

The ultimate effect on the balance of current payments of the initial autonomous rise in export demand can thus be calculated as $(\Delta E - \Delta M)$.[3] With this aim, we can rewrite equation (4):

$$\Delta M = \Delta E. \frac{m}{[1 - c(1-t)] + m} \tag{5}$$

where the term in square brackets is positive, being equal to the

---

[2] The rise in imports includes the import content of both the extra export and consumption demand:

$$\Delta M = \frac{m}{1+m}\Delta E + \frac{m}{1+m}\Delta C$$

$$= \frac{m}{1+m}\Delta E + \frac{m}{1+m}c(1-t)\Delta X$$

$$= m\frac{[1-c(1-t)]}{1+m}\Delta X + \frac{m}{1+m} \cdot c(1-t)\Delta X$$

$$= m.\Delta X - \frac{m.c(1-t)}{1+m}.\Delta X + \frac{m.c(1-t)}{1+m}.\Delta X$$

$$= m.\Delta X$$

[3] However, the calculation is subject to two reservations: the existence of a balance of payments disequilibrium may necessitate further government action; the level of exports has been assumed to be unaffected by the multiplier process.

sum of the marginal propensity to save (s) and the marginal liability to tax (t) out of national income. Hence:

$$\Delta M < \Delta E$$

since $(t + s)$ is positive. The intuitive explanation of this is that if $(t + s)$ were zero, the rise in national income would continue until the leakage of spending into imports rose to equal the autonomous injection of export demand—but since $(t + s)$ is positive, the rise in national income and so in imports will stop short of that point (refer figure 14.2).

FIGURE 14·2   THE NATURE OF THE MULTIPLIER PROCESS

In a non-trading economy the nature of the income multiplier process consequent upon a sustained rise in investment demand in an unemployed nation can be interpreted as follows:

Initially planned investment exceeds planned savings. Investment can be called an 'injection' of spending while savings are a 'leakage' inasmuch as they measure the part of income that is not spent on home-produced consumer goods. Equilibrium can only be regained when planned savings equals the higher level of investment. This is achieved by the multiplier process, which by raising national income also raises savings (which are a function of income) until finally leakages have risen to equal the injection of investment demand.

In a trading economy an exact analogy can be set out if the injection is a rise in export demand (instead of investment) and the leakage is imports (there being no savings or taxation).

Then once again the injection of higher export demand sets in train a multiplier process. Market equilibrium will not be regained until national income has risen sufficiently for spending on imports (leakage) to have risen to equal the initial injection of export demand. Hence in that market equilibrium the change in exports and imports will be equal.

In reality, since savings and taxes are also leakages from income, imports will not need to rise·so high. So the ultimate equilibrium will be one in which the rise in imports is less than the rise in exports.

In order to develop the analysis let us return to the first model (figure 14.1) and modify it in two respects: first, by recognising that the volume of imports depends also on the ratio of import prices to home prices; second, by setting up the two policy aims of full employment and zero balance of current payments. We now have the demand block of a second model in figure 14.3.

FIGURE 14·3   DEMAND BLOCK WITH POLICY AIMS

$$
\begin{aligned}
C &= a + c(1-t)X \\
M &= g + mX - jP_m/P \\
X + M &= C + I + G + E \text{ in equilibrium} \\
X &= X_{FE} \\
E &= M
\end{aligned}
\qquad \text{policy aims}
$$

Constants: a, c, t, g, m, j.

In the first model of figure 14.1 the unknowns were C, M and X (on the left-hand side of the equations) and the known variables included the level of G. In this new model the status of some variables is changed: we shift X from the status of an unknown variable to a target level of X_{FE}, and to match this we shift G from the status of a known parameter to the status of a variable that can be controlled to achieve the full-employment target; similarly, imports M are shifted from the status of an unknown to equal a parameter E, and to match this we have a variable P_m that can be controlled to achieve this required parameter. (P_m is the market price of imports in local currency and including any tariff). Both G and P_m are called 'instrument variables' because they are variables that can be controlled as instruments to achieve the twin policy aims. The number of instrument variables must equal the number of policy aims.[4]

Exploring the properties of this model we calculate solution values of the two instrument variables, viz.:

$$
G = [1 - c(1-t)] X_{FE} - (a + I) \tag{6}
$$

$$
P_m = \frac{P(g + m . X_{FE} - E)}{j} \tag{7}
$$

which shows the level of government spending and of import price needed to achieve the policy aims.

An alternative way of exploring the properties of this model is to solve the first three equations (i.e. ignoring the policy aims) for the left-hand side variables C, X and M—or what is more interesting for X and $(E - M)$.[5] We can then ascertain the change of each of

[4] The instrument variables must also differ in the pattern of their effects: the income tax and the rate of interest do *not* differ in the pattern of their effects on employment and imports, and so do not satisfy this requirement.

[5] Of necessity I, G, E, P_m and P are parameters, if such a solution is to be obtained.

these variables with respect to change in G and P_m. The importance of this exercise is that it enables us to state the sign (i.e. direction) of response to the instrument variables. By substitution, we find the solution value:

$$X = \frac{1}{1+m-c(1-t)} \cdot (a + I + G + E - g + j \cdot \frac{P_m}{P})$$ (8)

Then:

$$\frac{\Delta X}{\Delta G} = \frac{1}{1+m-c(1-t)}$$ (9)

$$= \frac{1}{1 - \frac{c(1-t)}{1+m}} \cdot \frac{1}{1+m}$$

which is seen to be *positive*. Similarly:

$$\frac{\Delta X}{\Delta P_m} = \frac{1}{1+m-c(1-t)} \cdot \left(\frac{j}{P}\right)$$ (10)

which is *positive*. This latter result reflects the fact that a small rise in the price of imports (ΔP_m) causes a switch in demand, reducing the volume of imports and raising demand for home-produced goods. This initial switch in demand is measured (from the import function) by:

$$\Delta M = -\frac{j}{P} \cdot \Delta P_m$$ (11)

and there is then an income multiplier effect measured by equation (10).

Similarly, the balance of current payments:

$$(E - M) = E - g - mX + jP_m/P$$ (12)

So $\Delta(E - M)/\Delta X = -m$, and from the expression (9) for $\Delta X/\Delta G$ we deduce:

$$\frac{\Delta(E - M)}{\Delta G} = \frac{-m}{1+m-c(1-t)}$$ (13)

which is *negative*; i.e. when government spending rises, the balance of current payments deficit increases owing to rising imports. More-over from (12):

$$\frac{\Delta(E-M)}{\Delta P_m} = \frac{-m.\Delta X}{\Delta P_m} + \frac{j}{P} = \frac{-m}{1+m-c(1-t)} \cdot \frac{j}{P} + \frac{j}{P} \qquad (14)$$

On the right-hand side the last term designates the direct effect of the import price rise in reducing import volume, while the previous term designates the *secondary rise* in imports due to the initial price-induced switch in demand causing an income multiplier process. The remaining question is whether we can be confident that the sum of these two terms of opposite sign is positive. This is in fact the case since by simplifying:

$$\frac{\Delta(E-M)}{\Delta P_m} = \left[\frac{1-c(1-t)}{1+m-c(1-t)}\right] \cdot \frac{j}{P} \qquad (15)$$

the term in square brackets is seen to be *positive* and less than unity.

Some of the comforting results obtained in exploring the properties of this second model will not be found in other models. For example if the volume of demand for imports is unresponsive to a price rise so that expenditure (price times volume) on imports rises, then an import price rise would cause a diversion of the stream of spending from home-produced goods to imports, with internally deflationary results. If this were the case we must design a different model to describe it.[6]

4. The behaviour of imports near full-employment capacity production

Back in chapter 4 figure 4.3 it was pointed out that, near full employment, rising demand may result in a diminishing physical output response as an increasing proportion of each increment in demand is dissipated in rising prices. The effect is re-enforced in a trading economy by the possibility of an increasing proportion of each increment in demand also being dissipated in rising imports. This phenomenon warrants some examination.

In an economy that is on a long-term growth path, with aggregate spending rising at the same rate as the rate of increase in production

---

[6] For example an import function $M = [(g/P_m)+b]X.P$ complicates results considerably.

capacity (due to increasing work force and rising labour productivity), one may expect imports to rise in a fairly steady fashion along with rising demand; though it might well be found that, if the economy was operating at 99 per cent capacity rather than say 97 per cent capacity, imports would be a larger proportion of supplies because of bottleneck problems. But if spending spurts ahead of capacity production then this demand very largely cannot be met either by inventory run-down or by rising physical production, and so must be 'dissipated' in rising prices and rising imports. This last effect has come to be known as an 'import spill-over' in nations where it has posed a major threat to full-employment aims. This spill-over effect is illustrated for Australia in figure 14.4, in which the second line shows that a *sudden* rise in demand (i.e. a rise in demand ahead of capacity growth) can be expected to be met to the extent of around one-half—range of 0.49 to 0.6—by imports. This contrasts with the long-term growth of imports equal to around 13 per cent of the rise

FIGURE 14·4   RESPONSE TO INCREMENTAL CHANGE IN
DEMAND—AUSTRALIA

Percentage of work force unemployed *a*	5%	3%	1%
Short-term response; i.e. capacity output is constant			
Marginal output effect	0.34	0.27	0.18
Marginal import effect	0.49	0.54	0.6
Residual price effect	0.17	0.19	0.22
	1.0	1.0	1.0
Long-term response; i.e. capacity output rises at the same rate as demand			
Marginal output effect	0.9	0.87	0.83
Marginal import effect	0.1	0.13	0.15
Residual price effect	–	–	0.02
	1.0	1.0	1.0

Note: a   The 5%, 3%, 1% percentage unemployment are used to label demand/capacity ratios of 1.1, 1.17, 1.25 respectively. (Demand includes demand for all commodities, including imports.)

Source: B. Cameron, *Production, Employment and Prices* (Melbourne: Cheshire, 1967), page 53. (Since the price effect is the residual, this row is affected by any accumulation of errors.)

in demand. It is a corollary of this that the constant-price national income multiplier (or the employment multiplier) declines since a rising proportion of demand is satisfied by imported supplies.

5. Conclusion

The main lessons of this chapter may be set out. First it is not surprising to find that the government can expect to need as many measures (or 'instrument variables') as it has policy objectives. If the government seeks to control demand, it must have control over say the tax rate, which alters the level of demand. And if the government *also* seeks to control the balance of current payments, it must have control over say import quotas in order to control the share of imports in sales on the home market.

Secondly it is equally unsurprising that the government must choose measures that move it towards *all* its objectives. But one must keep in mind that this implies that the existence of demand-deficiency unemployment does not mean that tax rates should be cut (since there may be a balance of current payments deficit). Likewise the existence of a balance of current payments deficit does not imply that the nation should devalue, raise tariffs or cut money wage-rates (since there may be over-full employment due to excess demand).

Thirdly, the preceding section has shown that there is a limit to the generalisations that can be made about economic policy unless the functional relations in the economic system are numerically specified. Confident advice cannot be given to a government without reasonable knowledge of these relations, in particular here the specific nature of the influences determining the level of exports and imports. Thus the pursuit of economic policy requires not only analysis of the economic system but also the numerical specification of the relations comprising the system.

In review then, the main conclusion of this chapter is that if the government is seeking *two prime policy aims,* it must first list alternative measures that are feasible in the sense that they are consistent with the pursuit of both aims. This is the link with chapters 3 and 13, which pursued *a single prime aim.* Once such feasible measures are listed then further criteria can be introduced to choose between them. This further task has not been pursued in this chapter, having been adequately covered in chapters 3 and 13.

Summary

§1. In a trading economy the size of the real national income multiplier is affected because the process of rising national income may either depress exports (because of competing pressure of home demand for scarce goods) or stimulate exports (because rising demand for imports promotes prosperity in foreign nations purchasing our exports). As noted later, the size of the multiplier is also affected by rapidly rising demand spilling over into imports.

§2. There is no such thing as an 'internal' government measure (or an 'external' one) inasmuch as all measures taken by the government affect the economy both internally (e.g. employment) and externally (e.g. imports). It is valuable to classify government measures into two groups: fiscal and monetary measures, which cause employment and imports to move in the same direction; tariffs, quotas and other demand-switching measures, which cause employment and imports to move in opposite directions.

In seeking twin employment and trade aims, the government must choose a measure from the group that will move the nation toward both aims. Hence it does not follow that unemployment is to be eliminated by a tax cut (since there may be a foreign payments deficit), nor that a foreign payments deficit is to be eliminated by devaluation (since there may be an inflationary state of over-full employment).

§3. The statements just set out can be derived by a formal logical treatment of government measures.

§4. The Great Depression of the 1930s brought a political demand for a policy of high employment. Events in the 1950s showed that one threat to this high-employment policy is a sudden spurt in demand outrunning the nation's productive capacity and resulting in a rise in imports beyond the nation's capacity to pay from current export earnings.

§5. The main lesson of this chapter is that the pursuit of more than a single prime policy aim necessitates careful examination of *feasible* measures, i.e. of measures that are consistent with the attainment of all aims.

Further reading

B. Tew, *Wealth and Income* (Melbourne: Melbourne University Press, 1964).

P.T. Ellsworth, *The International Economy*.

J.E. Meade, *The Balance of Payments*, The Theory of International Economic Policy, Vol. I (Oxford: Oxford University Press, 1956).

T.W. Swan, in *The Australian Economy*, ed H.W. Arndt and W.M. Corden (Melbourne: Cheshire, 1963), ch. 24.

Questions

1. Explain the sense in which import quotas and tax cuts have 'asymmetrical' effects on employment and imports.
2. Is the real national income multiplier constant?
3. Do you think of exchange devaluation as an 'external' measure? If you do, give an example of an 'internal' government measure.

11. Write out the simplest possible form of foreign trade model that will allow you to obtain a solution for the level of national production and imports in a state of market equilibrium. Explain in words the meaning of the solution value for national product.
12. Is it true that a rise in investment demand results in a rise in production and a balance of payments deficit, whereas a rise in export demand results in a rise in production and a balance of payments surplus? Explain a situation in which the last part of this statement would not apply.
13. The following relation was obtained by an analysis of quarterly national statistics in $ million:

$$\text{Current value of imports} = 955 - 780\pi - 0.3D + 0.36\frac{D^2}{X^*}$$

where π is the ratio of the import price index to the home price index in the previous quarter;

D is aggregate final demand at current prices (i.e. actual spending);

X^* is current capacity production (valued for statistical reasons at the prices of the previous quarter).

(The negative coefficient 0.3 merely means that if demand were zero then imports would be negative, but in fact demand is always high enough to ensure that imports are positive). Consider the significance of the last term in the relation by supposing that there is a sudden rise in demand D in a period of time over which it is approximately true to assume that both π and X^* are constant.

14. In section 1, $h = \dfrac{m.m'}{1-c'}$. Comment on the size of h.

21. What measures would you advise the government to take if the high ratio of vacant jobs to persons unemployed indicated a state of 'over-full employment' and there was simultaneously a deficit in the balance of current payments?

22. In the situation just outlined, comment on proposals either to devalue or to reduce the national level of money wage-rates.

23. A nation has inflation due to excess home demand and has a balance of payments surplus. Would you raise tax rates or restrict bank credit?

24. Is it politically realistic to say that the government should not cut tax rates or raise public works spending to reduce unemployment when there is a balance of current payments deficit?

25. What sort of forward thinking is needed to ensure high employment and balance of payments equilibrium in an economy that is experiencing economic growth due to rising labour productivity?

Intervention in Trade

While international trade does bring potential gains to a nation there also can be disadvantage. Thus there is a motive to intervene in trade wherever it is believed that this will enable the nation to raise its real national income. Other motives stem from the desire to influence the distribution of the national income or to meet the desires of pressure groups within the country.

1. Introduction

In chapter 12 the gains from foreign trade were discussed. Why then do governments intervene in foreign trade? It is true, as discussed in chapter 13, that governments may intervene when there is a balance of current payments deficit, but in practice the scope of government intervention is far wider than that. The more important reasons for government intervention will now be listed.

One motive for government intervention is that commercial trade may be regarded as a vehicle for political or cultural penetration of another nation. A second motive is that a government may seek to assist the normal commercial activities of its exporters by providing such services as market research, financial aid with research and development, or co-ordination of exporters' or importers' activities to attain a strong negotiating position. The phrase 'Japan incorporated' has been used to describe this co-ordination of government and private enterprise towards a common national goal. Where a nation is seeking to increase her share of the world export market it would be surprising if the government did not provide support for the efforts of her exporters.

Third, a government may seek to act as a monopolist. Thus she may seek to force down the price she pays for imports by restricting the volume imported, or may seek to raise the price she receives for exports by restricting their volume. Although such opportunities may be infrequent they warrant discussion. Consider for example a dominant exporter of say diamonds (or it might be rubber, nickel or wool). By restricting the volume of her diamond exports she *may* be able to force up the world price so as to raise her real national income. While such a course of action may succeed, it may meet any of three difficulties. The first is that the government may have miscalculated and the world price of diamonds may only rise fractionally so that the real national income may actually fall. The second difficulty is concerned with the short-term response of other governments, which may cut their volume of imports of diamonds for either of two motives: first to discomfit the monopolist even at some cost in real income to themselves; second to force the monopolist to negotiate. If both parties adopt a strong posture, one possible outcome is that the volume of trade declines and all nations involved suffer a fall in real national income due to the reduction in the gains from trade. The third difficulty is concerned with the long-term response of other nations in seeking to reduce consumer and industrial demand for the monopolist's diamonds by seeking substitutes whether in the form of alternative sources of supply, alternative materials or by chemical synthesis.

The fourth motive is similar to the previous, namely a dominant purchaser forcing down the world price of her imports by using tariffs or other means to restrict the volume of imports. This possibility has assumed importance as the established manufacturing nations of Europe and North America have pursued policies of agricultural protection, which have reduced their demand for the products of Southern Hemisphere agricultural exporting nations. The formation of a European common market strengthens the ability of the industrialised nations to behave as a monopolistic purchaser of raw materials.

A fifth motive for government intervention is the failure of a commodity market to work efficiently—as in the case of wheat, sugar and coffee. Production of these goods can be increased virtually at constant unit cost by a large number of producers in a number of nations. Thus a small rise in price for example may result in a large expansion of production, which could only be sold at a price below production cost for many producers. In this sense the market may operate inefficiently and so governments have sought to administer these markets. Since it is the producer who is hurt most when the market works inefficiently, it is not surprising that international commodity agreements tend to take the form of a cartel of producing nations, modified to a greater or lesser extent by the countervailing power of consumer

nations. Such international commodity agreements are usually administered by controlling stocks, prices or production–and each has
its problems. The buffer stock approach to stabilising the market,
apart from the costs of deterioration and of stock-holding, faces the
problem of forecasting the long-term price trend. Past experience
gives one no confidence in the ability of governments to do this—with
the result that buffer stocks can easily become a significant expense to
the taxpayer of the producing nation. The price approach may take
the form of setting maximum and minimum prices and even, as in the
case of wheat, agreeing on minimum quantities that producers and
consumers will sell and buy within this price range. The difficulty of
forecasting long-term price change which still exists in this case,
merely reflects the basic inability to control price levels when the
volume of production itself is not controlled. The third approach of
setting national production quotas does go to the heart of the problem
but faces severe practical difficulties—not least of which is that (as
with any cartel) any producer who stands outside the agreement can
gain by expanding his own production for sale at the high price set by
the cartel. The difficulties listed help to explain the chequered history
of international commodity agreements.

A sixth motive for government intervention in trade lies in the
international spread of depression from one nation to another. So
long as a nation feared that trade with other depression-prone nations
could cause harm, it was rational to seek to reduce this disadvanatge
of foreign trade, e.g. by setting an upper limit to one's dependence
on export markets.

A seventh motive is concerned with income distribution. For
while foreign trade brings gain in the form of a higher real national
income, those gains may be unevenly spread through the community
and indeed some members of the community may actually be worse
off. For example a nation that moves rapidly from no-trade to becoming a major agricultural importer may find her farmers absolutely
worse off though the urban proletariat have a much higher real
income. It was the application of this argument to an agricultural
exporting nation that was used to justify the establishment of Australian import tariff. Rather than eliminate a balance of current payments deficit by devaluation, which would raise the incomes of farm
exporters, the government chose to set up tariffs on manufactured

imports in order to protect the income share of the urban factory worker.

An eighth motive is the infant economy argument attributed to Friedrich List. This argument justifies the introduction of tariffs on manufactured imports of an underdeveloped nation on the basis that it provides a forcing-ground for the development of advanced scientific and technological skills among the population. The specific justification for this policy is the assertion that the benefits to society in the form of a superior labour force exceed the benefits accruing (as profit or surplus) to the protected industry—and this discrepancy between private and social gain justifies a tariff. In effect the tariff aids the nation in an effort to overtake the technology of the industrialised nations by generating an increase in resources in the form of human skill, knowledge and inventiveness.

A ninth reason for government intervention is to be found in sectional interests within a nation, such as where a specific industry seeks some form of protection by tariff or subsidy either to shield it from the competition of imports or to help it penetrate export markets, or perhaps simply to provide an income subsidy. The arguments that have been advanced to bolster such claims are legion: defence; industrial decentralisation; survival of a regional community; infant industry; risk in establishing a new industry; protection because of management's inexperience with new technology, because labour is unskilled or uneducated, or because it takes time to establish a profitable market, or because the market is small, or because the firm is giving the nation the advantages of industrial diversity, or because there is unemployment, or (if all else fails) because foreign competition is unfair.

In summary, motives for government intervention in external trade are as varied as motives for intervening in the operation of an economy that has no foreign trade at all. The ensuing sections examine some of the more important instruments of government intervention: import tariffs, export subsidies, and customs union.

2. Import tariffs

The significance of introducing a uniform tariff on imports has already been explored. Inasmuch as full employment of resources can be ensured by using fiscal or monetary measures to raise aggregate final demand, the choice of a uniform tariff rather than devaluation as a means of achieving balance of payments equilibrium must be based on its effects on the productivity of resources, on a desire to allocate resources in a specific way, or on effects on income distribution. In practice any of these three effects may be relevant, as we may now briefly explore.

The argument for a tariff advanced by Friedrich List is in effect a claim that, by providing tariff protection for manufacturing industry, human skills are stimulated and so labour productivity is increased. It is an argument that may well have validity when an underdeveloped nation is making a forced march into advanced technology in a hostile international environment.

Likewise a tariff on imports that are predominantly manufactured goods may be regarded as desirable because it helps allocate resources into industry that can increase the nation's defence capacity. Or tariffs on imports that are predominantly agricultural may be regarded as desirable because they promote decentralisation of population. (However, these are arguments that are advanced more commonly for non-uniform tariffs.)

Thirdly, a uniform tariff may be chosen because the devaluation alternative would result in a distribution of income that is regarded as politically unacceptable. This has already been discussed.

The introduction of a *non-uniform* tariff on imports brings a new dimension into the analysis. There are perhaps three quite different motives for the introduction of a permanent non-uniform tariff. The first is the decision of a government not to levy tariffs on imports that are not produced at home. Now, so far as imports of final consumer goods (not produced at home) are concerned the effect of this is merely to distort consumer spending, and secondly to levy revenues not by import tariff but say by income tax. But so far as imports of raw materials and other intermediate goods (not produced at home) are concerned, the effect of levying no tariff is to give higher protection to the industries using the raw materials, without appearing to raise the amount of tariff protection. Thus such a decision by the government is likely to be motivated by window-dressing, i.e. a desire to appear to have a lower tariff than is in fact the case (see figure 15.1).

A second motive for not levying a tariff—or for levying a lower-than-average tariff—is to exercise control over local monopolistic

FIGURE 15·1   EFFECTIVE TARIFF PROTECTION

The *nominal tariff rate on a commodity* produced by an industry is to be distinguished from the *effective tariff rate on the productive process.* The latter measures tariff protection *to the industry.*

Finished cotton textiles		at world price	at actual price with 50 per cent nominal tariff	
			uniform tariff	duty free materials
		(1)	(2)	(3)
Value of output	$	100	150	150
Materials used	$	50	75	50
a Value added (wages, profits)	$	50	75	100
Index of value added	%	100	150	200
Index less 100 (i.e. effective rate of protection)	%	—	50	100

Note: a This line is obtained by subtraction.

Example: Duty free entry of materials

The example illustrates a situation in which there is a uniform 50 per cent tariff, applying here to imported finished cotton textiles. Home-produced textiles can now be sold at prices 50 per cent higher than world prices. However, in column (3) the raw materials that the home industry processes and which are imported are admitted duty free (perhaps on the ground that there is no home-produced alternative). For arithmetic simplicity it is assumed (see column 1) that raw materials account for one-half of the total costs of the industry, valued at world prices.

In the last line it is seen that a truly uniform tariff (column 2) records an effective rate of protection of 50 per cent on the textile-making process, and is equal to the nominal rate on the commodity. But duty free admission of raw materials raises this effective rate of protection to 100 per cent: it is as if the tariff on the materials had been given to the textile-making industry as an additional subsidy.

industry. A firm that might make a high profit under a uniform tariff by preventing competitors from entering the industry can have its profit cut by a reduction in the tariff that protects it. This is a rational course of action by a government whose powers to regulate monopolistic practice are constitutionally weak.

The third motive for establishing a non-uniform tariff—or for levying higher-than-average tariffs—is to provide special assistance to individual industries. With minor exceptions such as defence and decentralisation, the common element of such arguments is a desire to satisfy the demands of some sectional interest or political lobby at the expense of the real national income. For high tariffs plainly involve the uneconomic use of resources in industries that could not otherwise survive. It is here that a nation's tariff may involve substantial loss of real national income through inefficient use of resources. For once the principle of non-uniform tariffs is established it becomes easier for a firm to seek tariff protection than to seek the level of efficiency needed to survive. The fact that some industries have succeeded in obtaining protection of 100 per cent or more in some nations is evidence of the misallocation of resources. Similarly the frequent desire of industries to be protected from technological change can be a major source of national loss. It is easy to envisage the loss of real national income if the candlemakers of the world had been successfully protected from the results of the work of Faraday, Henry and Edison. More prosaically it is of interest to examine the performance of nations, such as Sweden, that largely refuse to avoid problems of adjusting to technological change.

It is appropriate to add here that an import tariff may be regarded as a subsidy on home-produced import-competing goods. This is illustrated in the resource-transfer diagram figure 15.2.

FIGURE 15·2   RELATIONSHIP BETWEEN AN IMPORT TARIFF ON WHISKY AND A SUBSIDY ON HOME-PRODUCED WHISKY

50 per cent Import Tariff

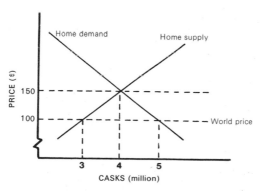

A 50 per cent tariff on imported whisky raises the home price from $100 per cask to $150. At this price home demand is 4 million casks and home producers are able to obtain the whole of this market.

33⅓ per cent Home Subsidy

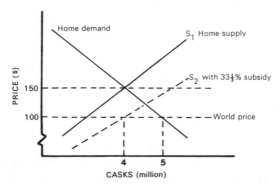

A 33⅓ per cent subsidy on home production lowers the home supply schedule by one-third. The home price remains equal to the world price of $100 per cask. At this price home demand is 5 million casks. Home producers sell 4 million casks, the remainder being imported.

Summary: An import tariff and a subsidy on the home-produced competing product are not equivalent because the difference in home price affects consumer demand. But one can choose rates of tariff and subsidy (here 50 per cent and 33⅓ per cent) that result in the same volume of home production.

Summary

Uniform tariffs are an alternative to devaluation as a means of eliminating a balance of current payments deficit. Such a uniform tariff may affect:
— productivity of resources (F. List);
— resource allocation;
— income distribution.
Non-uniform tariffs can be regarded as an alternative to uniform tariffs. Non-uniform tariffs may be motivated by:
— window-dressing (i.e. reduce apparent height of tariff);
— control over monopoly (lower tariff to encourage competition from imports);
— special assistance to an industry—involving a potentially serious conflict between sectional and national interest.

3. Export subsidy

Export subsidies affect both resource allocation (and hence real national income) and the distribution of national income. Since export subsidies are typically non-uniform, their effects are comparable with the effects of non-uniform tariffs on imports (since these can be regarded as having the effect of a non-uniform subsidy to import-competing industry).

Export subsidies involve a loss of real national income in as much as they support industries that could not otherwise continue to produce at the level made possible by the subsidy. (There is a qualification to this in a 'second best' situation outlined below.) Export subsidies may also affect income distribution by providing an income subsidy to producers. Consider two examples of this.

One motive for giving an export subsidy is to raise the incomes of marginal (i.e. high-cost) producers in an industry producing an agricultural crop for export. As the resource-transfer diagram (figure 15.3) shows, the effect may be for most of the subsidy to go to non-marginal (i.e. low-cost) producers. In such a situation the subsidy

FIGURE 15·3   COMMODITY SUBSIDY TO AVOID RESOURCE TRANSFER:
BUTTER

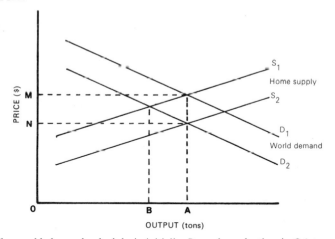

The world demand schedule is initially D_1 and production is OA tons. A change in tastes away from butter, causing a shift in the demand schedule downwards to D_2, shifts the intersection of D_2 with S_1, the home supply schedule, so that price falls and production falls to OB tons.

An export subsidy MN causes the home supply schedule to shift down from S_1 to S_2. Marginal producers can now expand production from OB back to OA. However, most of the subsidy accrues to non-marginal producers, i.e. MN times OB; only an amount equal to MN times AB accrues to marginal producers.

may be criticised both because it keeps uneconomic marginal producers in production, and because it subsidises low-cost producers who do not need such a subsidy. A more appropriate government approach could be a combination of social welfare legislation to prevent individual hardship through temporary loss of income, together with capital and retraining grants to shift labour and resources to other industries.

Another situation in which the government subsidises an agricultural export industry is where producer nations also hold up the world price. The result is that the commodity, although its production is subsidised, is then accumulated in unsold stockpiles. Figure 15.4 illustrates a situation of this kind, which might apply to a commodity such as wheat. The resulting unsold stockpiles represent a more drastic waste of resources than any resource allocation hitherto discussed.

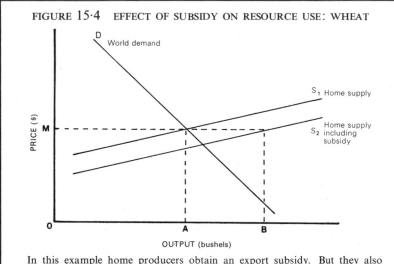

FIGURE 15·4   EFFECT OF SUBSIDY ON RESOURCE USE: WHEAT

In this example home producers obtain an export subsidy. But they also endeavour to maintain the world price at M dollars per bushel instead of letting it fall to the intersection of D and S_2. The result is an expansion of wheat production to OB, of which AB is unsold.

Summarising so far, we have seen that governments have been prone to three errors in export subsidies. The first is to subsidise some crops and not others—thus stimulating the farmer to produce the 'wrong' crops, involving a divergence between private and social gain. The second is to subsidise crops that are not saleable at prevailing prices. The third is to subsidise producers who do not need the subsidy, in order to subsidise those who do.

However, suppose that the nation already has a uniform import tariff. This is a 'second best' situation in the sense that the tariff has already caused a second best allocation of resources. The introduction of an equal uniform export subsidy may then be regarded as returning to a resource allocation that raises real national income. The net effect is equivalent to exchange devaluation.

The source of finance for export subsidies warrants comment. If the source is the income tax then there may be disincentive effects on taxpayers. If the export subsidy is financed by a high home consumption price (in effect, a tax) on home sales of that commodity, then the effect on real national income depends on whether the high home price causes consumers to switch demand to other goods. Sugar is a commodity whose exports have been subsidised by some nations by a high home price (supported by an import embargo).

Insofar as both import tariffs and export subsidies are motivated by a desire to influence the distribution of national income, one may question their efficacy by comparison with income taxes, income supplements and capital grants. For example Australia's use of an import tariff at an overvalued exchange rate is one way of 'taxing' exporters of wool and minerals, but it is an approach that causes a fall in real national income through resource misallocation. An alternative of devaluing together with taxes on incomes from land and minerals might avoid such misallocation. (Export taxes are of course used by such nations as Ceylon and Saudi Arabia.) Likewise the use of export subsidies for an ailing export industry ties up resources in that industry which could better be used elsewhere. The alternative of income supplementation (for example by a negative income tax or transitional aid) combined with capital grants could again avoid such resource misallocation.

4. Customs union

Two or more nations may decide to form a customs union in order to raise their real national incomes. Such a customs union has two elements: a common trade barrier between themselves and other nations; and the elimination of trade barriers between themselves.

The term 'trade barrier' includes not only tariffs, exchange control, export taxes and subsidies, and import quotas and restrictive 'health' regulations; it also includes subsidies given to specific home industries, inasmuch as these are equivalent to import tariffs.

The introduction of a common trade barrier might be achieved either by raising all tariffs to the highest, reducing all to the lowest, or some in-between formula. The effects of such a change can be examined by a detailed empirical enquiry. In the following analysis this will be avoided by assuming that both nations initially had identical tariff barriers, so no action is needed under this head. (For example two nations relying to a major extent on agricultural exports might well have the same uniform tariff on manufactured imports.)

Thus the essential element in forming a customs union is the elimination of trade barriers between the proposed member nations. There are at least four possible motives in doing this:

(a)   to achieve a more efficient allocation of resources;
(b)   to benefit from economies of scale in setting up larger plants for the expanded home market created by the union, and perhaps also providing a foundation for greater sharing of technical skills;
(c)   to give the union greater bargaining power *vis-a-vis* other nations and thus shift the net terms of trade in its favour, or force mutual reductions in tariff barriers with other nations;
(d)   to provide an economic basis for political union.

Each and all of these four motives may be important in practice. But it is the first that is the most complex and to which we now turn.

The effects of forming a customs union between countries *A* and *B* could be explored by considering a commodity 'cloth' that can be most cheaply produced in a third country *C*, and most expensively produced in our 'home' country *A*, with country *B* somewhere in between. Now if our tariff barriers are very high, say at 100 per cent, then we will currently home produce cloth; by forming a union with *B* we will shut down home production and import from *B*. In other words we switch from the most expensive source (home production) to the second-best producer *B*. This will mean a short-run dislocation problem in switching our resources out of cloth production into producing something else, but in the long run we expect to gain

Production cost $		Landed price $			
		100% tariff		20% tariff	
		no union	union with B	no union	union with B
in A	70	70	70	70	70
in B	45	90	45	54	45
in C	40	80	80	48	48

by more efficient resource use.

However, if our tariff barriers are rather low, say at 20 per cent, then currently we will be importing cloth from C; by forming a union with B we will switch our imports from C to B. In other words we switch from the cheapest source (C) to the second-best producer B. This does mean a long run switching to a dearer source of supply and so a lower real national income.[1]

It can be seen that a customs union brings both gains and losses. Our example suggests that the gains are likely to outweigh the losses if tariffs were initially high (because high tariffs suggest uneconomic home production exists). Also it seems intuitively that the gains are likely to outweigh the losses if the proposed union accounts for a high proportion of world production, since this would represent a major move towards efficient global resource allocation. In practice considerable tedious arithmetic is involved in calculating gains and losses, commodity by commodity. There are three aspects of such a calculation: first, where home industry is disestablished, transitional assistance may be needed in reallocating resources to other industries; second, there are the long-term gains and losses outlined above; third, if the calculations show that union implies a balance of payments disequilibrium to be corrected by a change in the exchange rate, then the long-term gains and losses must be recalculated at the equilibrium exchange rate.

In review, our four motives to form a union are little more than chapter headings for a complex practical enquiry. Moreover such an enquiry must be concerned, for political reasons, not only with

[1] There is a superficial paradox in that in the first case our home cloth industry is disestablished but this is not the case in which union causes us a loss of *long-term* national income. It is the second case in which we switch to a dearer source of supply that there is a long-term loss.

Summary

A customs union implies that the members of the union have a common trade barrier with the rest of the world and that trade barriers between members are eliminated.

Motives to form a customs union are:
— efficient resource allocation
— technical advantages, e.g. economies of scale
— greater bargaining power
— political union

As to the first motive (efficiency in resource allocation), a customs union brings gain to a nation when it causes a switch to a cheaper source of supply (purchase from another member nation instead of producing at home). On the other hand customs union brings loss to a nation when it causes a switch to a dearer source of supply (purchase from another member nation instead of from the rest of the world). Calculation of such gains and losses can be made, commodity by commodity, at the *equilibrium* exchange rate.

As with other trade measures, the effects of a customs union on the distribution (as well as the size) of real national income must be analysed in any actual situation.

effects on the size of real national income but also with effects on income distribution within the nation.

Summary

§1. Governments intervene in foreign trade for many reasons: for political and cultural motives as well as to achieve such commercial aims as penetration of export markets; to take advantage of a monoply position; to control fluctuations in commodity markets; or to protect the home economy from foreign recessions. Almost all intervention in trade affects the distribution of the national income, and much intervention is primarily aimed at such a distributional effect. Other motives for intervening in trade range from the 'infant economy' argument of F. List to the special pleading of sectional interests.

§2. Import tariffs are a major instrument of government intervention, which affect both resource allocation and income distribution. Uniform and non-uniform tariffs should be clearly distinguished.

3. Export subsidies are another important government measure. Since they usually apply to a few chosen industries, their effects on resource use and income distribution can be analysed similarly to non-uniform tariffs.

§4. The formation of a customs union has complex effects. Effects on resource use can only be ascertained by statistical investigation of trading nations both within and outside the union. Once again the effects of such a customs union on income distribution within any nation are of political importance.

Further reading

P.T. Ellsworth, *The International Economy*.

Questions

1. What motives may a government have for intervening in the conduct of foreign trade?
2. Consider grounds on which a nation may introduce a permanent uniform tariff on imports.
3. Consider the effects of a non-uniform (rather than a uniform) tariff on imports.

11. Explain the concept of effective protection to an industrial process. Set up an arithmetical example showing how an increase in effective protection can be given either by increasing the nominal rate of tariff on the output of the process or reducing the nominal rate of tariff on inputs into the process. (Note that a subsidy on the input or output of the import-competing process has the same effect.)
12. An imported good has a landed price of $100 while the home-produced competing product can be supplied to the home market for $125. Compare the effect of a 20 per cent subsidy on home production with the alternative of a 25 per cent tariff on the imported good.

21. Analyse the effects of export subsidies.
22. Explain how customs unions may cause either gains or losses to a nation through resource reallocation.
23. Consider the view that government intervention in foreign trade reflects:

    (a) a conflict of interest between nations;
    (b) a conflict of interest between income groups within a nation;

(c) a failure of the market system (e.g. either because prices do not reflect resource costs; or because of an inefficient response mechanism).

What situations does this view fail to cover?

Economic Policy

1. The elements of economic policy

The *elements* of economic policy are, literally, the basic ideas that go to make up the concept of an economic system. For if there is no government economic policy then the economic system will generate certain levels of output, employment, prices and incomes. The nature of government policy aims is to *specify certain desired levels* of output, employment, prices and incomes—and then to cast around for measures whereby the government may intervene in the operation of the economic system so as to pursue those aims. In principle

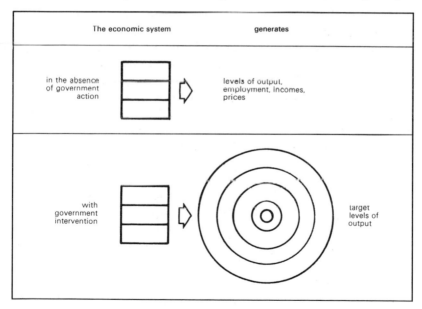

then, the basic idea of economic policy is starkly simple as a few examples will remind us:

— if labour is unemployed owing to inadequate demand, then

the government can achieve a high employment target by
raising demand;
— if unemployment is due to technological change, then the
government can facilitate resource transfers by retraining
and financial capital;
— if the distribution of income is considered inequitable, the
government can change it by inheritance or income taxes,
by subsidies, by controls over prices and restrictive practices,
by tariffs or devaluation, or by controlled inflation;
— if the market works poorly (say in mobilising resources for
war), then the government can take over physical direction
of resources;
— if living standards are too low, the government can raise
the nation's investment programme in order to increase the
amount of equipment per worker and so raise labour productivity.

However, the pursuit of one economic policy aim is often in conflict with some other aim. Thus measures to make income distribution more egalitarian may reduce incentives to produce—so that
it is a smaller pie that is more evenly distributed. Nowhere is this
conflict more vividly demonstrated than in capital accumulation—
since the cost of increasing the rate of growth of national product
is a higher savings-income ratio, i.e. lower consumption to-day.
Inevitably, therefore, the aims of government represent a *compromise*.
Familiar examples of such compromise are:
— how much of the nation's resources to divert from civilian
use to defence ('guns or butter');
— how much of the nation's resources to divert to communal
consumption in the form of schools, hospitals, roads;
— how high a proportion of the work force can be employed
without endangering foreign trade solvency owing to import
'spill-over' of demand.

The purpose of such compromise is to set out a *consistent* clutch
of policy aims. If such consistency were not achieved we would have
the spectacle of the government oscillating between mutually con-
tradictory aims. An example of this is when a central bank on the
one hand restricts bank credit to contain inflation and on the other
supports the government securities market in order to prevent interest

rates from rising.

Likewise it is to be observed that as a government's *aims increase in number* so its freedom to manoeuvre diminishes. Two examples may be given. First, imagine a developing fully-employed economy in which target aims have been set up as to the volume of investment (public and private), government consumption, and the size of the balance of current payments deficit. Does the government then have a choice as to the over-all tax rate? If the government also aims at controlling inflation, then in a basic sense the answer is negative. For the stated targets require the government to set the over-all tax rate at the level that will cut *private consumption* back to the level equal to the residual between capacity national product and the output already allocated to the targets. This is no idle matter—it implies that if the government subsequently undertakes to cut taxes in some area then it must compensate by raising tax rates elsewhere. The second example is the case of unemployment due to demand deficiency, which can be tackled by fiscal and monetary measures if the balance of current payments is in surplus: but if the government has the second aim of eliminating an existing balance of payments deficit then its freedom to manoeuvre is reduced inasmuch as those measures are initially inappropriate (since they would raise demand for all goods including imports).

It has been shown also how important is the distinction between the physical aims of economic policy and the financial measures commonly used to achieve those aims. Two errors to be avoided are: First, elevating a measure to the status of an aim (e.g. 'aim at balancing the budget'); second, passing judgment on the desirability of a measure as if there were an unconstrained choice between using that measure or not using it. This second case is illustrated by discussion of a tariff on imports as if the alternative were simply to have no tariff—the reality being that since one is constrained to achieve the aim of balance of payments solvency the alternative is some other measure such as devaluation or import controls.

Each of the points made in the past few paragraphs is of substantive importance. They do not, however, add up to a calculus for the solution of economic policy problems. The search for such a calculus is as doomed as the search for the philosopher's stone. For not only is the choice of measures to pursue a specified economic policy a choice between discrete options, but also those optional measures (like weapons systems) do not yield their fruits in the same proportions. Just as one weapons system is graded $A+$ on logistical support but $B-$ on crew training time, with no simple weights to apply to the two criteria—so also is this true of the alternative measures that can be used to achieve economic policy aims. The final decision to 'trade-off' a bit of one policy aim against another must be a political one and no calculus can avoid that. However, we do have a systematic method of tackling economic policy problems and this is an appropriate point at which to summarise that method.

2. The method of analysis

Economic policy aims are often proclaimed in ignorance of the full nature and magnitude of their implications. For example these policy aims

> balance the budget; maintain gold backing for the currency; full employment; better education; more immigration; self-sufficiency in food (or in petroleum, or in military procurement); equal incomes for all; military preparedness; promote manufacturing industry; protect low-income farmers;

vary in their degree of rationality, and have all been espoused at some time and often without full understanding of their effects. There is then a genuine need for a logical method that submits any policy aim to the same systematic scrutiny. Such a method was set out in chapter 13 figure 13.3 as three steps:

   (a)   specific policy aim (or group of consistent policy aims);
   (b)   alternative feasible measures to achieve the aim:
         (i) list the measures;
         (ii) analyse their effects, particularly on size, composition and distribution of national product;
        (iii) measure such effects where possible.
   (c)   state the criteria on which the alternative measures are to be judged, such as:
         (i) efficiency;
         (ii) economic policy criteria:
            — size of national product
            — income distribution
            — capital formation

— foreign trade solvency
(iii) non-economic criteria, such as:
  — military defence
  — political liberties

Such an approach can be used to analyse the pursuit of some *settled* policy aim such as high employment (as in chapter 14). The same approach can be used to analyse the pursuit of some *tentative* aim such as self-sufficiency in food production. In the latter case the task would be to analyse the effects that alternative measures (such as price supports, specific commodity subsidies, general farm subsidy, income supplements to low-income farmers, tariffs on imported foods) would have on the size and distribution of real national income. One possible outcome of such analysis is that any feasible measure would involve politically unacceptable effects and the policy aim is rejected.

In summary, we have sought to set out a method of analysing policy aims whether they be full employment, aiding oil exploration, or seeking foreign capital or foreign migrants. In each case the method is to consider alternative feasible measures by analysing how any measure would modify the operation of the three-block model of the economic system. In order to demonstrate how this can be done, we repeatedly set out the model and manipulated it in succeeding chapters. Once the effects of a measure have been ascertained then one can embark on the third step of applying agreed criteria. But, as already noted, a final judgment is necessarily political (i.e. an ethical or value judgment).

3. Epilogue

The simplest statement of a typical nation's economic policy aims is to raise living standards. It naturally follows from this that the nation should seek to reap the greatest possible physical benefits from increasing scale returns and from improved technology. While the pursuit of such benefits may have to be modified by ecological effects (i.e. the need to conserve exhausting resources or to avoid environmental pollution), it is nonetheless true that some nations do not rationally seek the benefits of increasing scale returns and improved technology. Three examples may be cited.

First there is the frequent attempt of an industry to protect itself from technological change and avoid resource reallocation which, while painful to it, is of net advantage to the community. In technological change it is common for the interests of the community at large to diverge from the interests of some individual established industry.

Second, a precisely comparable situation arises where trade unions and craft guilds seek to protect their membership by featherbedding or by slowing down the introduction of more efficient technology. Labour unions may reasonably seek to protect their membership by severance, superannuation and retraining benefits but not by methods that prevent the application of the main ultimate source of better living standards, i.e. technical change.

Third, increasing scale returns are significant in a variety of large-scale manufacturing processes (motor vehicles, chemicals). It is therefore of concern to find some nations limiting the benefits to be gained in this way, often in the name of 'competition'. Thus in recent years one national government has embarked on a programme of import replacement in the motor vehicle industry in a manner that has fragmented the annual home market of less than half a million new vehicles into four producers (plus several assemblers of other branded models). This is the antithesis of a rational import replacement programme—as indeed is any tariff level that is set high enough to allow competitive waste in the form of technical inefficiency or excess capacity.

There are perhaps two lessons to be learned from all this. The first is that social and private interests commonly conflict and it is a major task of central economic policy to resolve the conflict in favour of society. Second, the pursuit of a rational economic policy is not uncommonly obscured by slogans—such as 'competition', 'import replacement', 'balanced budget'—which confuse means and ends and so substitute myth for rationality.

Review questions

1. It is a commonly accepted precept in capitalist nations that if aggregate demand falls then the government should take measures to stimulate demand so that industry will be working to full capacity.

   Should this precept be applied to individual industries? For example if there is a fall in demand for the rubber fabricating industry, should the government take measures to stimulate demand closer to capacity?

2. An oft-accepted aim of economic policy is to maximise national income. Does this imply that in a socialised economy industry managers should aim at maximising the value produced (i.e. their contribution to national income) in their industry?

3. An individual may save because it appears desirable to him. Does it follow that a decision to save more made by a number of individuals is socially desirable? (Refer Bernard Mandeville, *The Fable of the Bees*, a book convicted by the grand jury of Middlesex in 1723).

4. 'As every individual, therefore, endeavours as much as he can both to employ his capital in the support of domestic industry, and so to direct that industry that its produce may be of the greatest value; every individual necessarily labours to render the annual revenue of the society as great as he can. ... By directing that industry in such a manner as its produce may be of the greatest value, he intends only his own gain, and he is in this, as in many other cases, led by an invisible hand to promote an end which was no part of his intention'; Adam Smith, *The wealth of Nations*, Book IV, chapter 2. Comment.

5. Consider a proposal for a government (with sovereignty over a large territory) to pursue self-suffiency in petroleum resources.

6. How would you formulate a policy attitude towards the inflow of foreign capital?

7. What policy issues confront a nation exporting mineral ores such as iron ore, bauxite?

Supplement:
Analysing Response to Change

This book has been written so that it can be read without any knowledge of differential calculus. But for the student who plans to go on with the study of economics, some knowledge of calculus is valuable. This supplement aims quite simply at showing how the reader can use calculus in economic analysis. Hopefully he will be stimulated to buy a *Teach Yourself Calculus* textbook and get a thorough introduction to the subject.

1. The basic argument

The reader is familiar with the concept of a functional relation, with the representation of a function by a graph, and with the fact

$y = f(x)$
where y is the dependent variable
x is the independent variable
reads: y is a function of x such that if the form of the function is known, then for a given level of x we can read off the level of y.

that a most important property of a function is its slope or gradient —which is readily observed in a graph. There is a choice of conventions in describing slope and we will here follow a mountaineering terminology so that in the sixth chart of figure 1 we say that the slope is 'steeper at A than at B'. Having thus stated that the slope at A is *numerically* greater than at B, we then give this number a *negative sign* because the line falls from left to right (and a positive sign if the line rises from left to right).

Our reason for being interested in the slope of the curve representing the function $y = f(x)$ is that this slope (i.e. the slope of the tangent to the curve at a chosen point) *measures the rate of change of y with respect to x.* Consider the example in figure 2 of a racing car that crosses the start line at Bonneville Flats at a velocity of b (say 100 feet/second) and constantly accelerates at a steady rate of c (say 5 feet/second per second) for a twenty second run. We can calculate the distance travelled as 3,000 feet as shown in the figure 2. What

FIGURE 1   GRAPHS PORTRAY ALGEBRAIC FUNCTION OVER PART OF RANGE

POSITIVE SLOPE (rising)[a]   NEGATIVE SLOPE (falling)[b]

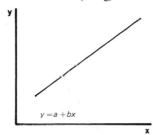 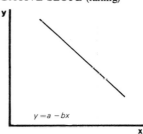

$y = a + bx$ $y = a - bx$

Constant slope: y is rising/falling at a constant rate relative to x.

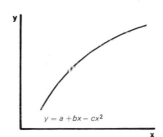 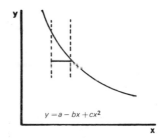

$y = a + bx - cx^2$ $y = a - bx + cx^2$

Diminishing slope: y is rising/falling at a diminishing rate relative to x.

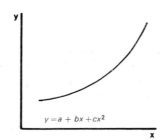 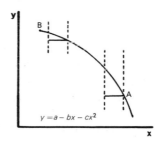

$y = a + bx + cx^2$ $y = a - bx - cx^2$

Increasing slope: y is rising/falling at an increasing rate relative to x.

Notes: a These graphs might reflect how consumption spending (y) rose as income (x) rose.
    b These graphs might reflect how the annual quantity of butter purchased (y) declined as the price of butter (x) rose.

interests us is that velocity is increasing throughout the run and that at any point in the run the velocity is measured by the slope of the tangent to the curve in figure 2. Moreover if we analyse the two

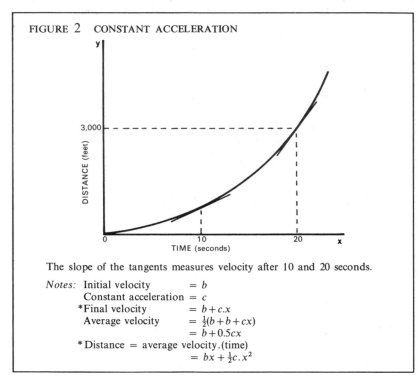

FIGURE 2   CONSTANT ACCELERATION

The slope of the tangents measures velocity after 10 and 20 seconds.

Notes: Initial velocity $= b$
        Constant acceleration $= c$
     *Final velocity $= b + c.x$
     Average velocity $= \frac{1}{2}(b + b + cx)$
                      $= b + 0.5cx$
  * Distance $=$ average velocity.(time)
                            $= bx + \frac{1}{2}c.x^2$

starred relations, it is seen that there is a family resemblance between: distance expressed as a function of time ($bx + \frac{1}{2} cx^2$) and the rate of change of distance with respect to time (i.e. velocity, $b + cx$). We now show that this resemblance is a general phenomenon.

Let $y = f(x)$, for example $y = a + bx - cx^2$ as in figure 3. Our aim is to *specify the rate of change of y with respect to x* in a function $y = f(x)$:

(1) ... The geometric equivalent of the rate of change is the slope of the curve describing the function $y = f(x)$, and this is measured by the *slope of the tangent* at the point concerned. The aim is to measure this (figure 3a). How then is the tangent slope obtained from a knowledge of the function?

FIGURE 3a

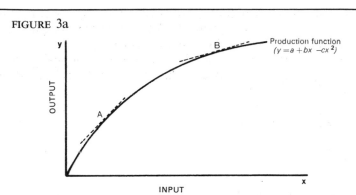

Rate of change of y with respect to x is measured by slope of tangent. Rate of change is high at A, low at B.

FIGURE 3b

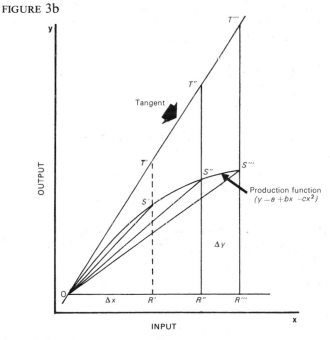

$\Delta y = RS;\ \Delta x = OR.$

The ratio of finite increments $\Delta y/\Delta x$ approaches the slope of the tangent OT as Δx is made smaller.

(2)   ... Using a diagram (figure 3b) for $y = a + bx - cx^2$, we see that the ratio of finite increments $\Delta y / \Delta x$ approaches the slope of the tangent as the size of Δx is made smaller.

(3)   ... So the slope of the tangent is seen to be the limiting value of the ratio $\Delta y / \Delta x$ as $\Delta x \to 0$, and this slope can be calculated as follows:

$$\Delta y = \{y + \Delta y\} - y \qquad \qquad \text{... (difference)}$$
$$= \{a + b(x + \Delta x) - c(x + \Delta x)^2\} - (a + bx - cx^2) \text{ ... (substitute)}$$
$$\frac{\Delta y}{\Delta x} = b - 2c.x - c.\, \Delta x \qquad \qquad \text{... (divide)}$$

Hence the

$$\text{Limit of } \frac{\Delta y}{\Delta x} = b - 2c.x \qquad \qquad \text{... (limit)}$$

as $\Delta x \to 0$

The shorthand expression for this limiting value is dy/dx, a single term (not a ratio) called the *first derivative* or differential coefficient.

By argument following the same steps, textbooks on calculus show that for *any power function* $y = a.x^n$

$$\frac{dy}{dx} \equiv \text{limiting value of } \frac{\Delta y}{\Delta x} = n.a.x^{n-1}$$
$$\text{as } \Delta x \to 0$$

2. Range of application of the basic argument

The fertility of this piece of reasoning is remarkable. For it indicates a way to analysing any situation where change is involved. Some areas of application may be listed:

(a) *Numerical application*

For example its numerical application to a case in which the relation between corn output (X) and addition of nitrogenous fertiliser (N) to a 100 acre plot of land is found to be:

$X = 20N - 0.008N^2$
X in bushels
N in bags

over the relevant range of fertiliser addition.

Then we deduce that the rate at which output is changing with respect to fertiliser input is:

$$\frac{dX}{dN} = 20 - 0.016N$$

which, as more fertiliser is added, is diminishing in a known way.

(b) *Estimating finite increments*

In economic analysis dX/dN in the previous example is called the marginal productivity of fertiliser; i.e. it is the rate at which output increases with respect to input of fertiliser. This expression for marginal productivity approximately measures the finite marginal product of a bag of fertiliser, provided our chosen unit of fertiliser (i.e. a bag) is sufficiently small. This follows from the fact that marginal productivity

$$\frac{dX}{dN} = \frac{\Delta X}{\Delta N} \text{ approximately}$$

if $\Delta N \rightarrow 0$.

So if a small unit of measurement of fertiliser is chosen, since $\Delta N = 1$:

$$\Delta X = \frac{dX}{dN} \text{ approximately}$$

where ΔX is the finite marginal product of fertiliser. Thus if the number of bags being applied to the 100 acre plot is 1,000, then the marginal product of a bag of fertiliser is readily seen to be approximately 4 bushels, since:

$$\frac{dX}{dN} = 20 - 0.016(1,000) = 4$$

The correct answer can be found to be 3.987984 bushels, but the extra accuracy may not be worth the calculating time involved.

(c) *Successive differentation*

Where, as in the previous example, the derivative:

$$\frac{dX}{dN} = 20 - 0.016N$$

is a functional relation of the independent variable, successive differentiation can be used to find the rate of change of the rate of change, usually called the second derivative:

$$\frac{d^2X}{dN^2} \text{ (i.e. } \frac{d}{dN} \cdot \frac{dX}{dN}) = -0.016$$

The most common example of this is the acceleration of a moving body: velocity is the first derivative of distance with respect to time and acceleration is the second derivative (i.e. the rate of change of velocity) with respect to time.

(d) Combinations of functions

If two variables are themselves functions of the same independent variable, then the same basic reasoning can be used to ascertain the rate of change of the sum (or product or quotient, whichever is of interest) of the first two variables with respect to the independent variable. The proofs for these, as also proofs for chain and inverse relations, are set out in calculus texts. The simplest example is illustrated by the first of the rules for derivation of combinations of functions.

The derivative of the sum (or difference) of two functions is the sum (or difference) of the separate derivatives.

Example: The only variable costs of a small mining company are labour costs, and the company experiences diminishing scale returns. Its total revenue (R) is a function of output (X) since the world price of its product is fixed; and of course output (X) is itself a function of labour employed (N). Total costs (C) are a function of labour (N). In summary:

$$R = f(X) = f(N)$$
$$C = \qquad f(N)$$
$$\text{Profits } V = R - C$$

Then the above rule states that the rate of change of profit as labour input rises, is:

$$\frac{dV}{dN} = \frac{dR}{dN} - \frac{dC}{dN}$$

So that if on a weekly basis the production function is:

$$X = 10N - 0.5N^2$$

and the wage-rate P_n is two dollars and the price (P) per physical unit of product is one dollar, then:

$$\frac{dV}{dN} = d\frac{(10N - 0.5N^2)}{dN} - \frac{d(2N)}{dN} = 8 - N$$

In summary, we have a quantitative expression showing how the rate of increase of profit falls as labour employment rises.

The rules for derivation of combinations of functions are summarised here for convenient reference. The proofs of these follow the same basic logic used to obtain the derivative of a power function.

Where $z = \phi(x)$, $w = u(x)$, and $t = f(x)$:

(i) Sum $\quad \dfrac{d}{dx}(z + w - t) = \dfrac{dz}{dx} + \dfrac{dw}{dx} - \dfrac{dt}{dx}$

(ii) Product $\quad \dfrac{d}{dx}(z.w) - w.\dfrac{dz}{dx} + z.\dfrac{dw}{dx}$

(iii) Quotient $\dfrac{d}{dx}\left(\dfrac{z}{w}\right) = \dfrac{w.\dfrac{dz}{dx} - z.\dfrac{dw}{dx}}{w^2}$

(iv) Chain $\quad$ If $y = f(u)$, $u = f(x)$ then:

$$\frac{dy}{dx} = \frac{dy}{du} \cdot \frac{du}{dx}$$

(v) Inverse $\quad \dfrac{dy}{dx} = \dfrac{1}{\dfrac{dx}{dy}}$ for single valued functions

(e) *Describing properties of functions*

Derivatives can now be used as a succinct way of describing the properties of functions. Thus in figure 1 the properties of the six diagrams can be summarised:

$y = a + bx$	$y = a - bx$
$\dfrac{dy}{dx} = b$ y rises at a constant rate relative to x	$\dfrac{dy}{dx} = -b$ y falls at a constant rate relative to x
$y = a + bx - cx^2$	$y = a - bx + cx^2$
$\dfrac{dy}{dx} = b - 2cx$ $\dfrac{d^2y}{dx^2} = -2c$ y rises at a diminishing rate relative to x	$\dfrac{dy}{dx} = -b + 2cx$ $\dfrac{d^2y}{dx^2} = 2c$ y falls at a diminishing rate relative to x
$y = a + bx + cx^2$	$y = a - bx - cx^2$
$\dfrac{dy}{dx} = b + 2cx$ $\dfrac{d^2y}{dx^2} = 2c$ y rises at an increasing rate relative to x	$\dfrac{dy}{dx} = -b - 2cx$ $\dfrac{d^2y}{dx^2} = -2c$ y falls at an increasing rate relative to x

The verbal statements in this layout refer to the range of values plotted in figure 1.

(f)   *Functions of two variables*

The above analysis of the process of derivation (i.e. ascertaining rates of change) is applicable without modification to power functions of two or more variables. In the production function:

$y = a . x^h . z^i$
a is positive
h, i are positive and less than unity

output y is a function of the input of two productive factors x and z —these being neither dependent on one another nor both functions of another independent variable.

To obtain the rate of change $(\partial y / \partial x)$ of output y with respect to the input of x alone, z *remaining unchanged at a given level,* we proceed with the derivation as before:

$$\partial y / \partial x = a . h . x^{h-1} . z^i = h . \frac{y}{x} > 0$$

This rate of change is called the *partial derivative* of y with respect to x and is given the distinguishing symbol $\partial y/\partial x$ to remind that the input of another vairable z is held constant.

Successive differentiation is likewise carried out as before:

$$\frac{\partial}{\partial x}\left(\frac{\partial y}{\partial x}\right) \equiv \frac{\partial^2 y}{\partial x^2} = a.h.(h-1).x^{h-2}.z^i = h\,(h-1).\frac{y}{x^2} < 0$$

And we may also ascertain the cross partial derivative:

$$\frac{\partial^2 y}{\partial x \partial z}\left(=\frac{\partial}{\partial z}.\frac{\partial y}{\partial x}\right) = a.h.i.x^{h-1}.\ z^{i-1} = \frac{h.i.y}{x.z} > 0$$

The meaning of these expressions is as follows: if x and z are respectively the inputs of land and labour producing wheat then $\frac{\partial y}{\partial x}$ is the positive marginal productivity of land, $\frac{\partial^2 y}{\partial x^2}$ the rate at which that marginal productivity falls with increasing input of land, and $\frac{\partial^2 y}{\partial x.\partial z}$ the rate at which the marginal productivity of land increases as the input of labour is increased.

(g) *Estimating finite increments when two or more independent variables change*

In (b) above, an estimate was made of the finite increment in production when one input alone changed by a small amount. Consider now the extension of this problem to estimating the increment in production when the inputs of *both* land (y) and labour (z) are changed by small amounts. If (x) represents output, then for the function:

$$x = f(y, z)$$

It can be shown that[1]

[1] The argument is as follows:

$$\Delta x = f(y + \Delta y, z + \Delta z) - f(y, z)$$

Now manipulate:

$$\Delta x = [f(y + \Delta y, z + \Delta z) - f(y, z + \Delta z)]\frac{\Delta y}{\Delta y} + [f(y, z + \Delta z) - f(y, z)]\frac{\Delta z}{\Delta z}$$

Consider the first term without the numerator Δy. It is seen that:

the limit of $\dfrac{f(y + \Delta y, z + \Delta z) - f(y, z + \Delta z)}{\Delta y} = \dfrac{\partial}{\partial y}.f(y, z + \Delta z)$
as $\Delta y \to 0$

which is the partial derivative, f_y, of x with respect to y at point $(y, z + \Delta z)$. As Δz approaches zero, this approaches the value of f_y at point (y, z). By repeating this reasoning it is seen that:

the limit of $\Delta x = f_y.\Delta y + f_z.\Delta z$
as $\Delta y, \Delta z \to 0$

$$\begin{cases} \text{the limit of } \Delta x = \frac{\partial x}{\partial y}.\Delta y + \frac{\partial x}{\partial z}.\Delta z \\ \text{as both } \Delta x, \Delta z \to 0 \end{cases}$$

or more compactly $= f_y. \Delta y + f_z. \Delta z$

where f_y, f_z are partial derivatives. To emphasise that this is concerned with *small* amounts of y and z we can write this result using the notation dy, dz for small increments:

$$dx = f_y.dy + f_z.dz \qquad (1)$$

This result states that an approximate estimate of the change in the value of a function, when there are small finite changes in two or more independent variables, is given by summing the products of the partial derivatives times the finite changes. Equation (1) is called the *total differential* of the function.

Example

$$X = 20N - 0.8\,\frac{N^2}{T}$$

$$dX = f_N.\ dN + f_T.\ dT$$

$$= \left(20 - 1.6\,\frac{N}{T}\right) dN + \left[0.8\left(\frac{N}{T}\right)^2\right].\ dT$$

Let $N = 1000$, $T = 100$; and let dN and dT each rise by one unit. Then our estimate is $dX = 84$. The correct figure can be calculated to be 83.4.

(h) *The relationship between the temporal rate of change of the dependent variable and the temporal rates of change of the independent variables.*

A further development from equation (1) is that if the growth of the factor inputs is a function of a fourth variable such as time (t), then it can be shown that[2]

$$\frac{dx}{dt} = f_y.\frac{dy}{dt} + f_z.\frac{dz}{dt} \qquad (2)$$

[2] Refer R.G.D. Allen, *Mathematical Analysis for Economists* (New York: St Martin's Press, 1964), page 333, or D. Huang, *Introduction to the Use of Mathematics in Economic Analysis* (New York: Wiley, 1964), page 92.

the rate of change of output equals the sum of the rates of change of the two inputs, respectively multiplied by their marginal productivities. Equation (2) sets out the *total derivative*.

Example:

In the previous example

$$X = 20N - 0.8 \frac{N^2}{T}$$

it is apparent that if X is output, and N, T are inputs, then this is a constant scale returns production function—for doubling both inputs will double output.[3] So if both N and T are increasing at 2 per cent per annum, then X should also be increasing at 2 per cent per annum. To confirm that this is so, using t for time:

i.e.
$$\frac{dX}{dt} = \left(20 - 1.6 \frac{N}{T}\right)\frac{dN}{dt} + 0.8 \left(\frac{N}{T}\right)^2 \cdot \frac{dT}{dt}$$

$$\frac{dX}{dt} = \left(20N - 1.6 \frac{N^2}{T}\right) \cdot \left[\frac{dN}{dt} \cdot \frac{1}{N}\right] + 0.8 \left(\frac{N^2}{T}\right) \cdot \left[\frac{dT}{dt} \cdot \frac{1}{T}\right]$$

so that if both terms in square brackets are 2 per cent per annum:

$$\frac{dX}{dt} = \left(20N - 0.8 \frac{N^2}{T}\right) [2\%] = X [2\%]$$

i.e. the annual rate of growth of output

$$\frac{dX}{dt} \cdot \frac{1}{X} = 2\%$$

In review, while the foregoing gives some taste of the power and scope of differential calculus it is only a beginning. For example the same basic logic that has been applied to power functions can be applied to logarithmic, exponential and trigonometric functions, though that is beyond the scope of the present discussion. However, there is one further major application that flows so naturally from the foregoing discussion that it seems a pity not to explore it briefly. This is done in the next subsection.

[3] If all the terms have the power of one, then the function is called homogeneous linear and it is characterised by constant scale returns. (Recall that $1/T = T^{-1}$.)

(i) *Ascertaining a maximum (or minimum) position from the specification of a zero rate of change.*

In figure 4*a* a philosopher at *A* is firing a cannon at a philosopher at *B*. The curve shows the flight path of the cannon ball, its height being a function of distance. Figure 4*b* shows a fighter pilot pulling out of a dive, height again being a function of distance. The two diagrams have one thing in common: a stationary point—but in the first case the stationary point is a maximum and in the second it is a minimum. By examining the two diagrams we can deduce the rules for specifying a maximum or minimum. The conclusion is that *a maximum position is specified when the first derivative is zero and the second derivative is negative.* Now consider the argument more fully: geometrically, the first derivative $f'(x)$ ($= dy/dx$, the slope of the tangent) at a point is the slope of the curve. If $f'(x)$ is positive at a point the curve is rising; if it is zero the *height of the curve is stationary;* if negative the curve is falling as x increases.

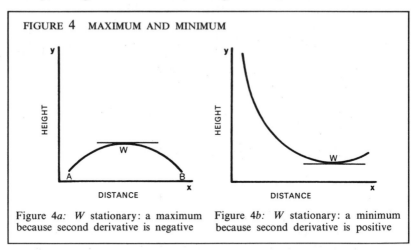

FIGURE 4   MAXIMUM AND MINIMUM

Figure 4*a:* W stationary: a maximum because second derivative is negative

Figure 4*b:* W stationary: a minimum because second derivative is positive

Geometrically, the second derivative $f''(x)$ ($= d^2y/dx^2$, the rate of change of dy/dx) gives the rate of change of slope of the curve. In everyday language if $f''(x)$ is positive at a point, the curve is convex to the x axis; if negative, concave to the x axis; and if zero, there is neither convexity nor concavity.[4]

[4] We need not consider this third possibility here. An inflexional value of the function $f(x)$ can only occur at a point where $f''(x) = 0$.

This leads to the following criteria for maximum (and minimum) values: For the function $y = f(x)$, if x is at a level at which the first derivative is zero, then that position is a maximum value of the function if the second derivative is negative (and is a minimum value of the function if the second derivative is positive).

Example: Production function for a small mining company (in physical units) displays diminishing scale returns:

$X = 10N - 0.5N^2$ X output

$P_n - \$2$ N labour input

                          P_n wage-rate

Fixed world price of product, $P = \$1$.

By differentiating profit (equals revenue minus costs) with respect to labour input, show that the most profitable scale of output is given by $N = 8$, $X = 48$; although maximum production attainable is given by $N = 10$, $X = 50$. If the factor price rises to $P_n = 3$, the most profitable scale of production is cut back to 45.5. Thus if the mining company is working numerous lodes yielding ore of different metallic content, a rise in factor prices may cause some sections of the mine to be shut down.

Example: A monopoly (e.g. diamond combine) has to reduce the price of diamonds in order to sell more and so faces diminishing value returns as it expands output. What output yields maximum profit?

Data: production function $X = 10N$
       demand function $X = 100 - 2P$
       factor price $P_n = 20$

Let G be profit; when dG/dN is zero (and d^2G/dN^2 is negative because the price has to be cut as output rises), the level of output X is 48, which (with $P = 26$) is the most profitable scale of production:

Profit $= XP - P_n \cdot N$

$$\frac{dG}{dN} = \left[(P)\frac{dX}{dN} + X\left(\frac{dP}{dX} \cdot \frac{dX}{dN}\right) \right] - P_n$$

$$= (50 - 0.5X)\,10 + X(-0.5 \times 10) - 20$$
$$= 500 - 5X - 5X - 20$$
$$= 480 - 10X$$
$$= 0, \text{ when } X = 48$$

The three terms on the right hand side reflect the fact that when the scale of output is raised, profit is affected in three respects: production costs rise; sales revenue rises on the extra output; but sales revenue on the old level of output falls because price has to be cut to sell more volume. Note that dP/dX is negative and expresses this rate of price fall. The term in square brackets may be called the marginal revenue productivity of the variable factor.

3. Uses of the argument in economics

Equipped with an elementary knowledge of the differential calculus of power functions, the student can handle a wider variety of functional relations than has been used in this book. In other words in setting up a model of the economy he can choose from a wider variety of algebraic forms in seeking to describe the structural relations defining the economic system.

Technology

To illustrate we consider the treatment of the technology of an economy. For example if there are three goods a, b, c to be produced and three activities[5] capable of producing each, then if we measure output in 'baskets' containing one ton of each good,

> *Example:* Scale returns are constant and 1 ton can be produced:
> of a by 5:1, 2:2 or 1:3, men:acres
> of b by 4:1, 3:2 or 2:4, men:acres
> of c by 4:2, 2:3 or 1:4, men:acres
> the commodities being demanded by consumers in equal physical proportions.

the technology of the economy can be represented by a convex envelope obtained by joining plotted activity-combinations (as in figure 5), each of which can produce one basket efficiently.

Now, it is natural to suggest that this convex envelope, which is a 'broken curve', can be approximated by a smooth curve. For then we can use functional relations that generate such smooth curves, and can use differential calculus to explore the properties of the economic system. We emphasise, however, that the use of such func-

---

[5] An *activity* is a productive process characterised by fixed amounts of each input per unit of output. In other words scale returns are constant and inputs are used in fixed proportions (i.e. no factor substitution).

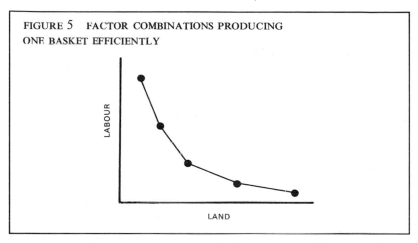

FIGURE 5 FACTOR COMBINATIONS PRODUCING
ONE BASKET EFFICIENTLY

LABOUR

LAND

tions is seen here as an aid to analysing the essential properties of
the economic system, not as a precise description of the nation's
technology.

Of the various algebraic forms available a popular one is the linear-
logarithmic or *Cobb-Douglas* production function relating the national product (X) to the input of labour (N) and land (K):

$$X = N^\alpha . K^\beta$$

where α and β are specified as positive constants less than unity.
The reader can satisfy himself that if $\alpha + \beta = 1$, then the nation's
technology is characterised by constant scale returns. Also, from
part (g) of the preceding section, we know that:

$$dX = \frac{\partial X}{\partial N}. \ dN + \frac{\partial X}{\partial K}. \ dK$$

where dX is the finite change in output and dN, dK are small finite
changes in inputs. If we let $dX = 0$, then:

$$\frac{dN}{dK} = -\frac{\partial X}{\partial K} \div \frac{\partial X}{\partial N}$$

This states that if labour and equipment are substituted for one another so as to leave output unchanged, then the rate of change of
labour with respect to equipment equals the reciprocal of the ratio
of their marginal productivities. And of course the curve has a negative slope. This is in fact the smooth convex curve that we wanted

as an approximation to figure 5. It is called an *isoquant* since output is constant.

The Cobb-Douglas production function can be incorporated in a model of the economy in order to explore such matters as production potential, capital accumulation and income distribution. For example in the case of income distribution we can set up the price formation block of equations (see figure 6) comprising:

— the cost account;
— the normal profit mark-up;
— the equi-marginal productivity condition (that, in order to be producing at minimum unit cost, the ratio of the marginal productivity of a factor to the price of the services of the factor must be the same for all factors employed in industry).

FIGURE 6   PRICE FORMATION

$$X.P = N.P_n + K.P_k + V$$
$$V = v(N.P_n + K.P_k)$$
$$\frac{\partial X}{\partial N} \div P_n = \frac{\partial X}{\partial K} \div P_k$$

P_n wage-rate
P_k land-rent

Assuming that the first, potential production, block of equations comprises our Cobb-Douglas production function $X = N^\alpha.K^\beta$ and a known supply of the two factors, one can deduce factor prices and income distribution as follows:

$$\frac{X.P}{1+v} = N.P_n + K.P_k$$

$$\therefore N.P_n = \frac{X.P}{1+v} - K.\frac{\frac{\partial X}{\partial K}}{\frac{\partial X}{\partial N}}.P_n$$

$$= \frac{X.P}{1+v} - K.P_n.\frac{\beta}{K}.\frac{N}{\alpha}$$

i.e. the wage share:

$$N.P_n = \frac{X.P}{1+v}.\frac{\alpha}{\alpha+\beta}$$

and the wage-rate:

$$P_n = \left[\alpha \cdot \frac{X}{N} \right] \cdot \frac{P}{(\alpha + \beta)(1+v)}$$

If we assume that $\alpha + \beta = 1$, which is the constant scale returns case, then the wage-rate:

$$P_n = \frac{\partial X}{\partial N} \cdot \frac{P}{(1+v)}$$

is a proportion $(\frac{1}{1+v})$ of the value of its marginal product. Thus if $v = 0.5$, the labourer receives two-thirds of the value of his marginal product.

Characteristics of consumer demand

A wide variety of demand functions can also be explored with the aid of calculus.

The demand for a consumer good or group of consumer goods will vary with the income of the purchaser, and with the price of both the commodity and of other competing or complementary goods.

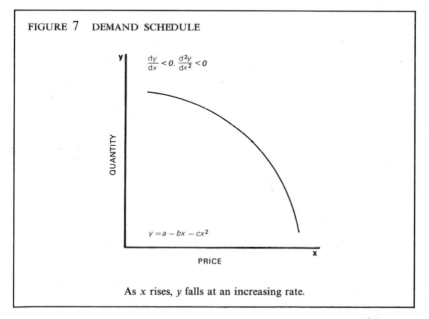

FIGURE 7   DEMAND SCHEDULE

$$\frac{dy}{dx} < 0. \quad \frac{d^2y}{dx^2} < 0$$

QUANTITY

$$y = a - bx - cx^2$$

PRICE

As x rises, y falls at an increasing rate.

Consider the relation between the demand for butter (C) in pounds weight, and the price of butter (P) in dollars per pound.

$C = a - bP - cP^2$ over a specified range. At any specified price level, what is the *responsiveness* of demand to price? One answer to this is to define responsiveness as the ratio of the incremental change in demand to the incremental change in price, i.e. $\Delta C/\Delta P$, when the price change is very small (approaching zero).

However, the figure thus obtained will vary according to whether we measure butter in lb., cwt. or centals, or price in £, $ or cents. A measure of responsiveness that is independent of units is:

$$\frac{\Delta C \div C}{\Delta P \div P}$$

i.e. a ratio of the proportionate (or percentage) changes in demand and price, instead of a ratio of absolute changes. This measure is called the *price elasticity of demand*. Since the value of $\Delta C/\Delta P$ approaches dC/dP as the price change approaches zero, we can measure the elasticity of demand (ε) in response to a small change in the price of butter as:

$$\varepsilon = \frac{dC}{dP} \cdot \frac{P}{C}$$

at the specified level P. It is useful to explore the cases of zero, unit and infinite elasticity, which respectively describe the situations where: the quantity demanded is constant and so unresponsive to price; expenditure (price times quantity) is constant; the quantity demanded is infinitely responsive to price so the demand curve is parallel to the quantity axis.[6]

The case of unit price elasticity of demand is especially useful as a mental reference point since it means that expenditure (price P times quantity C) is constant in the face of changing price. Thus the relation:

$$C.P = \text{constant } k$$

has unit price elasticity throughout the length of the demand curve $C = k/P$.

---

[6] It is common practice to assume in discussion that the price elasticity of demand is negative and to express the elasticity without regard to sign; e.g. 'If expenditure is constant, the price elasticity of demand is unity'.

Consider a more general relation:

$$C.P = 0.8Y$$

stating national expenditure on consumer goods (i.e. volume C times price P) is a constant 80 per cent of national income Y. Plainly if national income is held constant, this relation is of the same form as the earlier $C.P = k.$[7]

In more detailed discussion of consumer demand we need to subdivide consumer spending into groups (food, clothing etc.). For example suppose the division is into three groups of consumer goods b, c, g:

$$C_b.P_b = 0.1Y + h.P_b + k.P_c \qquad \text{inelastic, i.e. } \varepsilon < 1$$
$$C_c.P_c = 0.3Y - h.P_b - k.P_c - mP_c/P_g$$
$$C_g.P_g = 0.4Y \qquad\qquad\qquad + mP_c/P_g \qquad \text{elastic, i.e. } \varepsilon > 1$$
$$\Sigma C.P = 0.8Y$$

Looking at the first expenditure function for commodity b, observe that when P_b (the price of b) rises, then expenditure $(C_b P_b)$ also rises. This indicates that the price elasticity of demand is *inelastic*, i.e. is less than unity; in other words the percentage fall in quantity purchased must have been less than the percentage rise in price. This is confirmed by calculation:

$$C_b P_b = 0.1Y + h.P_b + k.P_c$$

$$C_b = 0.1\frac{Y}{P_b} + h + k.\frac{P_c}{P_b}$$

$$\frac{dC_b}{dP_b} = -0.1\frac{Y}{P_b{}^2} - k.\frac{P_c}{P_b{}^2}$$

$$\varepsilon = \frac{dC_b}{dP_b}.\frac{P_b}{C_b} = -\frac{0.1Y}{C_b.P_b} - k.\frac{P_c}{C_b.P_b}$$

$$= -\left[\frac{C_b P_b - h P_b}{C_b.P_b}\right]$$

---

[7] On the other hand it may equally well be that price P is a constant and income Y is a variable, in which case we know that when Y rises the 80 per cent rise in spending is wholly accounted for by a rise in quantity consumed.

It is important to note that we must specify which variables are held constant (called *parameters*) and which are free to vary.

which is less than unity, without regard to sign.

In comparable fashion the third expenditure function for commodity g shows that, as the price of g rises, expenditure on this commodity falls. This indicates that the price elasticity of demand is *elastic*, i.e. greater than unity, since the proportionate fall in quantity demanded must have been higher than the proportionate rise in price. Once again this can be confirmed by calculation:

$$C_g = 0.4\frac{Y}{P_g} + m.\frac{P_c}{P_g{}^2}$$

$$\frac{dC_g}{dP_g} = -0.4\frac{Y}{P_g{}^2} - 2m.\frac{P_c}{P_g{}^3}$$

$$\varepsilon = \frac{dC_g}{dP_g}.\frac{P_g}{C_g} = -\left[\frac{0.4Y}{C_gP_g} + \frac{2m.P_c}{C_g.P_g{}^2}\right]$$

$$= \frac{1}{C_gP_g}\left[\left(0.4Y + m.\frac{P_c}{P_g}\right) + m.\frac{P_c}{P_g}\right]$$

$$= -\left[1 + m.\frac{P_c}{C_gP_g{}^2}\right]$$

which exceeds unity, without regard to sign.

Finally, in order to illustrate the concept of income elasticity of demand, we consider another possible consumption function:

$C = Y^\alpha.Z$

where C national physical consumption of food grains

$\quad\quad\quad Y$ real income per head

$\quad\quad\quad Z$ population

Find the elasticity of demand with respect to the nation's real income per head.

$$\frac{\partial C}{\partial Y} = \alpha.Y^{\alpha-1}.Z$$

$$= \frac{\alpha}{Y}(Y^\alpha.Z)$$

$$= \alpha\frac{C}{Y}$$

Hence:

$$\varepsilon = \frac{\partial C}{\partial Y} \cdot \frac{Y}{C}$$

$$= \alpha$$

The income elasticity of demand is constant at α. Thus if $\alpha = 0.25$, this would mean that a 10 per cent rise in real income per head would result in a $2\frac{1}{2}$ per cent rise in quantity of food demanded.

Answers to Questions

Chapter 1

1. 'Economic system' refers to the collection of resources whose services are the inputs into the nation's industry, producing an outflow of commodities to satisfy final demand.
2. Economic analysis aims at explaining the determination of the volume, distribution and commodity composition of the national product. The method of analysis, as so far developed, is a systematic process of deduction from basic information on resources, technology, profits and final demand.
3. The sum of wages and surplus is $12,051m. The whole of output of $17,421m save for $1,568m sold to farms enters final demand, i.e. $15,853m.
4. For definitions see text. Old age pensions are a transfer payment, not a payment to factors for services rendered in producing the current year's output—hence they are not included in national income. Refer footnote 3.

11. Potential production is 4.5 million and wages are one-half of national income. Also, as discussed in chapter 3, equilibrium production is five times planned investment.

12. $$\frac{C.P}{P} = a + c\frac{[N.P_n.(1+v)]}{P}$$

   Then by introducing the cost account:

   $$X.P = N.P_n(1+v)$$

   where v is per cent profit mark-up, the consumption function can be simplified to read:

   $$C = a + cX$$

13. By setting up a complete set of accounts, we find the results are self-checking. Answers: 79, 2, 13.
14. $12m. Do not count the milk used as a raw material twice.

22. Major causes of secular growth of production, apart from population growth are: more capital equipment (through saving), more knowledge (through research), better and more widespread education.
23. No. Financial measures do not affect the fact that a proportion of the nation's physical resources will be diverted to military procurement from some other use such as consumption or capital formation.
24. The most urgent problems certainly differ. India depends on foreign trade, has difficulty feeding her population, has difficulty in obtaining savings for capital formation. All nations face a resource scarcity but India's problems are very different in degree from those of the U.S.

Chapter 2

1. Replacement; equipping addition to work force; raising living standards by raising equipment/labour ratio and furnishing the equipment that is a vehicle for new productive methods (innovation).
2. Ratio of value of plant and equipment to value produced (i.e. national product at the national level).
3. By cutting back consumption (i.e. saving), resources can be diverted to producing capital equipment (or reclaiming land) that, over its life, raises the output of consumer goods by more than the cost in terms of initial loss of consumption. This 'more' is a permanent rise in living standards (assuming old equipment is replaced). In formal terms: it is because the marginal productivity of equipment (net of replacement) is positive that living standards can be raised.
4. Not in a growing economy—because the investment being replaced is smaller than the ensuing stream of investment for which depreciation provision is being made.
5. Illustrate by considering a shipping line with 100 ships, each having a 20 year life, so that 5 replacement ships are built annually in the shipyards (the investment-goods industry). The ships carry consumer cargo and, so long as consumption is constant, cargo volume is constant and total investment is just the 5 replacement ships.

If consumer demand now rises 5 per cent annually, then the fleet must be increased by 5 (to 105 ships) to carry the 5 per cent rise in cargo since the capital/output ratio is constant. That is, net investment is 5 ships, which, added to 5 replacement ships, means that total investment is 10 ships this year, a rise of 100 per cent. (If the capital/output ratio $K/X=b$, then the marginal or incremental ratio $\Delta K/\Delta X=b$ also. This is called the capital coefficient since it shows the net investment ΔK needed to expand capacity to increase production by ΔX. Historically it has also been called the acceleration coefficient' because of the large percentage rise in investment just illustrated).

If the rate of growth of consumption next year falls back to 3 per cent, then net investment will fall back to 3 ships so that, adding 5 replacement ships, total investment activity falls back to 8 ships.

11. Savings-income ratio of 6 per cent compares with a ratio of 8 per cent required to maintain living standards. Options are in text.
12. Savings-income ratio of 10 per cent compares with a required ratio of 8 per cent to maintain living standards. Opportunity for raising equipment per worker.
13. Because the national income is rising more rapidly, the ratio of replacement to it declines.
14. The implicit assumption of constant marginal productivity of capital equipment allows one to assume that the capital/output ratio is constant. This is unlikely unless technical knowledge is improving so as to offset diminishing marginal returns to equipment. If in fact there are diminishing marginal returns, then the capital/output ratio rises, and the task of raising living standards is more difficult because a higher savings-income ratio is needed.
15. $868.
16. 8 per cent per annum; i.e. $40m annually for 25 years on $400m invested.

21. For a poor nation it may require a social upheaval to raise the savings-income ratio significantly. One strategy may be to hold national consumption absolutely constant in the face of rising

population by redistributing income from rich to poor. So long as this is done all net savings can be devoted to producing equipment to expand the capacity of the equipment-goods industries (and not expanding capacity in consumer industry). Thus the output of equipment grows while consumption is constant—a situation necessarily implying a rise in the savings-income ratio. This is only the first step of an operational strategy (and it faces disincentive problems).

22. Savings reflect the fact that some resources are not devoted to producing consumer goods and are available instead to produce equipment. If the savings-income ratio is too low, living standards may fall and complementary unemployment rise; while if the ratio is too high the possibility arises that all investible resources may not be used and so unemployment occurs owing to inadequate demand.

23. See text and previous questions.

24. (a) See text for explanation of discounting a stream of future prospective yields to equate the sum of their present values to the initial cost of equipment.

(b) Presumably there are more projects with a low rate of return over cost or 'marginal efficiency of capital' (m.e.c.). Hence graphing the value of planned national investment against m.e.c. would show a downward sloping schedule.

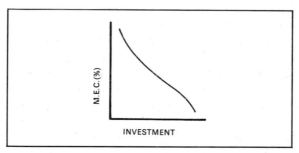

This suggests that the authorities could reduce the level of investment by raising the interest rate, and conversely.

25. It is a useful exercise to explore the impact of pollution, scale returns, saving, scientific knowledge, asset ownership and the like on living standards. But there is no simple answer to the optimum population question.

26. Different governments may choose to interpret the vague phrase 'living standards' as total real income, or total consumption, or income per head, or consumption per head. Other variations can be imagined. The more straightforward approach would seem to be 'real' consumption per head, for a specified income distribution', but even this ignores the relation between present and future living standards.

Chapter 3

1. The first is concerned with setting up national policy targets; the second tries to understand the collective behaviour of business enterprise in formulating its investment decisions.
2. The idea that, in order to expand production of consumer goods, one needs to invest in extra plant capacity is sound. But the quotation fails to recognise: surplus capacity; the need to invest before, not after, the rise in consumer demand; that the relationship may not be a simple proportional one dominated by a fixed capital coefficient.
3. The long-life of much equipment suggests that long-term influences (such as expectations of long-term growth) are important. It can be dangerous, however, to concentrate on one short-term influence and fail to recognise that others exist, e.g. the effect of short-term change in both interest rates and profits. A fall in the latter may neutralise a fall in the former so far as investment decisions are concerned.
4. If total demand is insufficient to clear the market of full-employment output.
5. The multiplier is based on the assumption that businessmen produce an amount equal to recent demand—which may be false if commodity stocks are excessive. Moreover the multiplier process is not instantaneous. In later discussion of foreign trade it will also be recognised: that the size of the multiplier is affected by the import leakage; and that the final position of market equilibrium may not be one of trade equilibrium. Finally, the real income multiplier is not constant at high levels of employment since rising demand is partly dissipated in rising prices.
6. A cut in tax rates raises after-tax income and so stimulates consumer spending; a rise in public works means more men are employed and their spending also rises.

A rise in public works spending has a multiplier effect on the national income and so income tax collections rise.

The choice between the options should be based on their efficiency (no time-lags) and on their effect on the use of physical resources (more consumer goods versus more hospitals and schools).

7. With a higher after-tax income, people spend more on canned beer and other goods using steel.

11. (a) 2.5; (b) 2 approximately, because the marginal propensity to consume home-produced goods out of national income is four-fifths of 0.6.

12. Because by the time one has allowed for taxes and undistributed profits and consumer spending on imports, the marginal propensity to consume home-produced goods can be as low as 0.5.

13. See figure 3.7.

14. $40m because the multiplier is 2.5.

In the second case the multiplicand or rise in consumer spending is 0.8 of $41.625m, and this is subject to a multiplier of 3, thus raising the income ultimately to the $100m target.

21. For a list see text.

Stabilising influences include: the tax system (which reduces the size of the multiplier); a reluctance of people to reduce their living standards (which squeezes savings); farmers smoothing out spending in accord with their 'normal' income.

Destabilising influences include: instalment credit (which means that when incomes fall, spending on consumption has to be squeezed in order to keep up the instalments); consumer pessimism engendered either by unemployment of others or by stock market fall (which may cause a desire to save more, i.e. spend less).

22. This elevates a financial mechanism irrationally to the status of a political objective.

23. The central government raises taxes in order to limit the purchasing power of private persons and firms. Thus in a recession with falling employment and a rising budget deficit, a rational government increases its spending or cuts its tax rates—and uses its central bank to foot the budget deficit. But if there is full

employment and inflationary rises in demand threaten, a rational government raises tax rates or reduces its own spending—even if it has a budget surplus. (The use of monetary measures will be discussed later).

24. Effective short-term economic management requires a close knowledge of time-lags so that crisis situations can be anticipated and avoided. This is a major justification for econometric studies of the economy.

Growing population indicates growing work force and productive capacity. So total demand must be planned to grow to match that expected capacity. (Refer Arthur M. Okun, *The Political Economy of Prosperity* (New York: Norton, 1969).

Technological innovation and automation raise for some the spectre of labour redundancy and mass unemployment. For such unemployment to be avoided two things are essential: to provide retraining programmes and associated financial assistance to unemployed workers; and to ensure that aggregate demand is growing at a rate to match the growth of the nation's productive capacity.

Chapter 4

1. Motives are: to finance transactions (since only money is generally accepted in exchange); and to hold as a store of value (since money, unlike many other assets, will not suffer a capital loss if one has to realise on one's assets hurriedly).

2. Fractional reserve banking refers to the cash reserve of a commercial bank being a fraction of its deposit liabilities. The limit to creating money is set by the need to maintain a minimum cash reserve ratio.

3. The sequence of events is detailed in section 2 for government spending financed by the central bank. Consider the similar sequence of events when the central bank buys securities on the stock exchange.

4. The equality of planned demand and supply can be equivalently restated as the equality of planned savings and investment. In disequilibrium, realised savings and investment are equal because realised investment is defined to include unintended stock change. This is equivalent to defining realised demand

and supply as always being equal by including unintended stock rise as part of investment demand in 'realised demand'.

11. $500m.
12. A recession, because planned production exceeds planned demand.

21. The criteria used are: (a) efficiency: time-lags, ability to forecast size of effect of measure, whether measures operate upwards and downwards with equal efficiency; (b) use of resources: for consumer goods, private investment, public goods for communal use (schools, defence). See also chapter 3, section 5.
22. The simple quantity theory proposed that the price level moves proportionately with the money supply. Refer analysis on page 92.
23. The frequent recurrence of high levels of unemployment in Europe, United Kingdom, and United States between say 1850 and 1940 suggests a basic scepticism about the efficacy of stabilising influences. Since 1940, economics have been more stable because governments have worked at it.
24. No. Higher interest rates will release idle money holdings for use in the transactions flow. The observed ratio of money supply to national product will then fall.
25. The capital market includes the array of financial institutions (banks, other lenders, stock market) engaged in financing: the nation's physical investment, the government budget deficit, and lending and asset formation overseas. Insofar as the capital market has historically failed to ensure that planned investment is always high enough to absorb the resources released by planned investment, it has from time to time served the capitalist economies badly. Its record in screening out low profitability projects is probably much better.

Chapter 5

1. See section 2.
2. Inflation is caused by excess demand, and by claims by factors for higher prices for their services, e.g. wage claims. Mechanism consists in the response of decision-making units, e.g. excess

demand for goods results in bidding up of wage-rates (one response) so that higher incomes result in higher consumer spending (another response).

Excess demand-caused inflation is cumulative; wage inflation is not cumulative unless a cumulative sequence is introduced, notably by cost-of-living adjustments.

The term 'spiral' suggest that a process is not only cumulative but also that it does not diminish (or converge to an ultimate finite price rise). Excess demand-caused inflation will slow down if some elements of demand are fixed in money terms—but the rate of slowdown may be slight.

3. No. Irrespective of the cause of the inflation, money wage-rates will rise.

4. Simplifications include:

    (a)   assuming constant profit mark-up;

    (b)   assuming volume of output is constant when, in reality, rises in demand result partly in rising output and partly in rising price—the 'demand dissipation' process;

    (c)   foreign trade not discussed;

    (d)   in reality there may be genuine difficulty in distinguishing the cause of inflation; i.e. whether the *lead* in the process is taken by excess demand or by higher wage claims.

11. The price level will rise at a steady rate of 5 per cent per period. The price index will read: 1, 1.05, 1.1025, 1.1576. (Initial investment must have been 200, which then rises by one-quarter to 250, which is a 5 per cent rise in total demand).

But if investment remains at 250, then the inflationary sequence will slow down—the price index will read 1, 1.05, 1.09, 1.122 in successive periods.

12. Applied to the lower part of table 5.3, this proposal would be: a multiplicand equal to 5 per cent of national product; a multiplier of 5 (since the marginal propensity to consume is 0.8); hence an ultimate price rise of 25 per cent.

The danger of such a formula approach is illustrated by the upper half of table 5.3—for the multiplicand (rise in investment) is not constant but rising. In other models, if part of consumer spending is fixed in *money* terms, it follows that the marginal propensity to consume will not be constant and the multiplier will be changing also. The approach is not recommended for a general analysis.

21. Possibly because of income distribution effects or conceivably long-term effects of saving—but most important in practice because of the adverse effect on the nation's ability to pay for its imports (which tend to rise, while exports tend to fall—see part III).

22. The action is rational given that the concern of the government is to prevent a foreign trade deficit. Indirect taxes only raise prices to home purchasers. More importantly, indirect (like direct) taxes can successfully slow down a *cumulative* inflation by reducing the purchasing power of consumers.

23. Because of the ability of businessmen to protect the profit share of the national income by applying a fixed profit mark-up to wage costs, it is open to doubt whether any successful wage claim has more than a transitory effect on the total wage share.

'Capacity to pay' at its worst is meaningless, at its best it suggests that workers should be paid higher in the high productivity growth rate industries. In practice this is likely to break down owing to 'pattern setting', i.e. emulation wage claims by workers in the low productivity growth rate industries.

'Productivity' may mean: (a) that workers nationwide should receive wage increases equal to the national rise in over-all productivity—in which case this is an alternative to lower commodity prices as a way of passing on the fruits of technical progress; (b) that workers in individual industries should receive wage increases matching the growth in productivity in their own industry—see previous comments on pattern setting.

'Cost of living.' The point of departure here is that if higher prices are paid, then they are also received. A second point is that higher wage-rates by powerful unions often mean higher cost of living for members of the less powerful unions. Third point is that cost of living clauses in wage contracts make wage-claim-caused inflation cumulative.

It is apparent that there are many more cases than the three listed. Inflationary price rises will be least if wage claims are based on a nationwide productivity criterion.

24. The logic we have pursued has been: (a) to treat the wage-rate as unit of measurement or numeraire (and unexplained); (b) explain *change* in the money wage-rate; (c) hence explain change in the price level. So we did alter the problem—because this seemed the politically interesting thing to do.

The reader who wants to 'explain the wage level' (and hence the price level), can use a modified quantity theory approach: in monetary equilibrium the supply of money (M) must equal the demand for money (M_d), which is proportional to the value of the national product ($X.P$) and inversely proportional to the interest rate; moreover the value of the national product is equal to the national income comprising the wage bill multiplied by a profit mark-up. In short, with i the interest rate, k a constant:

$$M = M_d = k.X.P/i = k.N.P_n.(1+v)/i$$

into which figures for M, k, N, v and i can be substituted to yield a figure for P_n. There is some doubt about the usefulness of such an exercise.

25. (a) The central bank has strong powers to control inflation due to excess demand; but it is debatable how far it is appropriate to use these powers to stop inflation due to wage claims. One could be paying a high price in unemployment when what is needed is a modification of social institutions; (each nation may have to develop its own unique solution—see the wage institutions of Sweden, Japan).

(b) A formula control for the money supply looks attractive. The first criticism is again that it seems a curious weapon to counter wage claims. The second criticism is that it seems to be in danger of setting up a financial measure as a political objective. A third criticism is that it fails to recognise that one can have quite a healthy inflation with no rise in the money supply at all—if interest rates rise to syphon idle funds into the transactions stream.

(c) This is ingenious. The notion is that budget deficits are fine if there is unemployment, and budget surpluses are fine if there is excess-demand-caused inflation, but that if one can avoid both pitfalls then the budget is to be balanced. The justification for the last might be a policy aim: (i) that unnecessarily high tax rates (yielding a budget surplus) *should not* exist at full employment because of disincentive effects; (ii) that the government *should not* have to plan savings in excess of its own investment (i.e. the budget surplus) at full employment, in order to enable private business to maintain its investment programme without causing inflation. Plainly this whole topic is a fertile field for debate—but it should not be forgotten that ultimately the criteria for choosing between financial measures are physical policy objectives.

26. There is a basic conflict between the central bank wishing to prevent excess-demand-caused inflation and wishing to maintain low (strictly, not-rising) interest rates. For example a businessman wishing to expand his investment programme may be denied a bank advance (because of a central bank directive to commercial banks), but he can sell some of his portfolio of government securities on the stock exchange to the central bank's buyer and thus obtain the necessary funds for physical investment. The central bank's buyer may be operating because otherwise the offer of the securities on the stock exchange would cause a fall in the market price, and so a rise in the market interest rate.

Judging by the Bank of England's March 1969 *Quarterly Bulletin*, the Bank was acting in the manner just described because of its concern for debt conversion—i.e. to let bond prices fall could create a fear of capital loss so that people would not convert into new securities as old securities fell due. If such securities to be redeemed by the United Kingdom Government had to be paid off with new money, this could be inflationary. So ran the Bank's thinking. But that does not overcome the basic fact that a policy of holding up bond prices is directly inflationary. The Bank has to handle its conversion problem by other means: achieving a better spread of maturities into long-term bonds; allowing interest rates to both rise and fall so that both capital gains and losses can be made on securities; introducing more imaginative securities, e.g. variable-interest-rate securities (or commodity-price-index-adjusted securities) for small buyers.

Chapter 6

1. The marginal product is the addition to total production resulting from increasing the input of the factor by one unit, the inputs of all other factors remaining constant.
2. Scale returns refers to a situation in which all variable inputs are changed equiproportionally. An expansion of the nation's fishing fleet could be expected to yield diminishing scale returns, while an increase in the size of tankers has yielded increasing scale returns.
3. Refer figure 6.1 and accompanying explanation. If the work force increases while other factors are constant then, if labour is imperfectly substitutable, output per worker will fall.
4. Find the loss of output in cutting back other processes (now in use) when resources are transferred.

11. Iron is obtained from the iron oxide haematite by heating it with carbon in the form of coke. The input of limestone converts silica or sand impurities in the iron ore into calcium silicate. In the blast furnace iron ore, coke and limestone are fed into the top and compressed hot air fed in at the bottom to melt both the reduced iron and calcium silicate slag. Technical coefficients vary with scale and quality of materials. For one period investigated, a group of blast furnaces used 0.18 tons of limestone and 0.58 tons of coke for each ton of iron ore, and produced 0.65 tons of pig iron. Other major inputs are blast furnace gas and labour.
12. This change in cheese technology alters relative demand for land and labour, with the result that the first method of producing beer is no longer competitive. Only the second method of producing beer would be used to maximise the national product.
13. Not at all. It is inefficient in as much as a combination of the other two activities can always produce a required output with fewer inputs.
14. Using the method of varying q, we find the solution value of q is two-thirds. The activities chosen will then be $A(3)$, $B(1)$ and (2) in relative scale 0.8375 and 0.1625, $C(3)$ and $D(3)$. The required figure is $4/131.5$ million tons of A at maximum production.

21. If population increased while all else remained unchanged— including capital equipment, knowledge—the concept of diminishing marginal productivity suggests that living standards would indeed fall. But in the past century there have been great increases in both equipment and scientific knowledge.

22. Choice of technology is important in a world in which knowledge is increasing and in which relative factor supplies (including equipment) are changing. But perhaps it is even more important to operate any chosen process efficiently. Other choices are concerned with the proportion of the national income saved, with income distribution, industrial location and foreign trade.

23. Not necessarily. A poor nation by definition is especially scarce of capital equipment, which it must use to best advantage. One likely strategy is to use its scarce savings to expand the capacity of the equipment-making industries, while for some years producing food with labour-intensive methods—since labour is the most plentiful factor.

24. Observe that, using the third meaning, the phrase 'minimising the cost of producing X' means producing X by means that leave the output of other goods in the economy as high as possible.

The cost of the nation's defence programme is the diversion of resources to the programme—when these resources could alternatively produce consumer goods. The method of finance among the local population leaves this cost unaffected. Thus the final proposition is false.

Economic policy is concerned with options and the cost of choosing one option is the transfer of resources from other options. Later, consider such issues as: the cost of a national immigration programme (diverting resources from consumption to investment needed to equip the immigrants); the cost of a high level of tariff protection (diverting resources from export industry to resource-expensive import-competing industry); the cost of self-sufficiency in food or fuel for a formerly food- or fuel-importing nation (same as the tariff).

Chapter 7

1. The marginal return from a dollar spent on any factor must be the same for all factors. If this is not so, unit cost is not minimised. Hence the manager will swap factors to achieve it.
2. Express all factor prices as a ratio of the wage-rate. Since the manager aims at minimising unit cost, factor prices so expressed can be interpreted as factor marginal products relatively to the marginal product of labour; e.g. for commodity i (inputs are labour and land), unit cost is:

$$[P_n . a_{ni} + P_l . a_{li}] \text{ in dollars}$$

i.e.

$$[a_{ni} + (P_l/P_n) . a_{li}] \text{ in wage-units}$$

and if unit cost is indeed minimised we can rewrite the expression:

$$[a_{ni} + (mp_l/mp_n) . a_{li}]$$

which is in physical terms, the measurement unit being the marginal product of labour.
3. The cost of producing a ton by the proposed process is 0.8 tons loss from existing processes.
4. This is the loss of production due to transferring factors from existing activities.

11. (a) Using the market simulation approach, we determine the demand for land acreage to be one-quarter the demand for labour; i.e. at full employment of labour, land demanded is $1\frac{3}{4}$ million acres.
    (b) Yes: with respect to those resources that are employed the search for minimum unit cost maximises the output those resources are capable of producing. (Of course, some other resources are idle).
12. Costing shows that this third activity will not be used.

23. The doctrine that self-interest and public interest always coincide is invalidated by the occurrence of restrictive monopolistic practice, and by environmental pollution, to name only two objections.

Chapter 8

1. Equality of mark-ups suggests competition. Absolute size is not a criterion unless some other form of comparison (e.g. international) can be made.
2. Population growth, especially in a rural economy, implies falling marginal productivity of labour relatively to land—accompanied by a fall in the ratio of the wage-rate to land-rent.
3. See text of chapter.

11. Profit share is one-third.
12. Price of beer is as already calculated. Because of 25 per cent mark-up, the land-rent is 80 per cent of the value of the marginal product of land.
13. (a) There is a time-lag in rising prices following a rise in wages, such that a $10m rise in the current quarter's wage bill results in a fall in profits of $7.3m.
    (b) If the wage-bill is constant over three quarters, then profits are 62 per cent of the quarterly wage-bill.
14. Commodity B is relatively labour intensive, as can be calculated from:

$$\frac{5(0.8375) + 3(0.1625)}{1(0.8375) + 4(0.1625)}$$

and compare the result with the other goods.

   If full employment of *all* resources is to be maintained, then a fall in the relative scale of output of the labour-intensive industry must be accompanied by a general switch to labour-intensive methods. (The market mechanism would be a relative fall in wage-rate). Calculation confirms that with the new composition of demand, the new technology is *A*(2) and (3), *B*(1), *C*(1) and *D*(2), which is in the direction forecast.

21. Inasmuch as the landowner has no alternative but to use the land, a tax on land-rent received by him may only affect the distribution of the national product and not affect technology or volume of production. The wage-earner does have the choice of work or leisure so that a tax on wages may affect the volume

of work and so volume of output. However, this is complicated in several ways:

(a) The introduction of a tax on the wage-earner both reduces his income (which may stimulate him to work more) and reduces his net receipts for an extra hour's work (which stimulates him to work less), so that the final result is uncertain.

(b) If the salary-earner's total income is received under an annual contract then such marginal considerations may not apply.

(c) Some income earners (e.g. stage performers) receive very high incomes, which are akin to land-rent—there is no alternative way in which they could earn such a salary and so the sole effect may be distributive.

22. Either by lower prices or higher wages.
23. Subsidies, tax concessions, deflation, devaluation.
24. The shift in the schedule portraying consumer tastes for land-intensive goods results in land becoming relatively scarce and labour relatively plentiful—land-rents rise relatively to the depressed wage-rate. There is then a general movement in all industry (both land intensive and labour intensive) to shift to less land-intensive methods of production. The ultimate effects are:

(a) because the content of demand has shifted, *all* industries move to more labour-intensive technology in order to absorb available resources;

(b) income distribution (before any taxes) shifts in favour of the land owner.

Chapter 9

1. 'Inefficiency' suggests an alternative more efficient situation. That alternative might be one in which more information is provided, in which individual small producers are restrained from following a course that is collectively irrational, in which even large firms are required to demonstrate that their action is consistent with national interest.

2. Refer sections 1 and 2.

3. Marginal utility of a commodity is the increment in total utility (or satisfaction) obtained from consuming one more unit of that commodity per period of time.

   The equi-marginal utility condition specifies a situation in which the ratio of marginal utility to price is the same for all goods bought by the consumer. In that situation he cannot increase satisfaction by switching expenditure between goods.

11. The rule of thumb measures the net loss as equal to the change in volume times one-half the rise in price. This assumes that there is a straight line demand curve, that the initial and final positions are equilibria, and that price can be used as an index of marginal utility.

12. The rise in money national income is superbly irrelevant. Nor is the use of a price index to calculate real national income the answer. The concept of national income simply breaks down as an indicator of welfare. In principle the national income is just a sum of factor incomes, not an index of welfare.

13. If resources remained unemployed the loss would be measured by the fall in production. Assuming aggregate demand is sufficient to ensure full employment, there will be a resource transfer and a welfare loss estimated at one-half the price rise times the fall in sales volume, i.e. $1m.

21. If consumers had a collective intelligence the thrust would have some point. But they don't and they are individually nudged by the market to a position that seems to them rational because it satisfies the equi-marginal utility condition, but which we know to be sub-optimal because the owners of industry *b* are using their monopolistic powers. But of course there is a clear conflict of interest between the owners of industry *b* and the rest of the community.

22. The two-part tariff seeks both to make people pay for what they use and to let them choose optimally by maintaining the same ratio of price to marginal cost for all goods. A broadcasting licence paid to the government broadcasting network is a two-part tariff in which the second part is zero, i.e. there is only an 'access price'; but there will be a second part if there are maintenance costs on the receiving equipment. Hydroelectric

power, telephones, driving on the road (the licence is the access price or it could be, and the petrol tax the usage price) can all be analysed in the same way.

23. This apocryphal directive to managers of socialist enterprise is open to criticism on three counts: First, it is a copybook fallacy of composition (similar to 'what is good for General Motors is good for America'). Second it does not stand up to analysis based on the argument in this chapter. Third, it could give quite lunatic results: imagine that the workers' demand for food was fairly unresponsive to price, and that the capitalists' demand for castles was quite responsive to price, then maximum value added by industry would be achieved by raising the profit mark-up on food and lowering the profit mark-up on castles—a good recipe for social revolution. (In reality the nature of tastes of the different income groups is more complex than suggested by this *reductio ad absurdum*).

24. The pursuit of maximum profit is one rational aim of a producer. If he does, then it is the task of government to ensure that he pursues this aim in an environment that *constrains* his actions to be consistent with community welfare, e.g. by ensuring that entry into the industry is not closed, or by ensuring that he does not pollute the environment.

The phrase 'maximum profit' has various interpretations. Thus in the industries subject to rapid technological change (petrochemicals, electronics) it seems typical for them to maintain standard profit mark-ups and pass on the benefits of lower costs (due to better technology) in an effort to expand sales volume as rapidly as possible. Firms in such industry are competing against each other but they are also competing against other industries for the consumer's dollar. Thus their drive for rapidly expanding sales volume seems a rational interpretation of the maximum profit objective.

Of course the guidelines for policy set out in the text still apply.

Chapter 10

1. Refer section 1.
2. Monopoly, exhausting mineral deposits, pollution.

3. Unemployment; living standards. Government initiative is needed in other areas, e.g. to establish the transport network, and public works needed to establish new cities.

11. No, inasmuch as the sum of all outputs is no longer constant at 100.

   The effect of a fall in P_w to 1, with income Y constant at 200 wage units and P_b still at 2, can be determined, by substitution in the demand schedules, as consumption of w: 90 physical units; of b: 55 physical units.

12. Infinite.

13. 40. New is $C_w = 60 - 10(P_w - k)$; compare figure 10.1.

14. Draw a diagram with land and labour inputs as axes; plot land: labour required to 'produce' $45 by growing: wheat (6, $1\frac{1}{2}$), oats (3, 3) and barley (2, 4). Draw in resource ratio line. Hence compute that the solution is to produce 36.67 tons of oats and 13.33 tons of wheat to earn from export $1,300. Now plot a fourth point showing that factor needs to 'produce' $45 by growing subsidised barley are (1.5, 3). Compute that the new solution is 34.3 tons wheat and 15.7 tons barley to earn $1,218 foreign exchange. Thus there is a national loss of $US82 foreign exchange due to resource transfer. Also there is a redistribution of income because any subsidy fractionally greater than $5 will cause farmers to switch from oats to barley; i.e. the subsidy of $15 is more than was needed to persuade the farmer to produce it.

21. Defence, decentralisation, income redistribution.

22. Actual examples are: embargo on the import of ships, and of sugar; legal requirement to colour imported margarine pink; more generally, import quotas and import tariffs that protect home industry as if by subsidy.

23. If commercial reafforestation reduces soil erosion and raises the water table, these effects may benefit other agricultural industry and so properly attract a subsidy. More commonly the activities of an industry cause additional costs to the rest of the community.

24. Since an indirect tax is a negative subsidy, the argument applies to both cases. Other criteria, however, may be relevant; e.g.

taxes on alcohol, tobacco, drugs, might be levied on the grounds
of danger to health (with implicit restriction on the individual's
freedom and/or ability to make his own choice).

25. An income tax alters the relative 'return' or satisfaction to work
and leisure. (But note that since work is often on a contract
basis as to length of time, e.g. 40 hour week, the individual may
not initially be in equilibrium with equal rates of return to both
activities). In such a problem it must usually be assumed that
a given tax revenue has to be raised. Hence the task is to *compare* the effects of the income tax with other alternative means
of raising revenue. Sometimes, however, other options are
relevant; e.g. the option may be either to have an income tax
to finance old age pensions or to have a national superannuation
scheme in which benefits are related to contributions (not taxes).
The first task is to specify feasible options, not to assume that
the alternative is an 'income tax or no income tax'.

Chapter 11

1. Improvement in technology may cause unemployment in either
of two ways. First, with rising real national income people
may tend to save a higher proportion of income than business
plans to invest—thus causing unemployment due to *deficiency
of demand*. Second, unemployment may arise because of *immobility of factors*, especially immobility (i.e. unwillingness,
and/or inability, to move) of labour as between locations, trades
or industries. Immobility must be treated as a specific problem.
In Sweden around 2 per cent of the work force are retrained
annually.

2. Yes, because with rising per capita real income the proportion
of that income spent on different goods will change.

3. First by maintaining its price at a high level, the surplus not
purchased in the usual way being bought by the government.
Second, by subsidising the product, thus reducing market price
and (hopefully) increasing the quantity purchased in normal
commerce.

11. Unit income elasticity means that say a $\frac{1}{2}$ per cent rise in income
results in a $\frac{1}{2}$ per cent rise in quantity purchased of a good. So

the probability of unemployment is greater if the income elasticity is less than one. (But any final answer also depends on changes in technology in the industry.)

12. A price elasticity of demand less than unity (i.e. 'low') means that a 1 per cent cut in price results in a less than 1 per cent rise in quantity demanded, and a zero price elasticity of demand means that a price cut results in no rise in quantity demanded. Comparable explanation can be given on the meaning of price elasticities of supply.

In the extreme case where both price elasticities are zero, no adjustment via the price mechanism is possible. Short of this extreme, it is also true that the lower the elasticities the smaller is the contribution of a given price fall towards equating demand and supply.

On the whole, evidence does confirm that price elasticities of demand and supply for farm products (including foodstuffs) are low—because of satiety in demand on the one hand, and on the other the unwillingness of the farmer to go out of production. (However, the farmers may switch fairly readily from one crop to another, given price incentives—while still maintaining total farm output.)

13. This illustrates a case where the price elasticity of demand is less than unity. It is one of the harshest realities of food production that a good crop may only be saleable for a smaller total return, so that the farmer's profit falls. The problem can be alleviated for many crops by storage, canning, drying, pulping, freezing and juice extraction.

21. Like other causes of unemployment, technological unemployment only becomes important if the problem is ignored. As the answer to question 1 showed, there is no reason why it should become important—nor is there any reason to consider the problem to be changed in kind by the appearance of automation. The problems of affluence should be the easiest economic problems to handle.

22. The genesis of 'the farm problem' lies in resistance by some politically powerful farm groups to contracting the resources used in farming, in order to spread the benefits of improved farm technology about the nation. It is a clear short-term con-

flict of interests.

The solution is neither to subsidise specific farm products, nor subsidise farm incomes, nor yet to have the government purchase unwanted production at artificially high prices. The solution is to plan a rational physical reorganisation of the industry and then to aim at implementing this by a combination of government purchasing of farms, retraining, and retraining grants. Compare the Mansholt plan for European farm reconstruction.

Any industry can face the problem of adaptation to technological change occurring either within that industry or in some other competing industry. The problem is more acute in farming (refer question 12) because the farmer is as immobile as it is possible to be (capital tied up in the farm, no nearby large city to get any other job, not trained for another job, and may not want to leave the land anyway).

23. If the aim of economic activity is to achieve 'the good life' then more concern might be given to leisure (longer annual vacations, a three-day weekend), pollution, reduction of health hazards in the factory, and making a higher proportion of jobs psychologically rewarding. Measures to achieve such aims include education, taxes and subsidies.

Chapter 12

1. Refer section 1.
2. Assuming that prices reflect resource costs, the difference in relative home prices indicates trade being profitable. The example in section 1 uses the concept of resource-transfers to illustrate this.
3. See section 3.

11. Relative home prices would be the same and so trade would not be profitable. Use resource-transfers to confirm this.
13. Fall of one-third (from 100/100 to 80/120).

21. Not unless you believed in the purchasing power parity theory. See section 4 for discussion.
22. This implies a serious reduction in national sovereignty. Suppose for example that there is a recession overseas, causing a

fall in demand for our exports. Thus we have a balance of current payments deficit, which is met by a run-down of the international currency held by our banks. Our banks then deflate, spreading the recession. The implications are: either one wants to reduce national sovereignty; or one assumes such a balance of payments situation will not arise; or if it does arise there will be planned capital movements to avoid the spread of recession.

23. In essence trade is advantageous because one can obtain some importable goods at a lower resource cost in exchange for exports than by producing them oneself. This will be the case if one's superiority is uneven, but if a nation is twice as efficient in producing all goods this condition is not met. See answer to question 11 above.

24. There is a basic internal conflict of interest in permitting trade: on the one hand the nation gains, but on the other hand the import-competing industry faces competition from imports. From a national viewpoint, acceptance of the clock-makers' argument would mean there was no trade.

Compare this conflict of interest with that explored in chapter 11.

Chapter 13

1. *Devaluation*, say of sterling, refers to a reduction in the amount of a foreign currency (e.g. marks) that a pound sterling will buy. *Deflation* refers to a recession in which real incomes, employment and also the general price level fall. *Drawing rights*, say with the International Monetary Fund, refer to a nation's right to buy or otherwise acquire foreign exchange from the Fund in accord with established procedures. *Gold standard* refers to an arrangement whereby in past time a number of nations pegged the price of gold in terms of their currency, thereby establishing a set of fixed exchange rates between their currencies: the real significance of this arrangement lay in the willingness of these nations to deflate when they had a foreign payments deficit, irrespective of the cause of that deficit and irrespective of whether they already had unemployment.

2. See section 2.

3. The fall in real incomes means people spend less on all goods including on imports; also imports become more expensive as the price of home-produced substitutes falls. In short there is a fall in total spending, and a switch in the composition of spending—both can help to eliminate a payments deficit by reducing foreign exchange spent on imports.

4. See section 3.

11. Compare figure 13.6. With a devaluation of 20 per cent, the index of export incomes jumps to 120 and a 17 per cent ($=20/120$) tax on exports cuts this index back to 100. The import price index is up to 120 and an extra tariff of 12 per cent (12 per cent of $120 = 15$ approx.) raises this index by 15 points to 135. All this could have been done by a 35 per cent tariff.

12. Starting at the vertical line, by moving one small step to the right we free one chunk of resources from import-competing industry, replacing their output by a rise in imports valued at 10 francs, and employ that chunk in export industry to earn an additional 15 francs from extra exports.

21. Danger points: low price elasticity of supply of exports; low price elasticity of foreign demand for exports; possible foreign retaliation; most importantly, possible inflationary effects including trade union reaction to a rise in the cost of living.

22. Not if there are given policy aims. It is perfectly logical to compare a situation in which there is a tariff with the same situation without a tariff—but such a discussion is likely to be *irrelevant* to the issues confronting a government.

23. Technically yes (see chapter 15, especially figure 15.2). But large scale use of subsidies raises questions of how to finance them. In practice, subsidies tend to be used where at a later stage of manufacture the produce is either exported or used by other home industries competing with imports. For example, subsidise fertiliser used by rural export industry, or subsidise cellulose acetate flake used by home industry competing with imported synthetic textiles.

24. See the concluding paragraph in the text.

Chapter 14

1. One changes the total level of demand, the other (quotas) changes the composition of demand.
2. No. As capacity output is approached the multiplier falls as a rising proportion of demand is dissipated in rising prices and in imports.
3. The important aspect of a measure such as devaluation is its effect on the pursuit of policy aims—devaluation has both internal (income) and external (trade) effects.

11. Figure 14.1 When demand equals supply in the commodity market, the national product equals the home-produced content of the constant components of final demand times a multiplier that equals the reciprocal of unity minus the marginal propensity to consume home-produced goods out of national income. The significance of this mouthful is clearer by considering what it states about *response to change*, equation (2) in section 3.
12. Generally, yes. However the last part would not apply if both the marginal propensity to save and marginal liability to tax were zero.
13. Imports rise at an accelerated rate under the influence of the squared term (analogous to the relation between distance and time for a projectile under constant acceleration). See answer to question 2; also figure 14.4 (top half).
14. If both the m arc in the range 0.05 to 0.25 and c' lies between 0.4 and 0.8, then h lies in the range 0.004 to 0.3.

21. Raise tax rates, reduce bank credit, to cut back spending on both home-produced and imported goods.
22. Devaluation would probably create inflationary increase in demand for home-produced goods, and if this were not contained then imports would resume their upward course. Both devaluation and a wage cut aim at reducing the structure of home factor prices compared with overseas—so the same comment applies to both. That is, the wage cut increases the demand for home-produced goods rather than imports—but the resulting inflationary sequence is comparable to the effect of devaluation. Hence these are inappropriate measures firstly because they

move the economy further away from the target of high employment without inflation, and because in themselves they are unlikely to solve the foreign deficit problem.

23. Neither, since they would both increase the foreign trade surplus. Propose to appreciate the exchange rate with deflationary effect and allowing imports to rise.

To assist in handling problems of this type, tabulate correct and incorrect measures in the following situations, as briefly illustrated:

Situation		*Correct measure*
unemployment, trade deficit	:	cut imports (quota)
overfull employment, deficit	:	raise income tax rate
unemployment, trade surplus	:	cut income tax rate
overfull employment, surplus	:	appreciate exchange rate

Chapter 15

1. Refer section 1.
2. Refer section 2.
3. Refer section 2.

11. Refer figure 15.1. Since an aim of policy is to make the best use of resources, it is the concept of 'effective protection' to a process that measures the effectiveness with which resources are used.
12. See parallel example in figure 15.2.

21. See section 3. Note particularly that export subsidies keep marginal producers in existence and fail to rationalise the industry's production, create a divergence between private and social benefit, and subsidise low-cost producers thus affecting income distribution.

22. See section 4.
23. The view suggested does explain the rationale of much intervention. However, there are cases where governments may intervene to their mutual benefit—possible examples are mutual reduction of tariffs, customs union and double taxation agreements to facilitate capital flows.

Symbols

a_{ni} $(= N \div X)$ labour input coefficient per unit of output
C consumption (volume)
D demand (expenditure; i.e. volume times price)
Δ an increment
E exports (volume)
G government expenditure on goods and services at constant prices
I investment demand (volume)
K stock of capital equipment
L land input
M money supply; M_d demand for money
N employment; i.e. labour input
P price; e.g. P_i price of commodity i
P_n wage-rate
P_l price of services of land; i.e. rent
P_m import price level
R replacement investment
S savings
T taxes
V profit (or surplus)
W work force
X volume of production
       X_c production of consumer goods
       X_i production of investment goods
Y national income
Y_d disposable income (after tax and other transfers)

In a few instances upper case symbols are given other meanings but these are clearly set out in the text.

Lower case symbols are used as constants and some symbols are necessarily used several times with different meanings. The following are some of the most common uses of lower case symbols in the text:

a a technical input coefficient
b capital/output ratio
i rate of interest
m equipment life in years

n growth rate of national production
p target rate of growth of output per worker; labour productivity
s average propensity to save; savings-income ratio
v profit mark-up coefficient
w growth rate of the work force

Index